The Psychology
of Prejudice

The Psychology of Prejudice

From Attitudes to Social Action

Lynne M. Jackson

American Psychological Association • Washington, DC

Second Printing, October 2013

Published by
American Psychological Association
750 First Street, NE
Washington, DC 20002
www.apa.org

To order
APA Order Department
P.O. Box 92984
Washington, DC 20090-2984
Tel: (800) 374-2721; Direct: (202) 336-5510
Fax: (202) 336-5502; TDD/TTY: (202) 336-6123
Online: www.apa.org/pubs/books
E-mail: order@apa.org

In the U.K., Europe, Africa, and the Middle East, copies may be ordered from
American Psychological Association
3 Henrietta Street
Covent Garden, London
WC2E 8LU England

Typeset in Goudy by Circle Graphics, Inc., Columbia, MD

Printer: The Maple-Vail Book Manufacturing Group, York, PA
Cover Designer: Mercury Publishing Services, Rockville, MD

The opinions and statements published are the responsibility of the authors, and such opinions and statements do not necessarily represent the policies of the American Psychological Association.

Library of Congress Cataloging-in-Publication Data

Jackson, Lynne M.
The psychology of prejudice : from attitudes to social action / Lynne M. Jackson. — 1st ed.
    p. cm.
 Includes bibliographical references and index.
 ISBN-13: 978-1-4338-0920-0 (print)
 ISBN-10: 1-4338-0920-6 (print)
 1. Prejudices—Psychological aspects. 2. Prejudices—Religious aspects.
3. Prejudices—Prevention. I. Title.

 BF575.P9J29 2011
 303.3'85—dc22
                                                    2010025103

British Library Cataloguing-in-Publication Data

A CIP record is available from the British Library.

Printed in the United States of America
First Edition

doi:10.1037/12317-000

For my students
and the wonderful gang of children
in my family

CONTENTS

Acknowledgments .... *ix*

Introduction 3

Chapter 1.   Defining Prejudice 7

Chapter 2.   Defining Differences 29

Chapter 3.   Evolutionary and Psychodynamic Approaches
              to Prejudice 47

Chapter 4.   Ideology and Prejudice 65

Chapter 5.   Development of Prejudice in Children 81

Chapter 6.   Intergroup Relations and Prejudice 103

Chapter 7.   Cognitive, Affective, and Interactive
              Processes of Prejudice 117

Chapter 8. Toward a Wider Lens: Prejudice
           and the Natural World 137

Chapter 9. Reducing Prejudice and Promoting
           Social Change 159

References 177

Index 213

About the Author 225

ACKNOWLEDGMENTS

Most of all, I am deeply grateful for my partner and husband, Patrick Callon, who has always believed in me and helped to make "life-while-writing" wonderful. To my parents, I owe a huge thank you. My mother, Lavoynne Jackson, read every word of the first draft of this book and provided insightful editorial feedback. She also taught me a great deal about the nature of speciesism, which has contributed to this book and enriched my life. My father, Gordon Jackson, provided the guidance, support, and role modeling that encouraged me to develop the career that has given me the chance to write this book. Friends, especially Diana Ruda and Cathy Chovaz, helped keep me well-rounded and happy during the process and provided much-appreciated enthusiasm about the book. Vicki Esses, my mentor and friend, has helped and supported me in my work in more ways than I can recount. Her ideas and inspiration are evident throughout the book, most especially in Chapter 6 (though any errors are entirely my own). My friend and colleague Imants Barušs was an encouraging mentor throughout the process of conceptualizing and writing this book. Thanks to my inspirational student Lisa Bitacola for reading and commenting on the original manuscript. I am indebted to everyone at APA Books, especially Maureen Adams, for sharing the vision of the book with me, and Susan Herman, for her expert editorial input. Two reviewers provided constructive input for which I'm grateful. Finally, King's University College at the University of Western Ontario provided me with my first sabbatical, so that I would have the time to write, and contributed financial support to some of my research cited in this book.

The Psychology of Prejudice

INTRODUCTION

This book is inspired by my work with university students. While studying prejudice and related topics, my students and I are always impressed by three things: the way that prejudice is entwined with many problems of social injustice, the profound role that religion plays in shaping prevailing social beliefs and attitudes, and the value of an open, self-critical, and forward-looking approach to scholarship. This book is aimed at satisfying those people, like my students, who want to learn about the state of knowledge regarding psychological aspects of prejudice while engaging with the connections between prejudice and broader social problems and acknowledging the importance of cultural variables, such as religion, in shaping attitudes. In addition, consistent with the value my students and I place on open, forward-looking scholarship, the book explores emerging ideas, such as the possibility that prejudice is entwined with people's relationship with the natural world.

The chapters that follow review key theoretical developments in the recent study of prejudice within social psychology, with an emphasis on those perspectives that situate prejudice in the context of intergroup relations. Throughout, I address research support for the theories, but the emphasis is more on theory than is often found in texts on social psychological topics. The priority placed on depth of understanding over breadth of coverage provides a strong educational tool, but it does mean that I had to make difficult choices about what material to include, and there is certainly excellent work I was unable to cite. Nevertheless, I attempt to provide an overall picture of the field as it currently stands while viewing it through a broad lens that captures the social context in which prejudice rests.

The book begins with an exploration of the meaning and forms of prejudice. In the first chapter, I show how prejudice manifests in myriad forms and also how it is embedded in aspects of the social context, such as inequality and privilege. At the end of the chapter, I use the example of audism (i.e., prejudice and discrimination against D/deaf people) to illustrate this issue.[1] The second chapter explores people's understanding of the nature of differences between groups. Using examples of race and sexual orientation, I explore biological and constructionist perspectives on difference and address the question of whether there is a connection between prejudice and explanations about how and why people differ. In Chapters 3 through 7, I examine causes of prejudice, starting with the most distal explanations and ending with the most proximal. In Chapter 3, I review evolutionary and psychodynamic theories that describe how and why people may be predisposed toward prejudice at the level of human nature. Chapter 4 considers how societies construct ideologies, such as political, religious, and social systems of belief that sustain inequality and promote prejudice. In Chapter 5, I show how, given this backdrop, children's cognitive and social development can reproduce prejudice in the next generation. In Chapter 6, I examine proximal explanations for prejudice, including theories of group competition and identity that explain why prejudice intensifies against some groups in some places at certain periods of time. The cognitive approach to prejudice is included in Chapter 7 on perpetuating factors. In this chapter, I cover the cognitive, affective, and interactive dynamics that serve to sustain those prejudices and forms of inequality that have become prevalent in society. The relatively new social neuroscience perspective is included here because, as I discuss, evidence has suggested that the way in which people's brains respond to social information is shaped, in part, by their social context and social goals.

In Chapter 8, I explore two ways in which an understanding of prejudice may be enriched by taking a broader view. First, the myriad connections between prejudice and the health of the natural environment are explored through discussions of environmental inequality (i.e., the disproportionate exposure to environmental toxins of minority groups), connections between intergroup and environmental attitudes, and influences of environmental

---

[1] That section of the chapter explains how the use of uppercase and lowercase D in the term D/deaf reflects different perspectives on deafness.

destruction on patterns of prejudice and group conflict. Second, after a discussion of how prejudice at times involves degrading parallels between humans and animals, I have included a section on speciesism in which I address the question of whether attitudes toward nonhuman animals ought to be considered a form of prejudice. Although some will find inclusion of this topic surprising, eminent scholars in other disciplines have argued that speciesism shares many parallels with other forms of prejudice (e.g., Dawkins, 2003; Singer, 2002). A psychological analysis of this proposal may deepen people's understanding of prejudice by situating it in the context of humans' relation with the natural world and by illuminating the pervasiveness of the human tendency to devalue the other. Chapter 9 concludes the book with a discussion of prejudice reduction and collective action, showing the movement from attitudes to social action.

Consideration of the perspective of disadvantaged groups is integrated throughout the book rather than included in a separate chapter. Although either approach has merit, it is my hope that by integrating this material throughout the book, the message that prejudice is an issue that influences everyone will become especially clear. Just as treating women in psychology as a separate topic from psychology in general falsely implies that "real psychology" is not about women, separating the target's perspective on prejudice from other issues risks misrepresenting the nature of prejudice by implying that members of advantaged groups can be understood with one set of principles and members of disadvantaged groups can be understood with another. This implication is false, as I hope becomes clear throughout the book. In addition, including discussion of the targets of prejudice throughout the book may best communicate the fact that it is often interactional dynamics between advantaged and disadvantaged group members that can sustain or challenge prejudice and inequality.

In each chapter, I consider the place of religion in potentially shaping people's beliefs and attitudes. Until recently, research on religion and prejudice has been conducted outside the mainstream study of prejudice, and the theoretical basis for the work (where it existed) tended to be ad hoc or derived from religion rather than psychology. For this reason, books on prejudice that include some discussion of religion tend to present it in a short, separate section. In my own work, I have argued that general theories of prejudice have much to say about connections between religiosity and prejudice, and so I have integrated discussion of religion throughout the book. The theme that emerges is that religion is an important social variable that needs serious attention in the study of prejudice.

Applications of the theories emphasize prejudice in Canada and the United States, although some international examples are provided throughout where they are especially useful in illuminating key processes of prejudice.

In addition, the work reviewed is primarily derived from North America and Europe. Although a genuinely international approach to the psychology of prejudice would be a welcome contribution to the literature, I felt that my hands were full with the task of describing and reflecting on local problems and scholarship. I hope that people who teach courses related to prejudice in these contexts will find this book to be useful reading for students and will themselves enjoy reflecting on the novel topics included and that anyone interested in the problem of prejudice may find the information discussed helpful.

1

DEFINING PREJUDICE

On November 4, 2008, the world watched as Barack Obama was elected president of the United States. Obama's messages of inclusiveness, hope, and genuine freedom and democracy apparently resonated with those in the American public who brought him to victory and also among others around the world who were inspired by the humanity of his vision. His election was significant not only politically but also symbolically because he is the first president of the United States of African heritage. His election appeared to galvanize hope that despite the history of slavery and exploitation of African American people in the United States and the current problems of ongoing economic and social inequality (Semyonov & Lewin-Epstein, 2009), the trend toward equal opportunity and intergroup respect continues. During his inauguration, Obama (2008) expressed optimism that "the old hatreds shall someday pass; that the lines of tribe shall soon dissolve; that as the world grows smaller, our common humanity shall reveal itself."

Just months before Obama's election, many Canadians were moved when Prime Minister Stephen Harper apologized to Canada's First Nations citizens for the abuses they endured in residential schools during the 19th and 20th centuries. In these schools, European settlers attempted to eradicate native culture. First Nations parents were forced (sometimes with threat of arrest) to give guardianship of their children to government-funded, church-run schools where the students would stay 10 months of the year. There, they were exposed to "industrial education" in which farm labor and domestic labor were mixed with education in Christianity and the English and French languages. Now, First Nations people in Canada face considerable economic and social disadvantage (Maxim, White, Beavon, & Whitehead, 2001), and they are faced with the existence of ongoing prejudice (see Esses, Haddock, & Zanna, 1993; Morrison, Morrison, Harriman, & Jewell, 2008).

During the apology, Harper publicly acknowledged the wrongness of the infamous goal of "killing the Indian in the child" and admitted that abuses of all sorts were endemic in the schools. The apology offered by Harper was emotionally significant for many Canadians because it acknowledged that First Nations people have experienced significant oppression for too long and it seemed to provide a sense of hope for positive changes among those listening to the apology. For some listeners, more powerful yet were the words of then Assembly of First Nations Chief Phil Fontaine, himself a survivor of sexual abuse in a residential school, who responded to the apology in the House of Commons. He spoke with pride of the voices of First Nations people who prompted the apology by exposing the extent and illegitimacy of the past abuses, and he affirmed the positive role that First Nations peoples play in shaping the Canadian identity (Diebel, 2008).

As the election of Barack Obama and the words of Harper and Fontaine make clear, positive change is occurring with respect to the denunciation of prejudice and movement toward equality and respect for all. Yet challenges persist. On July 16, 2009, police officers in Cambridge, Massachusetts, responded to a phone call about a possible break-in at a residential home. On arriving at the home, they confronted the man who had entered the home. After angry words were exchanged, the officer apprehended the man for disorderly conduct and took him into police custody. The man arrested was Henry Louis Gates Jr., a Yale-educated Harvard professor, winner of almost 50 honorary degrees and many awards for academic and social justice work, and director of the W. E. B. Du Bois Institute for African and African American Research. He was arrested in his own home, which he had entered with difficulty because the front door had jammed. Gates is a Black man, and the incident sparked much debate about racial profiling by police ("Henry Louis Gates, Jr.," 2009).

Although whether the arrest of Gates was appropriate or involved an element of bias is a matter of debate, there is no question that the ensuing reactions revealed the ongoing awareness of racial issues in the United States. Moreover, other events have shown that undeniable prejudice and troubled relations between groups persist in North America. For example, shortly before the election of Obama, controversy erupted when, after nooses were found hanging from a so-called White tree at a school in Jena, Louisiana, six Black teens were charged with attempted murder for beating up a White teen who had apparently been using racial insults. Although the charges were later reduced, all six boys were convicted in relation to the assault ("Jena Six," 2009). In Canada, although Harper and Fontaine spoke of healing in the relationship between native and non-native Canadians, First Nations people protested the lack of action by the Canadian government on unresolved land claims (in which non-native people continue to use and develop land that may be rightfully claimed by First Nations people) and First Nations people continue to face economic disadvantage and prejudice (Maxim et al., 2001; Morrison et al., 2008).

Around the world, conflicts between ethnic, religious, and national groups continue to erupt, and inequality between groups with respect to access to wealth, education, and health persists. Within communities, myriad manifestations of prejudice can be observed, such as the use of jokes that perpetuate stereotypes, the tendency of children to ostracize classmates who are different, insensitivity to cultural traditions that sometimes occurs in the workplace, and so forth. Such problems target people who are different not only in ethnicity but in numerous other ways as well, such as age, body size or appearance, education level, gender, intellectual ability, religion, physical ability, sexual orientation, and so on. The chapters that follow explore the nature and causes of prejudice and show how it is entwined with ongoing inequality and intergroup strife. In this chapter, the journey begins with an attempt to understand the nature of prejudice.

WHAT IS PREJUDICE?

Some forms of prejudice are easy to recognize, such as the venomous views of members of hate groups. More commonly, prejudice is subtle and varied in its manifestations, and people understandably disagree about what constitutes prejudice. Consider some examples of people's responses to gay men, lesbians, and bisexual people. Some people have respectful attitudes, some shrug off sexual orientation as unimportant, and others are open about holding disdain for sexual minorities. Some people claim to be nonprejudiced yet endorse stereotypes, such as the belief that gay men are effeminate and lesbians are tough. There are those who view such stereotypes as simplistic and hope to be nonprejudiced, yet feel awkward or nervous when interacting with people of sexual minority. For some people, sexual minorities raise concerns about the violation of religious values. Which of these responses involve prejudice? As the examples make clear, people's attitudes toward other people are complicated. They can be obvious or subtle, clear or ambivalent, passionate or dispassionate. For this reason, defining prejudice is not a simple task. Therefore, before attempting to do so, I discuss some characteristics of prejudice that recent research has revealed.

Prejudice Has Multiple Components

When asked to define *prejudice*, some people refer to the literal meaning of the word, "prejudgment." Making assumptions about others in the absence of knowledge about them—that is, *stereotyping*—is one aspect of prejudice. However, as the preceding examples of responses to sexual minorities make clear, attitudes toward others can also include emotional responses to people or concerns about ways in which groups may violate one's values. The various forms of responses that people sometimes have to others, such as stereotypic judgments, emotions, and concerns about value threat, are considered components, or different aspects, of prejudice (Esses et al., 1993). As discussed later, each of these aspects of prejudice involves some complexities.

Stereotypes

The term *stereotype* has been traced to 1798, when it was used to refer to the reproductions made by a printing press. In 1922, journalist Walter Lippman likened the mental images that people sometimes have of members of other groups to such reproductions—each member of the group is seen as the same, just as a printing press creates identical copies (Ashmore & del Boca, 1981). Stereotypes involve these images of groups. Specifically, they are beliefs that members of a group possess particular characteristics, such as personality traits, typical behaviors, interests, and so on.

Many stereotypes are consensual in nature, being widely endorsed within a culture. Even people who think that stereotypes are inaccurate can usually readily identify the content of major cultural stereotypes, such as images of men, women, ethnic minorities, elderly people, gay men and lesbians, and so forth because these stereotypes have been widely communicated within the culture (e.g., Devine, 1989). Stereotypes that purport to describe groups are referred to as *descriptive stereotypes*. For example, for many years Hollywood films have communicated a stereotype of Arab people as aggressive and threatening (Shaheen, 2009). Descriptive stereotypes, when widely endorsed, can lead to systematic forms of discrimination in which groups are treated differently. For example, it may be because the stereotype of Arab people as aggressive was already part of the culture that, after the tragedy of September 11, 2001, a majority of Americans supported profiling U.S. citizens of Arab background and requiring them to undergo special security checks at airports (Whitely & Kite, 2006).

In addition to providing descriptions of groups, stereotypes sometimes prescribe those characteristics that people think a group ought to have. For example, whereas descriptive gender stereotypes describe men as brave, prescriptive stereotypes imply that men *should* be courageous (Eagly & Karau, 2002). Prescriptive gender stereotypes imply that women should be kind, sexy, and so on. In fact, there is evidence that overweight women, compared with overweight men, are especially targeted for prejudiced attitudes and disrespectful treatment (e.g., Fouts & Burggraf, 2000). As with descriptive stereotypes, prescriptive stereotypes can be quite consequential. For example, people who endorse prescriptive gender stereotypes (i.e., the belief that men should be masculine and women should be feminine) tend to discriminate in work settings against women who show traditionally masculine qualities such as assertiveness and leadership ability (Gill, 2004).

Stereotypes can also shape how people perceive individual others. Stereotyping occurs when people's impressions of other individuals are colored by the lens of stereotypes. For example, consider different ways of understanding a simple behavior performed by a hypothetical person, Chris: After paying for lunch at a restaurant, Chris pointed out to the waiter that he had returned insufficient change.

What was your impression of Chris's behavior? Was it assertive? Was it complaining, or cheap, or reasonable? If people think that the behavior is assertive if performed by Christopher but complaining if performed by Christina, then the biasing effect of gender stereotypes on impressions of other people has been demonstrated.

Research has shown that stereotypes do shape how people perceive others, and the same behavior is sometimes seen differently depending on the identity of the person who engages in it. Some early work showed, for example, that White Americans interpreted a shove between two men as innocuous when a White man shoved a Black man but as violent when a Black man shoved a White man (Duncan, 1976). More recent work has shown that this sort of thing still occurs, and moreover, even seemingly nonprejudiced people who believe that stereotypes are inaccurate sometimes seem to be influenced by them in the way that they understand and respond to others (Amodio, 2008; Devine, 1989). That is, people who reject descriptive stereotypes as false or simplistic may still sometimes perceive individual people through the lens of these rejected stereotypes. For this reason, a theme in the current understanding of stereotyping is that cultural stereotypes can seep into people's consciousness in insidious ways and bias the impressions they form of others without people realizing it is occurring (Devine, 1989). Consequently, a good deal of current research on stereotyping has attempted to differentiate between relatively unconscious processes (that may involve stereotyping) and more conscious mechanisms (that can mitigate against stereotyping) involved in the task of forming impressions of people (e.g., Payne & Bishara, 2009). This research is examined in later chapters.

Emotions

Gay men and lesbians sometimes talk about the signs of nervousness they see in others when their sexual orientation becomes known. People with visible disfigurements at times have to deal with signs of discomfort from others. Elderly and disabled people may experience awkward pity. In 1954, Allport famously wrote, "Defeated intellectually, prejudice lingers emotionally" (Allport, 1954/1979, p. 328). He was responding to the theme that seemed to emerge in 100 essays written by university students about their experiences with minority groups. The majority of students, he noted, wrote about a conflict between their egalitarian values and residual, often emotionally based, prejudices. For example, one student is quoted as writing, "I try to see only the good points in Jewish people, but even though I try hard to overcome my prejudice, I know it always will be there—thanks to my parents' early influence," and another wrote,

> Intellectually, I am firmly convinced that this prejudice against Italians is unjustified. And in my present behavior to Italian friends I try to lean over backwards to counteract the attitude. But it is remarkable how strong a hold it has on me. (Allport, 1954/1979, p. 327)

Apparently, only one-tenth of the essays contained unrepentant prejudice. The remaining essays contained greater ambivalence, with half of the authors writing that they had critically examined their prejudiced beliefs and declared them to be unfounded, and most of these people discussing their desire to rid themselves of their prejudices.

Since Allport's time, researchers have identified a number of ways by which prejudice persists in the form of emotional responses to others (e.g., Smith, 1993). This work has shown that Allport (1954/1979) was correct when he claimed that prejudice that was "defeated intellectually" can "linger emotionally" (p. 328). In exploring how and why emotional prejudice may linger, some researchers look to brain systems that may explain persistent emotional reactions, whereas others look to aspects of the social structure that may shape how people respond emotionally to others, and still other researchers look at the interaction between these processes.

The relatively new research discipline of social neuroscience examines the brain processes involved in people's reactions to other people (Amodio, 2008). For example, some research has shown that emotional responses to members of other ethnic groups may reflect the conditioning of relatively ancient brain mechanisms that generate feelings of fear and surprise (e.g., Stanley, Phelps, & Banaji, 2008). This conditioning likely occurs early in life through exposure to negative media images of groups and so on. By implication, people may find that when they encounter others who are different, uncomfortable feelings arise spontaneously and seemingly inexplicably. Such feelings tend to taint interpersonal encounters because they can lead people to show awkward nonverbal mannerisms that are likely to be detected by others (Dovidio & Gaertner, 2004, 2008). Moreover, because there is no readily available explanation for the feelings, they may be attributed to the other (e.g., "Something about that person makes me uncomfortable") rather than the self ("Something about my history makes me respond in this way"). Related theory and research are examined in Chapters 3 and 7 of this volume.

A different line of research has suggested that the social status of groups, or people's perceptions of this status, may shape the emotional reactions people have to members of those groups (Fiske, Cuddy, Glick, & Xu, 2002). For example, sexism may involve feelings of resentment or hostility when it is directed at women in high-status careers but rather different paternalistic emotions when it is directed at women who work in supportive roles. Attitudes toward elderly people who no longer generate income have been shown to include feelings of pity, prejudice against welfare recipients sometimes reflects contempt for their social position, and so on (Fiske et al., 2002). This type of research has suggested that dynamics of social life, like inequality, may shape the emotional nature of prejudice. People may experience feelings such as admiration or envy in response to high-status groups but feel contempt or pity toward lower status groups (Fiske et al., 2002). It is helpful to recognize these patterns of emotional reactions because distinct emotional responses to groups generate predictable patterns of treatment (Cuddy, Fiske, & Glick, 2007). For example, people who react to others with resentment may endorse actively harmful responses (e.g., backlash against or harassment of groups that are gaining in status in the workplace), whereas responses of pity can generate more passive forms of harm or neglect, such as the exclusion of elderly people from places of work. Theory and research on this perspective are elaborated in Chapter 4.

Values

Attitudes toward other groups can also be experienced largely in terms of values and, more specifically, people's beliefs about how groups either uphold or threaten their ideals (e.g., Rokeach & Rothman, 1965). For example, some people express pleasure that immigrants promote the value of diversity, whereas other individuals are concerned that immigrants threaten their traditional cultural values. Similarly, some people believe that gay men and lesbians promote values such as freedom, whereas others express concern that these groups threaten conventional family values. The phrase *symbolic beliefs* refers to "all thoughts about the relation between social groups and basic values and norms"

(Esses et al., 1993, p. 147). Symbolic beliefs can be positive or negative. Positive symbolic beliefs involve beliefs that a group promotes one's values, whereas negative symbolic beliefs involve beliefs that a group threatens one's ideals.

Research has shown that people who hold negative symbolic beliefs about other groups tend to have more negative attitudes toward the group (Esses et al., 1993). For example, a study of Americans' attitudes toward Rwandan immigrants found that people who were concerned about threats to cultural values tended to report less liking and respect for and more resentment of Rwandans than did people who were not concerned about value-based threat (Stephan, Renfro, Esses, Stephan, & Martin, 2005). Similarly, people who have positive symbolic beliefs about gay men and lesbians (e.g., those who believe that they promote tolerance, acceptance, and freedom) have more positive attitudes toward these groups than do people who hold negative symbolic beliefs (e.g., the belief that gay men and lesbians block family values; Mohipp & Morry, 2004). In addition, the belief that gay men and lesbians threaten one's values has been found to be associated with a tendency to endorse discrimination against these groups in employment contexts (Jackson & Esses, 1997). Because symbolic beliefs are rooted in people's deeply held values, they are likely to be viewed as warranted by those who hold them. At the same time, they tend to be linked to other kinds of evaluative bias and to discrimination. For this reason, they have been described as one aspect of prejudice, along with stereotypes and emotional responses to groups (Esses et al., 1993).

Prejudice Can Be Indirect

Another characteristic of prejudice is that it may at times be expressed indirectly, for example, through attitudes toward social programs and policies that affect groups differently. Social programs or policies that are aimed at creating equality, such as affirmative action and same-sex marriage, tend to generate spirited debates. Psychologists who study prejudice have participated in such discussions by exploring the bases of people's attitudes toward these issues, with an eye to determining whether attitudes toward groups play a role in shaping attitudes toward programs or policies that affect groups.

One position is that opposition to programs that are aimed at creating equality results from prejudice against beneficiary groups (McConahay, 1986; Sears & Henry, 2003, 2005). From this perspective, some people experience a kind of prejudice that is rooted in negative feelings toward minorities that are socialized early in life and concerns that some minorities threaten conventional individualistic cultural values like hard work and initiative (Sears & Henry, 2003, 2005). At the same time, because most people either genuinely want to be nonprejudiced or at least want to avoid being seen by others as prejudiced, the prejudice is expressed symbolically in terms of the desire to protect conventional values. For example, people may explain their opposition to affirmative action as resulting from the desire to protect the conventional procedures of giving benefits like jobs or pay increases to those who have earned the most merit. Other politicized views, like the beliefs that inequality is a thing of the past, minorities are pushing too hard for change, and programs like affirmative action are not needed, have similarly been viewed as indirect expressions of prejudice (McConahay, 1986). The terms *symbolic prejudice* and *modern prejudice* have been used to describe the kind of prejudice that is said to be hidden behind other, more politically focused views.

A critique of this position is that people who are described as holding symbolic or modern prejudice are not prejudiced per se but rather tend to be politically conservative and so agree with political beliefs about the conservation of traditions (e.g., Sniderman, Piazza, Tetlock, & Kendrick, 1991). From this point of view, things like opposition to affirmative action and concerns about minority groups' demands for change are not expressions of prejudice but rather are principled objections to procedures that are thought to be unfair. It is argued that politically conservative people tend to strongly endorse conventional means of achieving social gains that emphasize individual merit, and so they see things like affirmative action as inappropriate. From this side of the debate, the constructs of symbolic and modern prejudice unreasonably label political conservatives as prejudiced.

Evidence has supported both perspectives. Evidence in support of the symbolic or modern prejudice perspective has shown, for example, that attitudes toward affirmative action correlate with a variety of indices of prejudice, with more prejudiced persons tending to be more opposed to it (Crosby, Iyer, Clayton, & Downing, 2003). Evidence consistent with the "principled conservatism" critique shows that people particularly dislike affirmative action programs that clearly deviate from the principle of merit in terms of the way in which they are implemented (e.g., Bobocel, Son Hing, Davey, Stanley, & Zanna, 1998), implying that nonprejudiced persons may oppose affirmative action not because of prejudice but because it is viewed as unfair procedurally.

Some recent evidence has suggested that such seemingly principled objections to affirmative action may at times be disguised reflections of prejudice, however. Blatz and Ross (2009) examined how willing people would be to support a social program, government reparations to victims of child abuse, depending on whether the victims were First Nations or European Canadians. They found that people who scored high on a measure of modern prejudice (i.e., those who believed that prejudice is a thing of the past, that programs like affirmative action are not needed) were less supportive of programs to aid First Nations people than they were of programs to aid people of European background. Because they opposed the social program only when it benefitted First Nations people, this research suggested that it was not merely attitudes toward the program that influenced endorsement of it but also views about the beneficiary group that shaped willingness to help people through the social program. Some people who strongly oppose programs to help underprivileged groups may, for example, be inclined to hold those groups in particular responsible for their problems and hence be unwilling to help them (Reyna, Henry, Korfmacher, & Tucker, 2006).

The fact that people's views on social programs can mask prejudice does not mean that they always do, nor does the view that conservative political ideas can be part of this mask mean that only people on the political right hide their prejudice, for at least two reasons. First, there is a difference between social conservatism (the desire to preserve traditions) and economic conservatism (preference for free markets and lack of government interference), and social conservatism more than economic conservatism seems to relate to prejudice (Roney, 2009; Roney & Alexander, 2002). Second, other research has made it clear that everyone has the potential for either prejudice or nonprejudice, but the way in which prejudice manifests tends to be shaped by people's political orientation (Gaertner & Dovidio, 1986; Son Hing, Chung-Yan, Hamilton, & Zanna, 2008). For example, Son Hing et al. (2008) found that people whose values tended to lean to the political right (toward political conservatism) were more likely than people whose values leaned to the political left (toward liberalism) to endorse beliefs that groups are inherently unequal. However, conservatives and liberals were equally likely to discriminate against a member of another group when they could do so under the guise of some legitimate-seeming justification.

The basic point is that prejudice can be hidden behind beliefs or actions that appear reasonable. Discussions about controversial issues, such as whether affirmative action should be supported, are difficult in part because people's positions can be shaped by fair considerations, prejudice, or both. This may be true of many issues of contemporary social debate, such as whether Sikh children should be permitted to attend public school carrying a kirpan, the ceremonial sword worn by devotees; whether Jehovah's Witnesses ought to be legally permitted to reject life-saving blood transfusions for their children; and whether immigrants should be expected to adopt mainstream customs and traditions.

Prejudice Rationalizes Inequality

Ask yourself this: What group is stereotyped as being more emotionally than intellectually inclined, in tune with nature, somewhat childlike, and better at following than leading? What group comes to mind? Women? Aboriginal people? Children? People with intellectual challenges? Hippies? Golden retrievers? All of these answers (including the last one) have been provided to me by students when I have posed this question, and all of them make sense. All of these groups are at times viewed as being more emotional and connected to simple things than intellectual and effectual.

This illustration raises two points about the nature of prejudice. First, many groups are stereotyped in similar ways. Women, natives, children, people with intellectual challenges, hippies (and even animals, such as dogs) tend to be viewed as more emotional than intellectual. Cultural stereotypes of other minority or disadvantaged groups have similarities as well. For example, African Americans in the United States and First Nations people in Canada are both stereotyped as aggressive and irresponsible. In many parts of the world, Asian and Jewish people are both stereotyped as hard working and competent, if sly. Elderly people and poor people are both stereotyped as lacking in competence (Fiske et al., 2002), and so on. Why are many groups stereotyped similarly? The answer rests in the second point of the example: All of the human groups included in the example I offered (women, natives, children, people with intellectual challenges, hippies) have less power, status, and respect in society than do other groups (and animals are typically viewed as less important than humans; see Chapter 8, this volume).

Why do groups that share a social status have similar stereotypes associated with them? One answer to this question could be that groups do actually differ in the ways described by the stereotypes, and so they end up with comparable social standing. For example, is it true that women are more interpersonally oriented than men and men more achievement oriented than women? If so, is that why men have higher average earnings than women? This explanation is challenged by evidence that many stereotypes do not jibe with reality. For example, evidence has contradicted the stereotype that women are more social and talkative than men. Researchers recently had several large samples of men and women in both the United States and Mexico wear recorders for several days that unobtrusively recorded their conversations. Contrary to the stereotype, women did not talk more than men. Both men and women used, on average, about 16,000 words per day (Mehl, Vazire, Ramirez-Esparza, Slatcher, & Pennebaker, 2009). Similarly, although women are very often stereotyped as being more emotional than men, research measuring emotions physiologically has shown that in fact men and women do not differ on average in their tendency to feel emotions (LaFrance & Banaji, 1992); they probably only show them differently. The extent to which various other stereotypes may contain a grain of truth is debated (e.g., Jussim, Cain, Crawford, Harber, & Cohen, 2009), but this type of evidence shows that some very commonly endorsed stereotypes are probably inaccurate.

Another explanation for the fact that groups who share a social status share a stereotype is that stereotypes are formed by people's need to explain and rationalize why some groups have lower status than others in terms of income, social power, and the like (e.g., Jost & Banaji, 1994). Recall the stereotype described at the opening of this section (emotional, childlike, in tune with nature). Although it has parallels with the stereotypes of many groups (women, natives, people with intellectual challenges, hippies), this was in fact the common stereotype of African American people during the time of slavery (Sampson, 1999). In a social system that would otherwise have been seen as absurd and cruel, this stereotype seems to have provided psychological justification. The belief that slaves were emotionally but not intellectually inclined rationalized their being denied education, the stereotype that they were in tune with nature provided justification for their exclusion to barnlike housing, and so on. From this point of view, the stereotype was part of the ethos surrounding slavery because it served to explain and justify an otherwise nonsensical and painful system.

Research has tended to support this position. In many countries, higher status groups are associated with stereotypes suggestive of an achievement orientation (e.g., efficient, responsible, productive, active, ambitious), whereas lower status groups tend to be stereotyped as having an interpersonal orientation (e.g., emotional, friendly, extraverted, ethical; Conway, Pizzamiglio, & Mount, 1996; Eagly, 1987; Eagly & Steffen, 1984; Jost, Kivetz, Rubini, Guermandi, & Mosso, 2005). Moreover, there is also evidence that people are more likely to stereotype groups in these ways when they feel a need to justify the social system. For example, Jost et al. (2005) showed that people's tendency to stereotype higher status groups as having an achievement orientation and lower status groups as having an interpersonal orientation became more pronounced after they were given information that suggested that their country was declining in its social and economic position relative to other countries. Apparently, when people were feeling that the value and legitimacy of their country was in question, they had a greater need to support it by accepting stereotypes that imply that status inequalities in their country are reasonable or fair. If stereotypes simply reflected reality, people in the research would have been no more or less likely to endorse them when their social system was challenged. Instead, the research showed that stereotyping served a psychological need—the need to justify inequality.

Prejudice Can Involve Attitudes That Seem Positive

Women are sometimes stereotyped as being kind, empathic, helpful, good at communication, and ethical (Eagly & Mladinic, 1989; Eagly, Mladinic, & Otto, 1991). Men are sometimes viewed as brave, calm, effective protectors (Glick & Fiske, 1999). Elderly people tend to be stereotyped as warm and likable, whereas Jewish and Asian people are stereotyped as being capable and industrious (Fiske et al., 2002). The positive nature of these attributes may seem, on the surface, to challenge the idea that stereotyping is problematic. Yet, for all the positive stereotypes that can be identified, there are also negative counterparts: Women are overly sensitive and tend to sexually tease and then control men (Glick & Fiske, 1996), men act like babies when they are sick (Glick, Lameiras, & Rodriguez Castro, 2002), elderly people lack competence, Jewish and Asian people are cool and competitive (Fiske et al., 2002), and so on.

Also, positive stereotypes may serve to perpetuate inequality. Stereotypes that depict women as supportive, kind, and nurturing have not shattered the glass ceiling, brought women's salaries on par with men's, or eliminated violence against women. Instead, these stereotypes imply that women are more suited to caregiving or teaching roles than to higher status positions of leadership (Eagly, 1987). This logic is true of positive stereotypes of other groups as well. For example, seemingly positive stereotypes of some ethnic minority men as athletic may limit their opportunities or bias their evaluations in nonphysical domains, such as academics.

It may be the seemingly harmless nature of such "positive" stereotypes that allows them to be continually communicated in a society and thus gives them their power to reinforce and reinvent inequality. In fact, it is not uncommon for people to express these kinds of stereotypes even about those they love (Glick & Fiske, 1996, 1999; Jackman, 1994). Because men and women love one another, live together, and depend on one another for survival, stereotypes of men and women seem on the surface to be harmless, yet they imply that each gender has deficiencies that are matched by the others' strengths. For example, the belief that women are weaker becomes framed in terms of affection and care in the view that women ought to be cherished and cared for materially, and beliefs that men are suited to domains of achievement and power fit well with the view that they are emotionally lacking and need women to hold them together.

Although the positive side of stereotypes may appear innocuous to some, people who are stereotyped are likely to see through their positive gloss. This was demonstrated by Czopp (2008) in an experiment in which African American and European American research participants observed videotaped recordings of interactions in which people discussed issues related to diversity. The video observed by half of the participants showed a White person endorsing a seemingly positive stereotype of African American people (that they are athletic); the video observed by the other half of the participants was identical except for the omission of this stereotype. Both White and Black participants rated the person in the video as less friendly and more prejudiced in the condition in which the positive stereotype was expressed. However, African American participants were especially likely to do so, and they were also more likely to view the person as being unconstructive with regard to relations between ethnic groups. Apparently, the double-edged sword of the positive stereotype is evident, especially to those who are stereotyped.

To summarize, prejudice has several characteristics that help to reveal its nature. Prejudice comprises a mix of stereotypes, emotional responses to groups, and perceptions of value differences or threat. People do not always admit their prejudices openly but sometimes express them in indirect or disguised ways, such as through policy attitudes, and people are not always aware of how their responses to others seem to reflect prejudice. Prejudice is related to inequality: Stereotypes can serve to rationalize and maintain the social status quo, and this may be especially true of seemingly positive beliefs about others. In a nutshell, prejudice is not just hate; it involves a complex mix of responses to others, aspects of which are quite prevalent.

A DEFINITION OF PREJUDICE

On the basis of this analysis of the characteristics of prejudice, I define *prejudice* as a disrespectful attitude toward or negative evaluative response to groups as a whole or toward individuals on the basis of their group membership. By defining prejudice in terms of disrespectful attitudes, seemingly positive yet problematic attitudes are included. For example, paternalistic stereotypes that imply that women are loving but not effective are not respectful because they imply that women are less capable than men. Because negative evaluative responses to a group are included in the definition, unpleasant feelings such as discomfort or anxiety are considered a form of prejudice even if they are subtle or coexist with positive beliefs about others or a desire to be non-prejudiced. Although emotions such as discomfort and anxiety are common, including them in a definition of prejudice is warranted because they involve ways in which people respond to others on the basis of group membership alone, and it also has the benefit of putting such experiences on the table for careful examination.

This definition of prejudice is silent with regard to the identity of the attitude holder and the target of the attitude with the exception that the attitude or response is directed at a group or an individual on the basis of group membership. Therefore, this definition allows for the possibility that majority-group members can be prejudiced against minorities, minority-group members can be prejudiced against majorities, and both minority- and majority-group members can even be prejudiced against their own group. Although the definition of prejudice offered here allows for the fact that it can exist in both advantaged and disadvantaged groups, it also points to the idea that prejudice is not independent of the nature of equality or inequality between groups. Rather, as is discussed throughout this book, prejudice and inequality are linked in many ways.

For example, disrespectful attitudes may be especially likely to develop toward disadvantaged groups because of people's exposure to their disadvantage, and this differential respect may contribute to ongoing discrimination (e.g., Jackson, Esses, & Burris, 2001). Moreover, prejudice among advantaged group members is especially consequential because it is more likely to sustain inequality than is prejudice among disadvantaged group members. A male executive may feel annoyed or hurt if he hears a sexist comment from a female employee, but she may be underpaid or without work if he allows sexism to influence his treatment of her. Although minorities can indeed be prejudiced against majorities, their power to influence the lives of majorities is typically limited (although not inconsequential) compared with the ability of majorities to influence the lives of minorities. For these reasons, it is important for prejudice to be considered in the context of the bigger picture that includes issues of discrimination and privilege.

DISCRIMINATION

Prejudice is perhaps most problematic when it manifests in *discrimination*, the differential treatment of groups or individuals on the basis of their group membership. Different forms of discrimination exist. *Interpersonal discrimination* occurs when individuals treat members of other groups differently because of their group memberships. The boss who negatively evaluates gay employees, the teacher who gives preferential treatment to children from affluent families, and the landlord who refuses to rent to certain groups all show interpersonal discrimination. Interpersonal discrimination persists in some shocking ways. For example, it has been documented in the medical system, with findings that ethnic minority individuals are less likely to receive needed treatments regardless of their ability to pay for them (B. D. Smedley, Stith, & Nelson, 2003). Apparently, some physicians are less inclined to offer referrals to specialists for minority people and more inclined to provide treatments of lesser quality. Sadly, research has shown that interpersonal discrimination exists even within families. For example, some parents discriminate against their children on the basis of their weight, being more willing to offer financial support for higher education to their slimmer children despite there being no reason on the basis of academic accomplishments or career aspirations (Crandall, 1991, 1995).

Another type of discrimination, *institutional discrimination*, involves policies or procedures in an organization that systematically disadvantage some groups. For example, the cosmetic company L'Oreal was recently found guilty of discrimination for their policy of excluding women of color from promoting their shampoo (Chrisafis, 2007). History provides powerful examples of institutional discrimination. The infamous Jim Crow laws in the United States between 1876 and 1965 prescribed racial segregation in schools and public settings, whereas in Canada before 1960 First Nations people were not legally permitted to vote in federal elections. Institutional discrimination is not a thing of the past, however. To give just two examples, religious profiling has been sanctioned at U.S. border crossings (e.g., Garcia, 2005), and in the Canadian province of Ontario, the two school authorities, public (secular) and Roman Catholic (Government of Ontario, 2009) receive public funding although other faith-based schools do not, a practice deemed discriminatory by the United Nations (Human Rights Committee, 2006).

Yet another form of discrimination, *cultural discrimination*, occurs when a dominant group defines those cultural values and norms that prevail and disadvantages some groups on this basis (Jones, 1997). A pointed example of cultural discrimination was revealed recently in the small community of Herouxville, Quebec, Canada, when the town council published a list of community standards and norms that immigrant families would be expected to uphold. An English translation of the original French document contained many statements suggesting limits on religious minorities' freedoms such as "No locale is made available for prayer or any other form of incantation." Others were deemed demeaning to Muslims in particular. For example, the proclamation that "the only time you may mask or cover your face is during Halloween" not only attempted to ban a religiously significant practice, but also demeaned Muslim people by equating this practice with the more frivolous custom of wearing Halloween masks. At the same time that it demeaned Muslim practices, the document promoted the public expression of Christian traditions, saying, for example, that in local schools, "You will possibly see Christmas Decorations or Christmas Trees" (Herouxville Town Charter, 2010, para. 12). Although the town council argued that the intent was to aid the successful integration of immigrants by providing information, the publication caused a stir internationally, and the standards were criticized as being ethnocentric and xenophobic (i.e., showing a fear or contempt of foreigners).

Cultural discrimination does not require its participants to be overtly prejudiced, however. Its importance rests in its effects. Regardless of the attitudes of the authors of the community standards (Herouxville Town Charter, 2010), it is clear that this document communicated cultural discrimination in the way it advantaged Christian traditions and disadvantaged others. In general, whether or not people are clearly prejudiced, they may participate in cultural discrimination if by virtue of belonging to a majority or advantaged group they have the ability to define what is considered normal, valuable, or good in their society. It is only in relatively recent years that communities in North America have become increasingly aware of the ways in which they have perpetuated cultural discrimination by giving special status to certain religious holidays, by producing media representations of the so-called normal family, and so on.

PRIVILEGE

Discrimination is important to recognize because it is part of the package within which prejudice and inequality rest. So, too, is privilege. In North America, as around the world, groups differ in their access to money, social status, health, and other resources (e.g., D. A. Green & Kesselman, 2006) and in their ability to define cultural norms, values, and practices. If some groups are disadvantaged in terms of access to finances, health, power, and ability to define and practice cultural traditions, then it follows that other groups must be privileged in these ways. The fact that women are underrepresented in board rooms means that men are overrepresented; the fact that people of color lack large supportive networks in positions of power in government has meaning because White people do have sizable supportive "clubs" that facilitate their success; if low-income families are at a disadvantage with respect to access to expensive higher education, children from higher income families must be at an advantage in gaining admission to university and college, and so on. In general, the existence of disadvantage has a logical corollary: Some groups must receive a disproportionate share of advantages.

Inequality has many implications for the material, physical, and psychological well-being of members of minority and disadvantaged groups (e.g., Ong, Fuller-Rowell, & Burrow, 2009). Less recognized are the implications for advantaged groups. By reflecting on her advantages as a White woman, Peggy McIntosh (2003, p. 191) came to think of privilege as "an invisible weightless knapsack of special provisions, maps, passports, codebooks, visas, clothes, tools and bank checks" that helps her navigate the world. Imagine traveling in a foreign country with a backpack full of maps, tips about places to stay and eat, language translation tips, and helpful contacts. Now imagine traveling without such help. This is the difference between having and not having privilege.

The essence of privilege is that it comes from mere group membership. Because privileges are inherited rather than earned, people tend to overlook them. For example, when I was a young woman, I was aware of gender inequality, but it was not until several years later that I came to understand the many advantages I have as a White person, a person of middle-class background, an able-bodied person, and so on. People may also be motivated to deny their own privileges. Acknowledging that privilege exists at a group level implies that one may have benefited personally from it. Recognizing this requires that one critically evaluate the belief that society functions fairly and also the belief that everything one personally has, one deserves. Perhaps for this reason, recognizing that one has been influenced by privilege has been shown to cause some psychological distress. Branscombe (1998) asked men and women to think about ways in which their gender group was either privileged or disadvantaged compared with the other group. She found that men felt worse about themselves as men after thinking about male privilege, but they felt better about themselves as individuals after thinking about the disadvantages men experience on the basis of their gender. Because thinking about ways in which one's group has been privileged may evoke guilt and other uncomfortable feelings, people may be motivated to deny it to avoid this discomfort. In fact, some evidence has shown that when people are challenged to think about their privileges, they show an increased tendency to express prejudice as a way of restoring a sense of the fairness of inequality, although this may occur only among people who are emotionally identified with their group (Branscombe, Schmitt, & Schiffhauer, 2007).

The discussion of prejudice so far has shown that prejudice is multifaceted and that some seemingly benign attitudes may be forms of prejudice. Also, it has been suggested that prejudice is entwined with related issues of discrimination, inequality, and privilege and that people often remain unaware of their advantages and others' disadvantages. In the final section of this chapter, I illustrate these various and related issues through an examination of the problem of audism.

THE CASE OF AUDISM

Recently, Eddy Morton booked a flight with Air Canada. The employee who took his reservation felt that because Mr. Morton is deaf and blind, he would require assistance during the flight. After consulting with the reservations department, the employee informed Mr. Morton that he would be required to pay for an attendant to travel with him and to assist him on the airplane. Mr. Morton disputed the decision because he travels capably on his own regularly (sometimes with an assistance dog) and has established ways of communicating effectively with strangers as needed (e.g., through manual spelling on his palm). In January 2009, the Canadian Human Rights Tribunal found that the decision made by the airline to require Mr. Morton to travel with an attendant and to pay for it himself was discriminatory because the decision process did not involve consideration of his individual capabilities, only his disabilities (Letheren, 2009). In fact, the employees who made the decision did not follow the Air Canada policy for handling reservations for people who may require assistance during flights, which was to refer the case to an occupational health department made up of health care professionals for individual consideration. Rather, it appeared the employees involved based their judgment on their beliefs about people with disabilities.

Several complexities in the nature of prejudice and discrimination are evident in Eddy Morton's experience. The Air Canada employees who judged that Mr. Morton would require assistance during a flight were probably well-meaning people who felt that they were making an appropriate decision based on concerns about his safety. However, the decision may reflect paternalistic prejudice—a kind of subtle, ambivalent prejudice that involves feelings of sympathy that correspond to stereotypes that a group lacks capability (Fiske et al., 2002)—because it appears to reflect the assumption that a deaf and blind person could not be capable of safe independent travel. This assumption may be incorrect. For example, in some contexts such as the workplace, Deaf people have a better than average safety record (Malkowski, 2009), and Mr. Morton, despite being both deaf and blind, traveled independently and safely on a regular basis (Letheren, 2009). The kind of paternalism shown by the airline employees is typical of attitudes toward people with physical challenges. For example, Deaf people report being treated as though they are not intelligent or not capable of doing things that they can do very well by relying on visual skills (e.g., driving or playing sports; Malkowski, 2009).

The Morton case also reveals the complexities of prejudice because it shows how paternalistic attitudes exist in the context of systemic forms of discrimination. Although the belief that a deaf and blind person could not travel safely alone is revealed on reflection to be paternalistic, it might be an assumption that most able-bodied people would make given that transportation systems (as with most public systems) are structured for those who hear and see. For example, safety instructions are typically provided verbally by flight attendants (without sign language translation) and in written form (without Braille). In addition, the airline policy of requiring people with disabilities to pay for their own attendants is arguably discriminatory because it creates a dual-fee structure in which people's physical attributes determine how much they pay for a service. Thus, the system is set up to advantage some people and disadvantage others. This, in turn, perpetuates inequality. For example, things like the dual-fee structure feed into the economic challenges already faced by people with disabilities, who are often underemployed (Layton, 2009).

The Morton case reveals the essence of "isms." Terms involving "isms" describe combinations of prejudice, discrimination, and inequality. Some "isms" are well known and widely deemed unacceptable, such as racism and sexism. Others are becoming known and starting to be challenged, such as heterosexism, which is the system of attitudes, policies, and practices that advantage heterosexual people. The term *ableism* refers to the systems of prejudice and discrimination that disadvantage people with disabilities. Eddy Morton's unfortunate experience revealed ableism and another lesser known "ism," audism.

The term *audism* is usually attributed to Deaf scholar Tom Humphries (Bauman, 2004), and it is generally used to describe prejudice and discrimination against people who are Deaf, deafened, or hard of hearing. Although it is not yet a widely recognized problem outside of the Deaf community, audism is pervasive and systemic, "woven into every facet of our society" (Malkowski, 2009, p. 28).

One of the most fundamental ways that audism is woven into the fabric of society is in the way that people define deafness—as a defect, a lack of hearing. People vary from one another in many ways with respect to their experience with hearing. Some people become hard of hearing during adulthood, some become deaf after developing spoken language, others are deafened very early in life, and others are born without hearing (Chovaz, 1998). These types of hearing differences are often understood in medical terms, with respect to a person's ability to detect and discriminate sounds. From this perspective, deafness is considered a problem to be fixed with hearing aids, cochlear implants (surgically implanted devices that generate sound in deaf people), and vocal training for deaf children. This medical understanding of deafness, as involving an absence of hearing, is denoted by using a lowercase *d* in the word *deaf*.

In contrast to this medical perspective, within the Deaf community it is common to understand Deafness in cultural terms. People who are culturally Deaf consider themselves to be part of a linguistic minority group (whose language is one of the sign languages such as American Sign Language [ASL]) that has a distinct social identity and set of cultural values, norms, and traditions (Chovaz, 1998; Woodward & Allen, 1993). Deaf culture has been described as one that places high value on group cohesiveness and collaboration, interpersonal reciprocity, and candid, forthright communication. Storytelling is valued, and the hands and eyes, as central vehicles of communication, are respected. In addition, many culturally Deaf people place great importance on their identification with the Deaf community and advocate for anti-oppressive policies such as access to education in sign language for Deaf children (Chovaz, 1998). Following convention, this cultural understanding of Deafness is noted with an uppercase *D*. Where both the medical and cultural understandings are relevant, the term *D/deaf* is used.

The medical understanding of deafness is inherently audist because it values oral communication over sign language, despite the fact that sign languages are complete languages with their own syntax and grammatical structure, like any of the spoken languages. The medical approach to deafness is also problematic because it gives rise to medical and educational practices that are geared toward changing deaf people to be more like hearing people, rather than, say, policies and practices that would require adaptation by hearing people by supporting widespread accessibility of sign language. Such one-sided practices are forms of cultural discrimination that privilege hearing people and can be very damaging to D/deaf persons (Bauman, 2004).

A very damaging implication of this linguistic cultural bias is the existence of policies that require that D/deaf children to be educated in oral language and that withhold education in sign language. Such policies have been prevalent to varying degrees during the past 2 centuries in both North American and Europe and unfortunately persist (Fishbein, 2002; Malkowski, 2006), although they are now being challenged in the courts (Malkowski, 2009). D/deaf children have often been placed in educational settings that emphasize speech training and education in speech (lip) reading and discourage children from using sign language. Although this oralist tradition is guided by the hope that skill with oral language will aid the integration of D/deaf people into the hearing community, it is problematic for D/deaf people for several reasons. It shows the essence of cultural discrimination because it assumes the superiority of oral language. It also requires D/deaf people to adapt to a language that is not natural for them and requires no adaptation by hearing people, despite the fact that hearing people face no barrier to using sign language.

Even more disconcerting, this cultural discrimination leads to systematic inequality because the cultural emphasis on oral rather than gestural language puts D/deaf children at a clear disadvantage in terms of their educational development. Because D/deaf children are often not enrolled in schools for the D/deaf that use sign language until after they have failed to adapt to oral educational techniques, they tend to be delayed in their language development (Malkowski, 2006). The most critical period for language development is during the early years, when many D/deaf children are understimulated because they are denied education in a language they can comprehend (Malkowski, 2009). Thus, young children who are taught with oral techniques despite not having the physical ability to use them are left with essentially no language, and by the time they receive education in sign language their educational development is behind that of other children. In fact, the D/deaf population has lower average academic achievement and lower literacy rates than the hearing population for this reason (Fishbein, 2002; Malkowski, 2005). However, this is not inevitable. There is evidence that early instruction in sign language fosters the later development of effective language skill in both ASL and spoken English (e.g., Musselman & Akamatsu, 1999), suggesting that support for education in sign language would not only reduce cultural discrimination but also ultimately reduce inequality by allowing D/deaf children to most effectively develop their potential.

In addition to cultural discrimination, D/deaf people face many other issues. D/deaf children experience much higher rates of sexual abuse than do hearing children (Malkowski, 2008), perhaps because of their vulnerability to exploitation by hearing adults. Moreover, D/deaf adults can be susceptible to homelessness and mental health issues given the myriad forms of discrimination they face (C. Chovaz, personal communication, August 13, 2009). This is complicated by the fact that, given their relative underemployment, access to mental health services can be out of reach for Deaf people. Moreover, there is a relative dearth of professionals qualified to work with Deaf people (cf. Chovaz-McKinnon, 2007).

Accessibility issues for D/deaf people are widespread. In North America, most government and private offices are not equipped for Deaf people, lacking visual fire alarms, specialized phones with text translation, sign language translators, and so on. Even doctors' offices and hospital emergency rooms, locations that surely ought to be accessible to all, are often inaccessible to Deaf people for similar reasons. Access to medical care is improving in Canada following a legal challenge in 1997, when the Supreme Court of Canada ruled that all federally funded health care facilities must provide services to D/deaf clients. Of course, implementation of this mandate is an ongoing challenge (Chovaz, 2009). The consequences of lack of care can be devastating because many D/deaf people are unable to effectively communicate with the majority of physicians, lawyers, or the very people in government who can change the policies that determine accessibility. As Bauman (2004) observed with regard to audism, "Once we start pulling up its roots, we see how vast and hidden are its systems" (p. 240).

Fortunately, there are signs of improvement, such as a recent United Nations Convention on the Rights and Dignities of Persons With Disabilities that upholds the right of Deaf people to education in sign language. Many countries, including the United States and Canada, now have government acts that support this, and failures to conform to this ideal are being recognized as discriminatory. An additional sign of progress is the increased interest in proficiency in sign language among hearing people. ASL is increasingly being offered to elementary and high school children as a language option, and there is a rise in the number of hearing students who enroll in graduate programs that are related to Deaf studies and conducted in ASL (Gallaudet University, 2009). Although there are many barriers yet to be broken, there is good reason why hearing and D/deaf people ought to address them. Hearing loss is the most widespread disability, and its prevalence increases with age, an important issue given the aging population (Canadian Hearing Society, 2007). As with reductions in any form of discrimination, challenges to audism make it possible for people to use their talents fully, something that benefits society as a whole.

The case of audism shows that some forms of prejudice are very subtle, such as common yet paternalistic assumptions about people with disabilities. It also shows how such prejudice both reflects and perpetuates a system of inequality that has significant consequences. Throughout this book, I examine both this type of subtle and common attitude and the more overtly hostile attitudes that are more easily recognized as prejudice.

2

DEFINING DIFFERENCES

For the past several years, a government-supported militia in the Darfur region of Sudan has been systematically attacking villages; raping women and children; murdering men, women, and children; and burning villages to the ground. When the atrocities first grabbed the attention of the Western media, they were described in ethnic terms. The largely Arab members of the militia were said to be attacking the non-Arab Black Africans in violent ethnic conflict. In fact, ethnic divisions in Darfur are blurry because of a history of intermarriage between Africans and Arabs, and before the government's intervention, relations between Arabs and Black Africans were relatively cooperative. Among the victims, the atrocities tend to be attributed to the government's use of Arab fighters as a means to maintain control through violence and oppression (Marlow, 2006). Depicting the atrocities as ethnic conflict thus simplifies the realities of group differences in Sudan and distracts attention from the role the government has played in the abuses. At the same time, it gives added power to those who might benefit from oversimplified notions of ethnicity in Sudan. Jen Marlow (2006), who spent time in Darfur filming the effects of the tragedy, wrote,

> The Black/African and Arab dichotomy that has been deployed to define the conflict in Darfur was first put forward by the government of Sudan

and quickly adopted by many in the West. This view is neither histori-cally meaningful to nor useful in helping the people of Sudan, as it inten-tionally obfuscates the underlying causes of the conflict. The promotion of this dichotomy has taken on very real meaning, however, as a means of organizing support by both the Sudanese government and those seek-ing to help the people of Darfur. . . . Organized activism in America by institutions with various political agendas utilizes the demonization of Arabs to play on the post-9/11 context . . . identifying Arabs with terror-ism, violence, and a clash of civilizations. . . . The politics of power in Darfur and Sudan cannot be rendered comprehensible by simple, ahis-torical notions of Arab and African. Understanding the conflict in Dar-fur requires acceptance of complexity. (pp. 254–259)

Apparently, both the government of Sudan and some Western organiza-tions make use of a simplistic notion of ethnicity in Sudan to mobilize support for their efforts. This is not an isolated case of the misuse of distorted notions of group differences. It is common for people to highlight and simplify differ-ences between groups during times of conflict or exploitation. For example, dur-ing the Holocaust religious and ethnic differences were expressed in faulty racial terms to reinforce anti-Semitism and to justify atrocities against Jewish people, suggesting that the way people understand the nature of differences between groups is malleable and has important implications for people's attitudes toward and treatment of others. In this chapter, I consider this malleability in people's understandings of difference and its implications for prejudice.

Examples such as the Darfur crisis and the Holocaust show that faulty or exaggerated understandings of difference are sometimes both common and consequential. This is important to recognize because the tendency to view people in terms of group differences is a pervasive characteristic of social per-ception. In general, the ability to perceive stimuli in the world in terms of cat-egories is necessary for people to detect regularities in the environment and successfully adapt to them (Allport, 1954/1979; Macrae & Bodenhausen, 2000). People perceive trees and people and food as separate entities because of categorization. *Social categorization* refers to the process by which people detect the category or categories to which other humans belong and respond accordingly. For example, when people recognize a person as a baby, they have categorized by age, and this may lead them to smile and coo or stick out their tongues playfully, things people would not ordinarily do to adults. As this example shows, categorization and its effects are often ordinary and even help-ful in terms of orienting people to the world. However, categorizing people by age, gender, ethnicity, religion, and so on can also lead to prejudiced responses, and this may be especially likely to occur if social categorization is shaped by faulty understandings of differences, as the example of early explanations for the Darfur crisis that simplified differences between ethnic groups implies.

People differ from one another in multiple ways and could conceivably be categorized along any number of dimensions. Yet people do not see the world in terms of tall people and short people, or people with pointy chins versus people with rounded chins. Rather, certain categories are especially likely to guide responses to others. Empirical laboratory research examining how people react to perceiving differences has shown that at a most basic level, people categorize between "us" and "them" (Perdue, Dovidio, Gurtman, & Tyler, 1990) by differentiating kin from strangers. Moreover, research conducted in North America and Europe has shown that people in these contexts have a habitual tendency to view other people in terms of age, gender, and so-called race (Brewer, 1988; Fiske & Neuberg, 1990). Contemporary research using the tools of neuroscience (e.g., brain imaging techniques) has demonstrated, for example, that when people look at a series of photographs of other people who differ on various dimensions, they show characteristic patterns of activity in the frontal areas of the brain when looking at people who are similar in age, race (Ito, Willadsen-Jensen, & Correll, 2007), and gender (Mouchetant-Rostaing, Giard, Delpuech, Echallier, & Pernier, 2000), suggesting that people tend to automatically categorize others on these dimensions.

The categories of age, race, and gender are often referred to as *basic* or *primitive* categories because this type of research tends to show that most people *relatively* automatically and immediately detect these attributes of others. It is a matter of some debate to what extent this phenomenon occurs because of attributes of the perceived or the perceiver (e.g., Ito, Willadsen-Jensen, & Correll, 2007; Wheeler & Fiske, 2005), however. Thus, it is important to consider whether these categories reflect essential differences between people or whether people tend to emphasize these differences over other, potentially equally meaningful forms of human variation. The early representations of the crisis in Darfur seem to illustrate that people may overemphasize ethnicity as a basis of categorization and exaggerate differences between groups by failing to recognize the fuzzy boundaries between them. Understanding how people view and define differences is relevant to understanding prejudice because views about the nature of differences have been shown to relate to attitudes toward others (e.g., Prentice & Miller, 2007). In the sections that follow, I consider the question of why particular markers of difference emerge as especially significant or basic aspects of social categorization, beginning with the example of so-called race.

THE EXAMPLE OF RACE

Before the 1500s, the term *race* was used primarily as a description of breeding outcomes for domestic animals (Jones, 1997). The extension of the concept from animal husbandry to human classification emerged soon thereafter in Europe to describe loosely defined group differences in lineage, social authority, customs, and religious beliefs. Linnaeus, often described as the father of modern taxonomy, provided scientific legitimacy for these vague ideas about race by developing a system for classifying people on the basis of superficial physical characteristics and social stereotypes regarding temperament. In his major work, *Systema Naturae*, Linnaeus (1758, as cited in Guthrie, 2004) described four primary racial groups: *Homo Europeaus, Homo Asiaticus, Homo Americanus,* and *Homo Afer* to describe European, Asian, Native American, and African people, respectively. According to this scheme, *Americanus* people were said to be tenacious and free, *Asiaticus* people were apparently inflexible and inventive, *Europeaus* people were described as haughty and opinionated, and *Afer* people were described as negligent and ruled by caprice (Guthrie, 2004).

Students of Linnaeus and other scholars subsequently developed variants on this system of classification but retained the theme that people can be categorized into discrete groups on the basis of salient visual markers. As with the system developed by Linnaeus, these categories were used not only to describe physical differences but also to depict the apparent character of racial groups, often in a way that appeared to justify institutions such as slavery. For example, leading academics in the late 1800s argued that African people were, by nature, animal-like and required subordination by Europeans to be civilized (Jones, 1997). As recently as 2005, psychologists Rushton and Jensen argued that the categories Black, White, and East Asian (they used the terms *Negroids, Caucasoids,* and *Mongoloids*) have legitimacy as genetically determined racial demarcations that connote group differences in both physical and intellectual attributes. This conception of race and the conclusions drawn from it have been criticized on several scientific grounds, however (e.g., Nisbett, 2005; Sternberg, Grigorenko, & Kidd, 2005; Weizman, Wiener, Wiesenthal, & Ziegler, 1991).

A variety of problems with this conventional perspective on race are evident. First, referring to a restricted number of races (e.g., Caucasian, African, Asian) to describe people who vary in skin color and feature shape artificially categorizes people according to variables that are continuous in nature. Skin tones range tremendously, and it is only at the extremes that people can be accurately described as White or Black. Moreover, such labels are often inappropriate. Look at a photograph of Colin Powell next to one of George W. Bush, and you will see that it is Bush, not Powell, who has darker skin despite the fact that Powell is labeled *Black* and Bush is labeled *White* (Dawkins, 2004). Of course, skin darkness is not the only marker of race; rather, combinations of skin tone, hair color and texture, and feature shape are typically relied on in determinations of race. However, the characteristics that are typically used to identify race do not always cluster together as conventional conceptions of race suggest but rather vary somewhat independently. For example, people with light skin may have wiry dark hair, skin folds above the eye are found among people with different skin tones and hair types around the world, and there are populations of people with very dark skin and light hair.

Second, the race to which people are thought to belong is not static across time or location. For example, as recently as a few decades ago, the term *Negro* was used to denote people from Africa and Pacific Oceana, but currently people living or originating in Pacific Oceana are described as Asian (Keita et al., 2004). In the United States, the most prevalent racial classification is the dichotomous Black–White distinction, and the distinction is used loosely in the same way in Canada. In contrast, in Brazil multiple racial designations are used, corresponding to variants in physical features (Jones, 1997). In some locations (e.g., Japan), the primary racial designation distinguishes the dominant group from minorities and foreigners. In parts of South Asia, occupational status is viewed in racial terms and is thought to reflect essential and immutable categories. In Zimbabwe, the relatively large group of people with albinism is viewed as racially subordinate (Sampson, 1999). As Fish (1995) noted, "Individuals can easily change their race by getting on a plane and flying from New York to Salvador or Port-au-Prince. What changes is not their physical appearance but the folk taxonomies by which they are classified" (p. 45).

Third, the criteria people use to assign racial categories do not follow logically from the wide physical variability among people. For example, people in different parts of the world vary not only in skin color (lighter or darker) but also in body shape (rounder or leaner) because of adaptations to geography. Just as skin color variations evolved in response to differences in sun exposure, rounded bodies such as those common among the Inuit in Canada emerged in cold climates to preserve heat, whereas lankier bodies such as those common among Tutsis in Rwanda developed in hotter climates to give off heat (Fish, 1995). Both skin color and body shape distinguish people on the basis of shared genetic lineage, and yet in North America skin color is viewed as a racial marker, whereas body shape is not. As Fish (1995) aptly noted, in North America, people consider body shape to be a type of variant among "white," "black," and "brown" people, but they could as meaningfully view "white," "black," and "brown" people as types of "roundeds" and "lankies" (p. 44).

Race as Human Genome Variability

Despite these complexities in the nature of differences, people do differ in systematic ways, and scientists now tend to use the Darwinian principle of common descent rather than race to describe people's shared genetic ancestry. All humans trace their origins to Africa, but people differ with respect to the diversity of geographical backgrounds in their family tree and the proportion of ancestors from various locations. Thus, scientists have called for a reconceptualization of human difference that rejects the categorical concept of race and instead identifies human genome variation (e.g., Royal & Dunston, 2004).

Compared with other animals, humans are remarkably homogeneous. Any two people, regardless of ancestry, share 99.9% of the same genetic information (Bonham, Warshauer-Baker, & Collins, 2005) in part because of events from human ancestral history. Consensus seems to be that contemporary humans originated in Africa some 150,000 to 200,000 years ago and that migrating groups traveled north roughly 30,000 to 50,000 years ago, ultimately separating into groups that moved toward what are now Europe, Asia, and India. However, the migrating population bottlenecked when it dwindled to small numbers (Dawkins, 2004), and although our species came close to extinction, it rebounded. The result is that modern humans can be traced back to a relatively small and homogeneous population, perhaps as small as 10,000 individuals (Caporael, 2007). Discussions of human differences must therefore be tempered by the knowledge that all people have a shared ancestral history, and genetic similarities outweigh differences by an enormous margin.

Although humans are genetically homogeneous, they are externally different in some superficial ways. Migration out of Africa took people to extremely varied terrains, habitats, and climates ranging from what is now northern Europe to the hot climates of south Asia and beyond. Selection pressures influenced those external body parts that were exposed to the elements. People in northern climates lived with low levels of light and needed light skin to absorb vitamin D, so natural selection lightened skin over time. In contrast, people in hot, sunny southern climates needed more melanin in the skin for protection from ultraviolet rays, and hence natural selection chose darker skin. Skin folds evolved as natural goggles over the eyes of people who lived in areas of bright light intensity (Dawkins, 2004; Pinker, 2002).

These superficial features are genetically transmitted, and therefore variations in these attributes correspond to patterns of gene flow, which is the exchange of genes across populations (e.g., through intermarriage in geographically close areas; Jorde & Wooding, 2004). The flow of genetic information across populations occurs for many characteristics, not just those superficial attributes that relate to adaptation to climate, and genetic material is not always expressed superficially, although it may reside in a person's DNA. Therefore, people who look superficially different may be quite similar at the level of the genome. For example, Europeans, because of gene flow, are the population most closely linked genetically to Africans despite differences in skin color.

Clearly, boundaries between groups of people based on ancestry are fuzzy at best. Genetic data have shown that there is a mixing of ancestry in all population groups (Jorde & Wooding, 2004). Moreover, there are no gene variants that exist in all members of one population group but none of another (Bonham et al., 2005). Most of the genetic differences between people exist between individuals within the same group: Approximately 90% of human genetic variation exists between sets of individuals within groups typically viewed as racial groups, and only about 10% of meaningful genetic variation exists in patterns of differences between these groups (Jorde & Wooding, 2004). Any two people of different races may be genetically more similar than any two people from the same race. To illustrate the fact that more genetic variability exists within rather than between groups, Dawkins (2004) pointed out that if all but one geographically local group of humans were wiped off the earth, the majority of genetic variability that currently exists in the species would remain.

Three conclusions can be drawn from this analysis. First, human genome variation does not give rise to categorical differences between people but rather a range of dimensions on which people vary, often by degrees. Second, genetic variations based on ancestry are not easy to detect using simple visual criteria like skin color and feature shape. Third, these simple visual characteristics that distinguish people mask the enormous similarity that exists beneath the skin. Given this complexity of human diversity, is a concept of race meaningful? At the scientific level, it may be meaningful to identify patterns of human genome variation, and doing so may benefit both pure knowledge and applications such as human health (because health is linked to genetics). In contrast, in common usage the term *race* is more misleading than helpful because it falsely implies that people differ categorically.

Visualize an elementary school classroom in a multicultural area of Canada or the United States. Some children have lighter skin, and others have darker skin. Some children appear to be of Asian background, and others appear to be Native North American. One can view this class in a variety of ways. One could look at the children as unique individuals, as boys and girls, as members of their respective ethnic or religious groups, as groups of friends, and so on. One could also perceive them according to traditional racial categories of White, Black, Asian, and perhaps First Nations. Imagine that the students arrange their seating according to these traditional so-called racial categories so that there are four groups in the room. Within each group are unique individuals who share some characteristics of skin color, eye shape, and so on. This is the conventional view of race, the one historically given scientific legitimacy by Linnaeus. However, if one was to see the genetic information written on each child's DNA, a different picture would emerge. If one identified patterns of genetic variants that distinguish the students according to their intergenerational heritage and had them sit in groups with similar genetic markers, some students would have to switch seats, and it would be a judgment call as to which group some children belong to. Groups would be differentiated to a degree according to some small fraction of their genetic material, and in each group would be people with lighter and darker skin, some with skin folds above the eyes and some without, and so on. This is the fuzzy picture of group differences suggested by recent research on human genome variability.

Race as a Social Construction

Despite the emergence of this more sophisticated view of human genome variability, when these students leave their recategorized classroom and participate in their daily lives, people will see them and sometimes treat them according to the traditional racial categories. The fact that people are classified by others according to superficial markers of difference reflects the social construction of race. The idea of race as a social construction refers to the idea that race is "a folk idea, a culturally invented conception about human differences. It became an important mechanism for limiting and restricting access to privilege, power, and wealth" (A. Smedley & Smedley, 2005, p. 22). In other words, culturally people create a set of meanings associated with something such as race in response to social rather than biological factors, and these social factors involve issues of inequality and privilege.

When the idea of human race emerged in scientific circles, inequality between groups was pronounced, and justifications of this inequality using stereotypes were normative. With the work of people like Linnaeus, erroneous ideas about race that reflected this social reality were given scientific legitimacy. As a scholar, Linnaeus had the credibility to shape public thought, a fact that was not unique to him but a reflection of the broad tendency whereby the ideas of people in respected institutions such as science, law, and religion have added power to influence cultural beliefs. The social constructionist perspective describes how because people in positions of leadership tend to be disproportionately from advantaged groups, it is the dominant groups' perspectives on concepts such as race that tend to become embedded in the culture (e.g., Jones, 1997), and such views serve the interests of the dominant racial group. For example, it benefited the Puritans to categorize Native American peoples as racially distinct barbarians because it justified the expropriation of land. The institution of slavery was also upheld in part by justifications that appealed to so-called racial differences in aptitude, and the Holocaust was justified in part by the use of racialized depictions of Jewish people.

A variety of social institutions, including the law, have supported ongoing social constructions of race. During the apartheid era in South Africa

(1948–1994), when the segregation and subordination of native Africans was legally supported, the local government formally sorted people into racial groups, the European (mainly Dutch) Afrikaners, or Whites (who at the time had relatively exclusive access to power and privilege); Bantus, or Blacks (native Africans); Coloreds (people of mixed heritage); and Indians (people from India). During this era, the racial distinction was used to justify the restricted legal rights of native Africans, who were stripped of citizenship, segregated on reservation lands, and restricted in access to voting, education, medical care, and government services. After the dismantling of apartheid, the courts filled with cases deciding on the appropriate racial designation for people of mixed parentage (Dawkins, 2003), a testament to the socially negotiated nature of race. Here the law, not clearly defined natural human differences, created categories of people.

Psychological processes also perpetuate such systems. This was demonstrated dramatically during the apartheid era, when psychologists Pettigrew, Allport, and Barnett (1958) conducted a study of the way in which Afrikaners and members of the Black majority in South Africa categorized people of mixed descent. Participants in their research were shown photographs of people of mixed heritage and asked to indicate their race. The researchers found that Afrikaners made the most restrictive categorizations, allotting people of mixed heritage to the most subordinate category (African) more often than did others. By assigning people of mixed background to the most subordinate group, Afrikaners psychologically preserved the exclusiveness of their more privileged category.

In North America, the idea that slaves were racially distinct and inferior also became entrenched in laws, and this persisted long after the abolition of slavery. For example, hypodescent rules of racial designation indicated that a person with mixed heritage was categorized according to the socially subordinate group (Deo, 2008). Rules of hypodescent emerged in the United States in the early 1600s to classify people with Black heritage as Black. Sometimes known as "one-drop" rules (Hickman, 1997), such systems determined that a person with any known Black heritage, no matter how little, was legally Black. This approach to racial classification became embedded in law and in government practices such as the collection of census data. In their early forms, rules of hypodescent served to determine who was and was not legally free from slavery and to protect the perceived interests of the White majority. Such laws also served to preserve racial boundaries. For example, the Racial Integrity Act of Virginia in 1924 made recording the race of all infants mandatory and prohibited interracial marriage (Deo, 2008). Contemporary racial classification in the census is controversial because despite its racist history and problematic potential, it is also now used for purposes such as allocating resources to education and health and to fund civil rights groups.

In Europe, before and during the time of the Holocaust, religion, another authoritative system, combined with law and science to create a racialized view of Jews. The racialization of Jews had a long history among early Christians, who associated Jews with the death of Jesus and sought to explain their resistance to conversion to Christianity sometimes by assuming that Jews were of a different and more malevolent origin. The Gospel of John declared, "If God were your father, ye would love me. . . . Ye are of your father the devil" (8:41–44). This notion of fundamental difference became racialized in some religious teachings. For example, Harris (2004) pointed to a Vatican-approved paper from 1880 that declared,

> Oh how wrong and deluded are those who think Judaism is just a religion, like Catholicism, Paganism, Protestantism, and not in fact a race, a people, and a nation. . . . For the Jews are not only Jews because of their religion . . . they are Jews also and especially because of their race. (p. 103)

Politically, the Nuremberg laws of 1935 furthered the racialized views of Jews by prohibiting marriage and sex between Jews and non-Jews in an effort to protect German blood. In the next year, the German Catholic Episcopate issued guidelines that stated that God gave Germans the trust of preserving race (Harris, 2004). Although there is debate about the relative roles of atheism and religiosity in the ideologies that contributed to the Holocaust, religiously rooted beliefs about race are evident. For example, Heinrich Himmler, the commander of the SS and the founder of the concentration camps, reportedly believed that Aryans alone were not human animals evolved through natural processes but rather were a special race derived from heaven (Harris, 2004).

Efforts among scholars of various disciplines also coalesced around the effort to define Jews as a distinct race and biologically inferior, and using the scientific tools and sensibilities of the day, they constructed theories that ranked the races of the world, placing Nordic and Aryan people at the top of the hierarchy. In this scheme, Jews and other victims of the Holocaust were marked as inherently biologically inferior, problematic, and threatening to other people. Therefore, when the Nazis came to power, their task was made easier by the scholars, religious leaders, and teachers who perpetuated these ideas. As Sampson (1999) expressed,

> When the Nazis came to power and avowed as part of their official policy to engage in the final solution to the Jewish question, they were not met by a shocked public, but rather a public who had been long prepared for just these ways of thinking. (p. 56)

As a whole, the biological and social constructionist perspectives on so-called race show that although it is possible to make loose distinctions between large groups of people in terms of degrees of genetic relatedness (Pinker, 2002), these distinctions do not correspond to conventional socially constructed categories of race. Indeed, it is the position of the National Human Genome Center that the term *race* is wrongly used and that "traditional 'racial' designations in humans are not bounded, discrete categories but are fluid, socially constructed constructs" (Royal & Dunston, 2004, p. 6). Such social constructions have developed in response to historical and cultural conditions that have oppressed some groups and privileged others, and they have been promoted by science, the law, and religion. As Jones (1997) aptly noted, the concept of race means nothing and it means everything. It means nothing in that the conventional conception of race is faulty from a biological point of view, yet it means everything in that the social construction of race has been enormously consequential, and "this four-letter word has wreaked more havoc on people in the world than all the four-letter words banned by censors" (p. 339).

Of the many ways in which people tend to be grouped—gender, age, ethnicity, religion, and so forth—the social category of race stands out in terms of its historical significance in retaining inequality. Similar arguments have been made about the use of categories of sexual orientation (e.g., Foucault, 1990). To further illustrate the biological and social complexities of human groupings, I next examine the example of sexual orientation.

THE CASE OF SEXUAL ORIENTATION

Scientific attempts to understand sexual orientation in psychology have tended to focus more on understanding the causes of people's relatively enduring attractions to members of the same sex than on exploring the nature of sexuality more broadly, a fact that points to the assumptions of scientists about normality and nonnormality because heterosexuality is generally taken for granted rather than explained. Early work that was inspired by psychodynamic and social learning theories tested whether a same-sex sexual orientation was shaped by early life experiences such as parenting style or peer group influences, and these efforts were met with unanimous failure. In a review of research on the causes of sexual orientation, Rahman and Wilson (2003) reported that there is a "dearth of evidence for any known psychosocial determinant of sexual orientation from the past 50 years of research" (p. 1342). More currently, efforts to understand sexual orientation have followed two prongs. Biological approaches study genetic and prenatal contributions to sexual orientation, and constructionist approaches critique the very notion of sexual orientation as a categorical distinction between people and study social and historical influences on people's understanding of the nature of sexuality.

Biological Approaches

Sexual orientation appears to be shaped by both genetics and prenatal developmental processes (for a review, see Rahman & Wilson, 2003). With respect to genetics, it tends to cluster in families. For example, gay men are 15% more likely than heterosexual men to have gay brothers, and lesbians are 10% more likely than heterosexual women to have lesbian sisters. Also, studies comparing the concordance in sexual orientation among identical and fraternal twins have supported a genetic interpretation because identical twins are more likely to be alike in sexual orientation than are fraternal twins. Overall research examining familial patterns of sexual orientation have suggested that about 50% to 60% of the variance in people's sexual orientation may be attributed to genetic influences.

Sexual orientation has also been linked with the level of androgens available in the womb prenatally. These hormones shape the sexual differentiation of the fetus. In the very early stages of pregnancy, the fetus has structures that can develop into either the male or the female form. In cases in which the fetus has a Y sex chromosome, androgens, especially testosterone, stimulate the development of the male pattern and the deterioration of the female pattern. In the absence of this testosterone-stimulated effect, the female pattern develops and the male pattern deteriorates. This sexual differentiation occurs for the internal and external sex organs and for the few areas of the brain that differ between men and women. Prenatal hormone theory proposes that lower-than-typical levels of testosterone in male fetuses may predict brain development associated with male homosexuality and higher-than-typical levels of testosterone in female fetuses may predict brain development associated with female homosexuality (Rahman & Wilson, 2003). Evidence for this view is indirect and mainly involves animal models. For example, animals artificially given atypical hormone levels often show same-sex behavior.

Constructionist Approach

The constructionist perspective does not purport to explain why people have the sexual orientation that they do. Rather, it critiques the very nature of the concept of sexual orientation. The constructionist analysis is that sexuality is complex and fluid and the notion that there are discrete categories of people (heterosexual, gay, bisexual) is misleading and potentially damaging because it forces people to categorize themselves and, by so doing, distorts their experience of their sexuality (Foucault, 1990).

Studies of people's sexual behaviors and interests have indicated that there appears to be a considerable gray area in many people's experiences. In surveys of people's attractions and sexual activity, many people have reported degrees of interest in both sexes. In Kinsey's famous early North American research (Kinsey, Pomeroy, & Martin, 1948), almost half of the men interviewed could not be categorized as exclusively heterosexual or homosexual on the basis of their interests and behavior. More recent work has shown that about 20% of people report having some degree of same-sex desire or contact (e.g., Bagley & Tremblay, 1998), and much smaller numbers actually identify themselves as gay. Approximately 2% to 5% of men and women report that they are exclusively gay (Rahman & Wilson, 2003), which suggests that sizable numbers of people who feel that they are heterosexual have some sexual interest in members of the same sex.

Also, analyses of sexual behavior across time and cultures reveals many variations and many examples of sex between same-sex partners among people who do not identify as gay. Sexual contact between men was common in ancient Greece and also in Japanese Samurai culture, in part because of a belief that the battlefield fate of men who were bonded by sexual intimacy would be enhanced because of partner loyalty and protection (Adriaens & DeBlock, 2006). Other cross-cultural comparisons are well known, such as the case of the Sambians of New Guinea, among whom sexual contact between older and younger men is deemed to be a necessary component of male sexual development. Cross-culturally, bisexuality is much more common than is strict homosexuality (Adriaens & DeBlock, 2006).

In addition, sexuality has not always been understood in categorical terms in Western culture. The emergence of the idea that there is a type of person who is homosexual and another type who is heterosexual is typically traced to social changes that occurred during the 18th and 19th centuries associated with urbanization and industrialization (Adriaens & DeBlock, 2006; Foucault, 1990). Around this time, medical and religious authorities arguably became concerned that increased access to nonprocreative sex in urban settings might threaten population growth, and so their social goal of maintaining reproduction could be met by labeling nonprocreative sex as abnormal. As a consequence, the understanding of sexuality changed. Whereas previously people who engaged in same-sex acts were simply thought to be engaging in certain behaviors, now people who engaged in same-sex sexuality were labeled as a certain type of person and pathologized or deemed ill (Adriaens & DeBock, 2006).

In Foucault's (1990) terms, "Western societies thus began to keep an indefinite record of these people's pleasures. They made up a herbal of them and established a system of classification. They described their everyday deficiencies as well as their oddities or exasperations" (p. 64). Religious notions of sin became expressed in medical terms related to normality and pathology. The idea of types of people was created so that one type could be critiqued. In so doing, those labeled *heterosexual* became above reproach. This tendency to pathologize a certain category of people took hold in many ways in professional circles and persisted until very recently in the mainstream. For example, homosexuality was formally deemed a medical illness between 1952 and 1973 in the *Diagnostic and Statistical Manual of Mental Disorders* used by psychiatrists and psychologists.

In summary, evidence on the nature of people's sexual experiences suggests a degree of fluidity. At the same time, sexual orientation appears to have a genetic underpinning. As with race, the reality of sexual diversity appears to be complexity. Yet, also as with race, authoritative systems such as religion and science have not always acknowledged this complexity, and this has no doubt shaped people's views of differences between people on the basis of sexuality (e.g., Hunsberger & Jackson, 2005). Perspectives on differences are important in part because they are linked to people's attitudes toward and treatment of different others, the topic I turn to next.

IMPLICATIONS OF UNDERSTANDINGS OF DIFFERENCE

The preceding analyses of so-called race and sexual orientation showed that institutions that have historically disadvantaged people have been supported with faulty understandings of difference and also that in this context people's attitudes toward and beliefs about others tended to mirror those of these institutions. What does this tell us about the nature of people's beliefs about differences in contemporary society? Are current views about differences similarly problematic? These questions are addressed in contemporary research on the construct of *essentialism*—the tendency to view categories as "having deep, hidden, and unchanging properties that make members what they are" (Prentice & Miller, 2007, p. 202). Essentialism involves ascribing to categories an invariant essence. For example, in North America people typically essentialize the social categories of gender, ethnicity, race, and physical disability (Haslam, Rothschild, & Ernst, 2000) by viewing these categories as meaningful, discrete, and biologically rooted. In other cultures, patterns of essentialism differ somewhat. For example, in India social class is essentialized by many people through the belief that the traditional caste system reflects inherent, unchanging, and inevitable differences between groups (Mahalingam, 2003).

Essentialism may be communicated subtly in one's culture yet remain consequential. Imagine listening to a public service announcement that gives a simple message about group differences in health, such as the claim that different treatments for heart disease have been shown to be effective for Black and White people. Would this message influence your thoughts or feelings about the nature of group differences? Researchers Condit, Parrott, Bates,

Bevan and Achter (2004) wondered just that, and so they had a sizable group of American students (the large majority of whom were White) listen to a bogus health announcement about heart disease and genetics that either did or did not claim that White–Black group differences in treatment effectiveness exist and then complete a variety of questionnaires, including a measure of prejudice. People who listened to the announcement indicating that specific treatments were effective for Black people subsequently reported higher levels of prejudice against African Americans than did people whose message did not refer to group differences. Apparently, the message subtly communicated an essentialist view of differences between European and American people and, despite its subtlety, led White participants to psychologically distance African American people from themselves.

This finding is consistent with a considerable body of evidence that has shown that essentialist views are related to prejudice. A number of empirical investigations in different contexts show that people who view so-called racial and national or ethnic groups in more essentialist terms tend to be inclined to stereotype those groups and to be more prejudiced against them (for a review, see Prentice & Miller, 2007). Essentialism also appears to perpetuate inequalities as the social constructionist analysis describes because evidence has shown that people who view others in essentialist terms tend to be less motivated to engage in intergroup encounters and less interested in working to change inequality than are people who do not essentialize these group differences (Williams & Eberhardt, 2008).

A variety of other research findings have linked essentialism to prejudice, discrimination, and the perpetuation of inequality. In a review of the content of hate-related Web sites, Holtz and Wagner (2009) found that especially hostile attitudes toward Jewish people and African people reflected essentialist notions. In a study of attitudes toward immigration issues, Pehrson, Brown, and Zagefka (2009) found that people who tended to essentialize minority groups were more inclined than others to support negative treatment of them, such as antagonistic measures against asylum seekers. Finally, laboratory research has shown that exposure to essentialist ideas tends to increase people's tendency to accept inequality by viewing it as natural, acceptable, or unlikely to change (Morton, Postmes, Haslam, & Hornsey, 2009; Williams & Eberhardt, 2008).

A key position of the constructionist analysis of differences is that essentialism may be used strategically by members of advantaged groups. Some evidence has supported this claim. For example, Mahalingam (2007) showed that in India, where caste differences involve significant differences in social status, it is members of the highest status caste that are most likely to essentialize caste differences. If essentialism is a social tool that advantaged group members use to justify or reinforce inequality, it ought to be relied on especially in circumstances that imply that social inequality may be unstable. In a laboratory study of this issue, Morton et al. (2009) asked people in Australia and the United Kingdom to read information about gender inequality that either suggested that it was stable or that it was changing. They found that endorsement of essentialist views about gender was related to sexism, but only among men who read that gender inequality was changing. Apparently, in a situation that could be perceived as threatening to male privilege, essentialism was used as a tool among sexist men to justify inequality. These researchers also found that exposure to essentialist ideas about gender increased men's tendency to accept discriminatory practices, suggesting that essentialism may also be an effective tool in maintaining injustice.

Essentialism is not always associated with devaluation of other groups, however. At times, it may reflect a positive affirmation of a socially devalued identity. For example, proponents of gay rights may emphasize the biological underpinnings of sexual orientation as a way of communicating the legitimacy of a gay identity. In fact, people who think that sexual orientation is biologically rooted tend to have more positive attitudes toward sexual minorities than do people who think that it is a chosen lifestyle (e.g., Jayaratne et al., 2006; Whitley, 1990), and they are also more inclined to support gay rights (Wood & Bartkowski, 2004). Similar logic may at times be true for other minorities. For example, among biracial people, believing that race is biologically meaningful has been found to enhance the psychological value of contact with other biracial people (Sanchez & Garcia, 2009). Verkuyten (2003) suggested that people may use either essentialist or nonessentialist language to emphasize either oppressive or progressive goals. For example, minority ethnic groups may essentialize aspects of culture if their valued identity is threatened by assimilation, yet they may tend to reject others' essentialist views of culture that appear to be linked to discrimination. Thus, essentialism may be used strategically by members of minority groups and of advantaged groups.

As a whole, evidence has suggested that the link between essentialism and intergroup attitudes is not fixed but may depend on the target group at issue and also whether people are oriented to protect or challenge inequality. These findings, together with research and theorizing on the nature of differences, have shown that people view other people through the lens of culture, history, and personal motives. As described at the beginning of this chapter, social categories such as age, gender, and race have been labeled as basic or primitive to reflect people's habitual tendency to detect these differences. Yet, the remainder of the chapter has shown that to a degree, the history and nature of relations between groups determines which differences will be marked as significant and hence become a habitual focus of attention. Moreover, the contemporary nature of relations between groups is likely to shape and be shaped by people's views about the nature of group differences. Although the analysis in this chapter highlighted so-called race and sexual orientation to reveal these tendencies, similar critiques can be made of other differences, such as ethnicity, age, and gender. For example, as shown in the opening of this chapter, it was exaggerated conceptions of ethnic group differences that were used to distract public attention from the government's role in perpetuating the violence in Darfur. To recognize the influence of historical and social factors in shaping perceptions of difference is not to deny that differences exist, it is to caution that differences must be understood in their complexity.

3

EVOLUTIONARY AND PSYCHODYNAMIC APPROACHES TO PREJUDICE

Recently, I had a window replaced at the back of my house. One of the men working on the job pulled a yellowed piece of newspaper published in 1945 from the wall. The first headline that caught my eye read "Fool Ducks Too." The article, which turned out to be about the multiple functions of GI camouflage suits worn by soldiers during the war, started with the sentence "Stalking ducks, coyotes, and rabbits after the war won't be as thrilling or satisfying as hunting Japs" ("Fool Ducks Too," 1945, p. 10). Startled, I scanned the rest of the paper and found it to be full of sentiments that would be deemed prejudiced and inappropriate today. Why would comments considered inappropriate today be sufficiently normative just more than 60 years ago as to appear in a newspaper? Have people changed, or has the way that people express prejudice changed? Did cultural norms favor prejudice at that time? Was it the war that brought out these hostile sentiments? In short, what causes such prejudice?

When I pose this question to groups of students, the usual reply is that people learn to be prejudiced (or not) from parents, the media, friends, and so on. This socialization perspective certainly has merit. There is no doubt that attitudes are communicated within families, within peer groups, and through television, music, the Internet, and the like. However, this begs several

47

questions: Why are some parents, friends, and media writers prejudiced? Why were those who taught them their attitudes prejudiced? How does it all begin? This puzzle suggests that although socialization factors clearly play a role in the transmission of prejudice within a culture, they do not really address the core causes of it. Clearly, researchers need to explore additional explanations to understand why prejudice is part of the human experience at all.

Explanations for prejudice that address the background factors that predispose people to become prejudiced and attempt to address issues of ultimate causation are known as *distal* explanations. They explain those factors that make the experience of prejudice possible and likely. Here, I discuss two distal perspectives: *evolutionary* and *psychodynamic*. In addition, I briefly describe *terror management theory* (Pyszczynski, Greenberg, Solomon, Arndt, & Schimel, 2004), which draws on both evolutionary and psychodynamic perspectives.

Evolutionary perspectives are enjoying a tremendous growth of interest and attention among prejudice researchers and are sure to guide much theorizing and empirical work in the years to come. In contrast, psychodynamic perspectives, including Freud's classic psychoanalytic view as well as post-Freudian dynamic theories such as object relations theory (Fairbain, 1952), do not currently enjoy much attention from the majority of prejudice researchers. However, they are worth review because of the many (often unacknowledged) parallels between the assumptions of psychodynamic theorists and more contemporary views of prejudice. One parallel is that they share the assumption that prejudice is part of human nature. I now turn to a discussion of the way in which the evolutionary perspective describes human nature and what this teaches us about prejudice.

EVOLUTIONARY PERSPECTIVES

The devaluation or social exclusion of some individuals and groups appears to be relatively universal across time, culture, and even animal species (Kurzban & Leary, 2001). According to evolutionary psychology, psychological phenomena—typical ways in which people think, feel, and act—that are common across many cultures may have been designed in the past by natural selection. The assumption is that people whose genetic material prompts them to think, feel, and act in ways that help them to survive and to attract the opposite sex will have more children than others. Because these children inherit their genetics from their parents, those genes that lead to adaptive behaviors will become more and more representative of humans over evolutionary time. Therefore, any common psychological phenomenon, including prejudice, can potentially be understood as an outcome of the process of natural selection. In this sense, evolutionary accounts of prejudice are distal explanations because they explain how natural selection has shaped human nature to be predisposed toward prejudice.

Humans were shaped by natural selection in important ways when early hominids emerged. Modern humans evolved during the middle to late parts of the lengthy Pleistocene era (roughly 1.8 million to 12,000 years ago). Humans are thought to have developed in ways that allowed for adaptation to the environmental challenges of the time, and so this time frame is sometimes referred to as the *environment of evolutionary adaptedness* (EEA). Because humans emerged so long ago when life conditions were very different from what they are now, understanding the past is "the key to the present" (Buss & Kendrick, 1998, p. 983). Many biological and psychological phenomena that persist today reflect adaptations that aided survival and reproduction during the EEA.

The human brain was shaped by natural selection, just as the rest of the human body was. Adaptive behavioral patterns are thought to have become part of human nature through the shaping of neurological systems that regulate experiences and behavior in the same way that neural circuits give rise to basic biological processes, such as food preferences and eating behavior (Tooby & Cosmides, 1992). Arguably, people's brains have evolved many specific systems that give rise to information-processing patterns, emotional experiences, forms of motivation, and so on that lead to adaptive behavior related to specific environmental challenges. Hunger modules regulate food intake and direct interest in certain types of food, sexuality modules regulate mating behavior and direct people's interest toward particular mates, and so on. Even some attitudes and social behaviors are thought to have their origin in such functional modules. Specifying these mental modules in specific neurological terms is an ongoing task for researchers; however, a variety of types of evidence support the modular depiction of the brain.

Mental modules are thought to have been shaped during the EEA to regulate behavior in a way that would have been adaptive in that context. Thus, contemporary behavior is regulated in some ways by ancient brain systems. What was adaptive during the EEA may be less adaptive now. Many people struggle with their cravings for high-sugar and high-fat foods because during the EEA food sources were often scarce and so seeking high-sugar and high-fat foods was adaptive, whereas in the current era in which such foods are plentiful, these cravings are no longer especially adaptive. The question for evolutionary theorists is, therefore, whether humans evolved mental modules that, although once adaptive could, in modern times, manifest in the problem of prejudice.

A collection of observations and research studies suggest that mental modules for recognizing kin and treating them preferentially may have evolved. The ability to recognize relatives is consistent across many species of animals, and in humans this ability is underscored by a specialized brain area that is devoted to facial recognition (Johnson, 2001). During early human development, the ability to recognize kin likely allowed people to cooperate especially with family members in the tasks of survival. During the EEA, people lived in hunter–gatherer societies in which communal living and cooperation led to greater safety and fostered effective access to food and other resources (Johnson, 2001; Kurzban & Leary, 2001). Indeed, sociality and group living seem to be universal and may be humans' primary survival strategy (Neuberg, Smith, & Asher, 2000). A particular tendency to cooperate with biological relatives is especially functional in an evolutionary sense because family members share some genetic material (Hamilton, 1964). Helping family is parallel to fostering one's own genetic survival. The tendency to recognize and orient toward kin may be one prerequisite of prejudice because of a tendency to focus on "us" versus "them."

Moreover, because family groups formed cooperative alliances within bands, a psychological sense of a broader family, clan, and society—that is, a psychological sense of "we-ness" or ingroup—could emerge (Johnson, 2001). Neurologically, people are wired to recognize kin on the basis of physical attributes. However, people are also socially conditioned to use these brain mechanisms to ascribe kinship to loosely related or unrelated others. Through vehicles such as language (e.g., the metaphoric use of terms such as *sister*, *brother*, and *motherland*; Johnson, 2001), myth (e.g., religious teaching about oneness or group belonging), and politics (e.g., national boundary identification), people come to respond to weakly related or unrelated others as to family. Although such vehicles are social in nature, they depend and build on people's evolved ability to detect and respond to kin.

Most people feel especially warmly toward members of their own family or group, and this does not necessarily imply prejudice against others. However, favoritism toward ingroups often does lead people to discriminate in favor of members of one's own group which by definition does disadvantage outsiders (Brewer, 1999). Also, it is clear that people have inclinations toward both cooperation with and favoritism toward some people and devaluation of others (Neuberg et al., 2000, p. 36). To explain this, evolutionary theories point to conflicts of interest. Just as other people are one's best source of protection, they are also one's primary competitors for resources (Goetz & James, 2001). Conflicts of interests are widespread because some of the resources needed for intergenerational survival (e.g., land, food) are scarce or difficult to access. Consequently, the corollary of cooperation with kin is wariness of, and concerns about, competition with those deemed to be outsiders. According to Johnson (2001), cooperation is the route "through which allies and enemies are recognized" (p. 20).

In modern times, contact between people of different backgrounds is much more likely than it was during the EEA. As such, concerns over competition for resources are likely to emerge. In this type of situation, ancient neurological mechanisms may become active and sensitize people to potential competitors. Indeed, some research has shown that when people are exposed to members of other ethnic groups simply by observing photographs, a part of the brain known to be involved in fear and aggression (the amygdala) often becomes active (e.g., Hart et al., 2000). Precisely why this occurs is not known, but it does show that a relatively ancient brain system—the amygdala is part of the limbic system in complex vertebrates, including humans—is associated with intergroup responses.

Schaller (2003) proposed that during human evolution people developed a propensity to be vigilant in detecting and avoiding outsiders who represent a source of threat. Indeed, empirical research has shown that people tend to be vigilant in the detection of both differences and negative information (J. M. Olson & Janes, 2002; Pratto & John, 1991). Schaller (2003) suggested further that stereotypes of outgroups as dangerous or untrustworthy reflect this vigilance and function to promote avoidance of those who are perceived to be a threat. His intergroup vigilance theory describes how some situations or social cues may activate the vigilance mechanism. For example, Schaller suggested that negative stereotyping of others is more likely to occur in situations of ambient darkness in which ancient self-protection mechanisms may be cued, as they would tend to be at night. Moreover, he argued that people with a strong tendency to feel fearful or believe that the world is dangerous are likely to respond especially unfavorably when situations evoke wariness.

Schaller, Park, and Mueller (2003) demonstrated empirical support for these predications. In their research, they had White Canadians who were known to vary in terms of their tendency to believe that the world is dangerous engage in a task that measured their tendency to stereotype others on the basis of ethnicity while in a room that was either dark or bright. Consistent with Schaller et al.'s theorizing, research participants who more strongly believed that the world tends to be dangerous were more likely than others to show evidence of ethnic stereotyping—in particular, associating people of color with dangerousness and threat—when in a dark room than when in a bright room. According to the theory, the dark room was a cue that would elicit, probably unconsciously, the intergroup vigilance mechanism.

This kind of research has shown that deeply rooted fearfulness of outsiders may contribute to some kinds of prejudice. In many cases, however, prejudice occurs against insiders, or against members of an ingroup. For example, in contemporary North America, prejudice is common against low-income people, people with HIV/AIDS, people with mental illness, homeless people, unattractive people, and so on. People who share a nationality, ethnicity, gender, or any other group marker may nevertheless show prejudice against other group members with such stigmas.

Evolutionary theorists have also claimed to explain stigmatization and prejudice even when it occurs within groups or families. According to Kurzban and Leary (2001), stigmatization reflects the evolution of brain mechanisms that give rise, relatively automatically, to negative emotional responses to people who pose specific threats to well-being. In particular, they proposed that people are vigilant to detect not only outsiders but also ingroup members who may pose a threat by cheating in apparently cooperative efforts or by transmitting illness. Thus, they suggested that prejudice against people with mental illness may reflect evolved wariness of people whose behavioral unpredictability lessens confidence in cooperative potential, prejudice against low-income or homeless people may reflect evolved suspicion of people who may be ineffective contributors in cooperative efforts, prejudice against people with illnesses such as AIDS or with physical blemishes that could indicate illness reflect evolved wariness of people who may transmit viruses, and so on. In evolutionary terms, stigmas mark people and elicit negative responses because there is adaptive value to selective avoidance and sociality (see also Neuberg et al., 2000).

Adaptations thought to give rise to prejudice presumably operate unconsciously or in a way in which the roots of the experience are hidden. According to Neuberg and Cottrell (2006), evolved mechanisms for selective avoidance of others work through emotional, cognitive, and behavioral reactions to others. Moreover, they postulated a "functional specificity" to responses to others. For example, a person whose appearance or behavior cues concerns that he or she may be a poor cooperative partner (e.g., a low-income person) may elicit emotional reactions such as contempt, cognitions such as stereotypes that the person is dishonest or lazy, and behavioral reactions of avoidance. In contrast, a person whose appearance or behavior cues concerns that he or she may be a source of competition for resources (e.g., an economically successful immigrant) may elicit anger, stereotypes about ruthlessness, and more directly antagonistic or aggressive responses. Such responses are deemed to be "functional prejudice syndromes" (Neuberg & Cottrell, 2006, p. 171) because they elicit behavioral responses that are self-protective.

In summary, evolutionary accounts of prejudice have proposed that during the EEA, it was adaptive for people to cooperate especially with relatives, be wary of outsiders who might be competitors for resources, and avoid people who would be poor cooperative partners or likely to transmit illness. Because these tendencies would have aided survival and reproduction, the biology underlying them (genetic information, neurological systems) was shaped in the course of natural selection. Contemporary humans are influenced by such ancient mechanisms, although they are probably no longer adaptive. Emerging evidence has tended to be supportive of this perspective on prejudice. There is no question that evolutionary influences are but one factor shaping prejudice, and few would question the fact that they work in concert with cultural causes. Nevertheless, they do provide a compelling account of the persistence and prevalence of prejudice.

PSYCHODYNAMIC PERSPECTIVES

Evolutionary and psychodynamic accounts of prejudice share the assumption that people are often not aware of why they think, feel, and act as they do. As Moghaddam (2008) wrote, "the proposition that genes causally influence intergroup behavior, acting like a whispering within . . . implies that people do not consciously recognize the real factors shaping their behavior" (p. 51). Psychodynamic theorists are joined together by their shared emphasis on the nature of these unconscious processes. Freud, whose psychoanalytic theory of personality has been pivotal in psychodynamic theorizing, was influenced by Darwin's evolutionary theory in that he saw humans as being driven by their biological imperatives. However, he built on this idea in unique ways that suggest distinct influences on prejudice.

Psychodynamic ideas have filtered into popular discourse in many ways. For example, the commonsense idea that people are prejudiced because they are insecure or have low self-esteem, although in some ways contradicted by contemporary research, owes a nod of acknowledgment to psychodynamic thinking. At the same time, researchers are often wary of psychodynamic perspectives for good reasons: They often lack theoretical clarity and contain untested or untestable assumptions. For these reasons, an open-minded yet critical stance toward these views is advisable. With that caveat in mind, I turn to Freud, whose work has shaped more current developments in psychodynamic theorizing.

The Classic Psychoanalytic Theory of Sigmund Freud

Freud's primary focus was on personality and psychopathology, but he applied his theorizing to issues relevant to prejudice in several of his works, including *Group Psychology and the Analysis of the Ego* (1921/1967), *Civilization and Its Discontents* (1929/1961), and *Moses and Monotheism* (1939/1955). Freud's assumption that prejudice reflects fundamental aspects of human nature may have arisen from his use of his theory of personality to understand group phenomena such as prejudice. He saw prejudice as a reflection of the way in which people grapple with unconscious feelings and motivations. This is consistent with his theory of personality, which especially emphasized the inner dynamics of the psyche. Where he drew links between inner experience and the outer social world, he viewed social dynamics as reflections of the individual psyche rather than the reverse. This stands in contrast to other major historical thinkers (e.g., Karl Marx) who felt that people's inner experiences are shaped in fundamental ways by the social conditions in which they live.

Freudian theory of personality is often visually illustrated by an iceberg to highlight the importance he placed on unconscious determinants of personality and behavior. People's sense of their personality and inner experience is just the tip of the iceberg that is visible above water, whereas the substance of a person's full personality remains hidden, like the bulk of an iceberg under water, in unconscious emotions and motives. What, in Freud's view, lurks in this unconscious stew? He viewed the content of the unconscious as both idiosyncratic and shared. Idiosyncratic material relates to details of individuals' lives, such as emotionally significant events (e.g., a person who experiences abandonment during infancy might hold unconscious feelings about this), whereas shared experiences involve themes that cut across people. For example, with a tip of his hat to Darwin, Freud reasoned that all people are motivated by primal instinctive drives (sexuality, aggression) and that all people show evidence of these themes in the content of their dreams, their hopes and fears, and so on. It was these shared themes that most notably guided his theorizing.

In Freud's analysis, one shared unconscious motive is the libido, a powerful instinctive force with obvious evolutionary significance. In his words, the libido is "sexual love with sexual union as its aim" (Freud, 1921/1967, p. 22). Unsurprisingly given the Victorian era in which Freud did his work, he was aware of the discomfort that issues of sexuality could generate, and he acknowledged that some people find sexuality to be "something mortifying and humiliating to human nature" (p. 23). He proposed that motives and emotions that would cause distress should they be consciously acknowledged are often hidden from conscious awareness. The full potency of the libido was thus presumed to lurk in the unconscious, slipping out indirectly in dreams, slips of the tongue, and so on.

Like a pot of boiling water with a lid on it, instinctive drives push for expression. Freud reasoned that people's psyches handle the conflict of having both drives that need expression and a conscious aversion to those drives by distorting or masking their expression. In addition to manifesting in dreams and other symbolic form, the libido is often indirectly experienced as a variety of forms of uncontaminated love. As Freud (1921/1967) wrote, it is experienced as "on the one hand, self-love, and on the other, love for parents and children, friendship and love for humanity in general, and also devotion to concrete objects and to abstract ideas" (p. 22).

For Freud, much of conscious experience and behavior reflected individuals' unique indirect expressions of shared unconscious material. People may outwardly seem quite different—a woman who appears to be a natural mother may focus her libido on parental love for her children, whereas an independent free spirit may focus her libido on love of art—despite having the same unconscious push toward life. Manifest experiences and behavior, for Freud, often reflected translations of more basic shared unconscious and instinctive forces.

In addition to primal drives, Freud (1921/1967), like his student Jung, reasoned that humans carry other types of shared unconscious material, specifically traces of events from their ancestral past in the form of unconscious feelings and related motives and wishes. Drawing loosely on a Darwinian hypothesis that early humans were horde animals ruled by a dominant male with associated status hierarchies and struggles, Freud proposed that people (and here he seemed to focus on male people) carry a profound unconscious ambivalence toward their fathers because of historical traces of competition with the "primal father" or the dominant male of a group. He speculated that "the fortunes of this horde have left indestructible traces upon the history of human descent" and that core to these traces was "the killing of the chief by violence" (p. 54). Consequently, in Freud's thinking, people's (particularly men's) relationships with their fathers are characterized by ambivalence. On the one hand, most men have conscious wishes for identification, connection, and love with father figures. On the other hand, these feelings exist in conjunction with unconscious traces of animosity and competition with the primal father. It was this description of the basic human need for identification, connection, and love combined with unconscious traces of competition and hostility, and the assumption that unconscious material often seeks indirect expression, that formed the basis of Freud's thinking about prejudice.

With respect to prejudice, Freud (1921/1967) saw as his task explaining the behavior and thinking of people who felt some emotional connection to a group and evidenced prejudice against those outside the group. Like others before him, Freud presumed that membership in a group shapes people's behavior and mental and emotional states in many negative ways, including generating negativity toward outsiders. Perhaps as a consequence of witnessing the destructive behavior of military groups during World War I, writers whom Freud noted, such as LeBon and McDougall, claimed that when people identified emotionally with their group, a collective mentality or *group mind* emerged. This group mind was thought to involve the suppression of individuality and surfacing of an uncritical state in which people are open to social influence within the group and are inclined to behave in an emotionally driven and capricious manner. Prejudice and hostility against outsiders was presumably consistent with this state. For Freud (1921/1967), such behaviors reflected the emergence of shared unconscious material in the group context and a consequent "revival of the primal horde" (p. 55).

Freud thought that it was significant that this sort of group dynamic often occurs in groups with a clear leader. He claimed that the leader symbolized the primal father to group members and that many groups are held together by a central illusion—that the head of the group loves all the members. He gave special attention to the Catholic Church, pointing out that the central illusion for Christians was that Christ (a symbolic father figure) loved all group members. For Freud (1921/1967), because the group leader is a substitute father figure, all the emotional power of related libidinal ties and unconscious ambivalence toward this figure emerges in the group context.

First, Freud reasoned that one consequence of people's need for an emotional connection with a father figure is a binding to the group and a generation of obedience to the leader and conformity among group members. Moreover, the fear of cessation of emotional ties with the father figure causes behavior to be geared toward maintaining ties to the group, which gives the group the power of social influence so that any norms that emerge in the group—including prejudice—are absorbed by the members. Not only are they absorbed, they are strengthened by the power of the group bond. Because of the unconscious potency of the need to maintain libidinal ties within the group, the group mentality moves toward consensus and sharpness. It apparently goes "directly to extremes; if a suspicion is expressed, it is instantly changed into an incontrovertible certainty; a trace of antipathy is turned into furious hatred. . . . It is as intolerant as it is obedient to authority" (Freud, 1921/1967, p. 10). People's need to cement a feeling of connection with a father figure—although healthy in its own right—can, in Freud's view, have the surprising effect of leading them to be submissive to their groups, giving leaders the power to perpetuate prejudice.

In addition, targeting outsiders also protects libidinal ties with the father figure when outsiders may be viewed as a threat to the integrity of the leader. For example, members of other religions, because of their different beliefs, may be seen as threatening the validity of the father's teachings. Such outsiders are thus convenient targets for redirected negativity. The unconscious need to protect libidinal bonds is powerful in Freud's analysis. He wrote, "A religion, even if it calls itself the religion of love, must be hard and unloving to those who do not belong to it," and as a result "cruelty and intolerance toward those who do not belong to it are natural to every religion" (Freud, 1921/1967, p. 30). Indeed, it is the very strength of the within-group love that necessitates such prejudice.

Second, unconscious ambivalence toward the father figure was presumed to further strengthen prejudice against outsiders among group members. For Freud, echoes of competitiveness with the primal father lurk in the unconscious as remnants of people's ancestral past. Indeed, he presumed that ambivalence characterizes all relationships, just as love sometimes coexists with strong antipathy. In Freud's view, relationships with a group leader and other group members were no exception. However, negative feelings cannot be experienced directly without creating anxiety. Consciously recognizing hostility toward one's group leader—a symbolic father figure—would be emotionally parallel to admitting hatred of one's real father and could threaten one's status as a group member. Because this possibility is often too frightening for most people to endure, the negativity is expressed indirectly—it is displaced (redirected) onto an emotionally safe target, the "other." From this perspective, prejudice against outsiders is a necessary outcome of the need to maintain connection within a group despite feelings of ambivalence toward it.

In summary, Freud viewed prejudice as an outcome of shared unconscious themes pertaining to the need for libidinal connections with others and ambivalence toward father figures. Needs for connection bind people to their groups and make group members vulnerable to social influence. Unconscious animosity toward father figures is expressed indirectly by projecting it onto outsiders. If people cannot tolerate the inevitable feelings of ambivalence that arise in relationships—or if their groups do not allow for expression of such complex feelings—they may unfairly target others with misdirected negativity.

Freud's ideas about prejudice have proven difficult to substantiate empirically. Efforts to test psychodynamic interpretations of prejudice (e.g., Adorno, Frenkel-Brunswik, Levinson, & Sanford, 1950) have been fraught with methodological challenges and are generally viewed as inconclusive. However, some of Freud's core ideas have been elaborated in different forms and subjected to empirical tests. For example, the idea that unconscious processes play a role in prejudice has received considerable research support, as I show in Chapter 7. In addition, Freud's observation that love attachments to one's group underlie prejudice is a foundational idea of a contemporary approach to prejudice, social identity theory (Tajfel & Turner, 1986); this theory and related research are described in Chapter 6. Thus, some foundational assumptions made by Freud (e.g., the role of unconscious process and group identification in prejudice) have been tested and found to contain degrees of truth, whereas the specific details of his analysis of prejudice (e.g., the roles of ambivalence toward father figures and misdirection of libidinal impulses in prejudice) are probably best viewed as unsubstantiated hypotheses.

Other Psychodynamic Views

Freud's legacy is indisputably widespread. With respect to work on prejudice, his enduring influence is most evident in work on the authoritarian personality (Adorno et al., 1950), object relations theory (Fairbain, 1952), and the frustration–aggression hypothesis (Dollard, Doob, Miller, Mowrer, & Sears, 1939).

The Authoritarian Personality

Theodor Adorno worked as a psychologist at the University of California, Berkeley, around the time of World War II. He and several colleagues were concerned with what they viewed as a prefascistic authoritarian personality that they thought could lead people to undermine democracy and engage in destructively hateful acts similar to those that occurred during the Holocaust (Adorno et al., 1950). In this view, a person with an authoritarian personality tends to be submissive to authority, conventional, accepting of aggression, and inclined to use simplistic stereotypic thinking. This person is prejudiced by his or her nature.

Adorno et al. (1950) drew insights from Freud in order to attempt to understand the development of this personality type. In essence, they argued that the dynamics described by Freud in his group psychology were especially likely to occur among people raised in families in which the father was punitive yet emotionally remote. In these contexts, children would learn to repress any feelings that were threatening to them, including impulses that would meet with parental disapproval such as anger at parents. Instead of experiencing these feelings directly, they would be projected onto safe targets. Prejudice, and a propensity to submit to authorities who might oppress scapegoats, was presumed to be the result of this process.

Although Adorno et al.'s (1950) attempts to test their ideas about the familial influences on authoritarianism have been widely criticized as inconclusive, a more recent related body of work has described the authoritarian personality and its correlates. In a sustained program of research, Canadian Bob Altemeyer has developed a measure of right-wing authoritarianism, showing it to be a meaningful descriptor of a personality type. Authoritarian individuals tend to be aggressive, submissive, and conventional. Moreover, people with an authoritarian personality tend to be prejudiced against a wide range of groups (Altemeyer, 1982, 1988, 2006). Altemeyer rejected the psychodynamic interpretation of the origins of the authoritarian personality, however, and explained it in terms of socialization, showing that authoritarian parents tend to raise their children to be similarly authoritarian. Drawing on both psychodynamic and socialization perspectives, recent research has shown that socialization that leads people to be conforming and to believe that the world is a dangerous place encourages the development of an authoritarian ideological orientation (Duckitt, Wagner, du Plessis, & Birum, 2002).

Object Relations Theory

Object relations theory is an extension of classic psychoanalysis that describes how people's self-concept is rooted in and shaped by relationships (Fairbain, 1952; Klein, 1949). Early in life, attachments to caregivers are critical to the formation of a child's sense of self. Young children cannot understand that people and relationships can be good and bad at the same time. As a consequence, they tend to split these emotions and represent others in their life in discrete terms, as all good or all bad. These representations become internalized "good objects" and "bad objects." The need that people have to establish bonds with a good object and to avoid hurts from a bad object shape subsequent social relationships. People may perpetuate an emotional splitting during adulthood by idealizing some people while derogating others, by feeling unduly threatened by ordinary hurts by loved ones, and so on. The theory helps to explain how and why individuals have more and less healthy interpersonal relationships, and it has also been used to explain difficulties people have in relating to other groups (e.g., Aviram, 2006; Friedman, 2007).

Aviram (2006) proposed that early relationships with family "provide a template for identifications with in-groups" (p. 6). People whose emotional experience is strongly shaped by the splitting of representations of others into good and bad objects are likely to feel both a strong need to satisfy attachment needs and a clear need to avoid dependency on a potentially hurtful bad object in an interpersonal relationship. Consequently, people who carry such needs from childhood into adulthood are said to be likely to identify especially strongly with their ingroups, so that strong identification with one's group can "compensate for the experienced inadequacy of the infantile character" (Aviram, 2006, p. 6). According to Aviram (2006), the need for a sense of emotional safety can be achieved "by idealizing the in-group, and blurring the distinction between the self and the in-group" (p. 10). At the same time, separating the self from emotional threat by projecting bad objects onto outgroup members is thought to lead to prejudice.

As with Freudian theory, object relations interpretations of prejudice have not gathered much empirical attention, and so the validity of the theory as an explanation for prejudice is unknown. Some clinical case studies have provided insights seemingly consistent with the theory (e.g., Aviram, 2006), yet given the potential for varied interpretations of people's myriad emotional experiences, such evidence is not conclusive. However, object relations theory has proven very helpful in understanding interpersonal relationships, and so it may in the future prove to be similarly useful for contributing insights regarding prejudice.

Frustration and Aggression

In 1939, around the time that Freud's ideas were making their mark, Dollard et al. published a book called *Frustration and Aggression*. In it, they drew on the Freudian idea that inner tensions are energizing and often prompt people to express them in indirect form. They proposed that animosity against the targets of prejudice can result from the frustration that people feel when they inevitably face some barriers in their efforts to meet their various goals. This frustration, they reasoned, leads to a motive to aggress against the source of the frustration. For example, an employee who is denied a promotion may feel a motivation to express aggression against the employer. However, in many circumstances it is difficult to target the source of the frustration. Just as one ought not to express aggression against an employer, it is inadvisable to express aggression against loved ones and impossible to express aggression against life circumstances. Therefore, following the Freudian notion that motives can be expressed indirectly, Dollard et al. (1939) proposed that people often target scapegoats such as vulnerable groups to release their frustration. The employee denied a promotion might find him- or herself lashing out with prejudice against innocent bystanders as a result of his or her frustration.

Some striking evidence initially appeared to be consistent with this view. For example, Hovland and Sears (1940) used the frustration–aggression hypothesis to explain a horrific manifestation of prejudice in the American South in relatively recent history—the murder of African Americans by lynching. They speculated that poor White Americans might have aggressively scapegoated Black Americans as a result of economic frustration. Indeed, they found that between 1882 and 1930 in the southern United States, there was a strong correlation between the number of Black Americans who were murdered by lynching and the price of cotton. When prices were low, suggesting economic downturns, the number of lynchings was high. This was often interpreted in line with the frustration–aggression hypothesis; economically frustrated people may have lashed out at an especially vulnerable group.

Despite the striking nature of this evidence, other examinations of relations between economics and prejudice have failed to show clear links between economic downturns and general increases in prejudice and intergroup aggression. D. P. Green, Glaser, and Rich (1998) tracked the number of hate crimes that were perpetrated against minorities (racial, religious, ethnic, or sexual orientation) in the New York area between 1987 and 1995 and assessed whether they corresponded to the unemployment rate. Although levels of hate crimes and the unemployment rate both varied, they did not fluctuate together. Also, most contemporary work on frustration and aggression has shown that when links between frustration and aggression do occur, people tend to respond with hostility primarily against those who are deemed responsible for the frustrations rather than against neutral scapegoats (Berkowitz & Harmon-Jones, 2004; Esses & Jackson, 2008), indicating that although links between frustrating situations and prejudice sometimes emerge, prejudice and aggression against other groups is not a result of a psychodynamic process of scapegoating as the frustration–aggression hypothesis proposed. An alternative explanation is offered in Chapter 6.

In summary, psychodynamic perspectives offer a range of rich and speculative ideas about the origins of prejudice. Although little research evidence has clearly supported any of the perspectives in their entirety, some core ideas have been enormously influential in shaping contemporary work on prejudice. The ideas that unconscious processes, identification with groups, family relations, personality, and difficult frustrating situations play a role in prejudice continue to stimulate developments in theory and research, and I explore many of these issues in later chapters.

TERROR MANAGEMENT THEORY

Terror management theory offers an intriguing explanation for prejudice: People are prejudiced because they are afraid of death. Psychologists Solomon, Greenberg, and Pyszczynski (1991) developed terror management theory in an effort to provide an integrative account of social motivation and behavior. Their influences include psychodynamic perspectives, evolutionary theory, and existential philosophy. From psychodynamic perspectives, they borrowed the idea that much behavior is unconsciously motivated and shaped by defensive responses. From evolutionary theory, they drew on the notion that people are centrally motivated to survive and reproduce. From existential philosophy, they viewed the inevitability of death as a prod that motivates people to seek meaning in life.

The central tenets of the theory are as follows. Human beings, because they are shaped by evolution, are motivated to preserve their lives and to reproduce. Because humans have complex brains and consciousness, they have the ability to anticipate the future, which includes inevitable death. Awareness of one's mortality generates anxiety, which is dealt with through the development and enhancement of *cultural worldviews*: "humanly created, shared beliefs that provide individuals with the sense that they are valuable members of an enduring, meaningful universe" (Solomon, Greenberg, & Pyszczynski, 2000, p. 200). Through participation in cultural worldviews, people gain a sense of immortality. This immortality may be assumed to be literal (e.g., religious beliefs in an afterlife) or symbolic (e.g., immortality through identification with enduring aspects of a culture).

Because people apparently assuage existential terror through involvement in cultural worldviews, threats to them generate anxiety similar to the terror of death. If one's worldview is proven to be mistaken, one's emotional defense against the terror of death is destroyed. As a consequence, compensatory dynamic defense mechanisms are used to keep the anxiety at bay. Fear of death is repressed, and negativity is projected outward. Prejudice—especially derogating people who threaten one's cherished worldview—is one such response because people with different beliefs can challenge the validity of one's own anxiety buffer. According to terror management theory, "the ongoing ethnic strife pervading human history is in large part the result of humans' inability to tolerate those with different death-denying visions of reality" (Solomon et al., 2000, p. 201). Moreover, the theory describes how people with low self-esteem, whose sense of value and purpose is already vulnerable, ought to be most inclined to defend against death and insignificance by emphasizing the positive value of their own cultural and religious groups and devaluing others (Pyszczynski et al., 2004).

A substantial body of evidence in support of the theory exists. Most relevant are studies that examine the effects of temporary events that make mortality salient (e.g., viewing video footage of a death scene or writing about one's thoughts about death) on people's defensive responses. Research has shown, for example, that people who have been led to think about death report more positive attitudes toward those who bolster their worldview and more negative attitudes toward those who threaten it. For example, a manipulation of mortality salience led Christians to report more positive evaluations of Christians and less favorable evaluations of Jews (J. Greenberg et al., 1990). In addition, researchers have found that mortality salience increases people's tendency to express sexist ideas (Fritsche & Jonas, 2005). People given reminders of death are also more accepting of racist others (J. Greenberg, Schimel, Martens, Solomon, & Pyszcznyski, 2001). Moreover, although there is some mixed evidence, generally people low in self-esteem are those most inclined to show these effects, as the theory predicts (Pyszczynski et al., 2004). The idea that the threat of death is unconscious is supported by evidence showing that outgroup derogation occurs in response to death-related stimuli presented to people below the threshold of awareness (e.g., too quickly to be consciously recognized; Castano, 2004). Overall, evidence is fairly convincing that people's tendency to orient more strongly toward their own and to reject others who are in some way threatening functions, in part, to alleviate existential anxiety.

Taken as a whole, the evolutionary and psychodynamic perspectives provide valuable insights and speculations about the distal origins of prejudice. Human nature and the human brain appear to have evolved to lead people to be wary of potentially threatening others and to respond to them with a degree of alarm and caution. Thus, prejudice may be pervasive and persistent in part because of its basis in survival mechanisms in humans' biology and ancestral past. It may also reflect deeply seated existential needs characteristic of human nature. Freud speculated about how the very development of groups, especially cultural and religious groups, can serve needs for meaning and identity, and research based on terror management theory has shown that similar existential needs can underscore prejudice against people who are seen to threaten the legitimacy of these cultural and religious groups. These contributions help to explain why prejudice remains powerful even though the circumstances of human lives have changed enormously over the millennia. Other perspectives, addressed in the next chapter, add to these insights by showing how contemporary social conditions can shape how prejudice manifests and serve to further perpetuate it.

4

IDEOLOGY AND PREJUDICE

In medieval Europe, many people unlucky enough to be mentally ill, old, unattractive, or widowed endured persecution and torture, and roughly 50,000 were murdered. The culprit was *belief*. Common folklore included a belief in witches, "covens of pagan dissidents, meeting in secret, betrothed to Satan, abandoning themselves to the pleasures of group sex, cannibalism, and the casting of spells upon neighbors, crops, and cattle" (Harris, 2004, p. 87). People believed to be witches were shunned, tortured, and subjected to brutal murders, such as being burned alive.

During the Holocaust, more than 6 million Jewish people were tortured and murdered, along with scores of others who were killed because of their ethnicity, disability, sexual orientation, or religion. Children were subjected to torturous experiments, including amputations and chemical injections into the eyes. People were crammed into freight trains and taken to extermination camps, where they suffered brutal treatment until their deaths in gas chambers. The causes were numerous and included economic and political factors, yet arguably beliefs played a role by providing legitimacy to the Nazi movement. Some of the beliefs that supported the culture of anti-Semitism were secular in nature. For example, part of the impetus for the Holocaust was the ideological attachment among Nazis to the conspiracy theory that pitted a Jewish agenda to control the world against a similar vision among Aryans. Yet the ethos of anti-Semitism was undeniably linked to religious ideology as well, given Christian notions that Jews were responsible for the death of Christ and depictions of Jews as children of the devil. Research by Pargament, Trevino, Mahoney, and Silberman (2007) on the attitudes of American Christians has shown that even today a sizable minority of Christians view Jews as a threat to Christian values, and these feelings of threat predict anti-Semitic attitudes.

Beliefs (both secular and religious) shape intergroup responses in many ways. During the past 2 decades, the role of particular types of beliefs—*ideologies*—in shaping prejudice and discrimination has received increased attention. When clusters of beliefs coalesce around central themes such as political or religious principles and serve to influence how people understand and respond to events, they are deemed to be ideologies (e.g., Jost, 2006). For example, political and religious conservatism or liberalism can be viewed as ideologies because they all involve sets of beliefs held together by common assumptions, and they tend to motivate people to behave in particular ways.

Perspectives on prejudice that examine the role of ideologies in sustaining or creating prejudice can be viewed as mid-range theories that build on distal explanations. Whereas distal explanations primarily look at fundamental aspects of human nature that can play a role in shaping attitudes, mid-range theories especially emphasize how common beliefs often arise in communities that support prejudice. Although some mid-range theories acknowledge original causes and precipitating factors, they do not stress them. Rather, they give particular emphasis to the kinds of beliefs that are associated with prejudice and how and why people develop these beliefs.

In this regard, societal factors such as the degree of inequality between groups are emphasized. Several contemporary theories view prejudice as part of an ideology that emerges in society as a way of perpetuating inequality to the benefit of those at the top of the social heap. The notion that people form and hold beliefs that serve to perpetuate social arrangements has a long history, having been examined by thinkers such as Plato and Aristotle around 300–340 BCE, Machiavelli in the 1500s, Marx and Engels in the mid-1800s, Weber in the early 1900s (Zelditch, 2001), and numerous contemporary theorists. Central to many of these analyses is the idea that beliefs linked to prejudice perpetuate inequality because they provide a sense of legitimacy to the social system (Jost & Major, 2001).

SOCIAL DOMINANCE THEORY

Social dominance theory (Pratto, 1999; Sidanius & Pratto, 1999) draws on diverse intellectual traditions like Marxist theory and sociobiology. The theory rests on two observations. First, group hierarchies—differences among social groups in access to power, status, and wealth—are persistent and universal. Although the strength of inequality among groups varies considerably around the world, social hierarchies of some degree appear to characterize virtually all human societies regardless of political system, dominant religion, or complexity of social and economic arrangements (Pratto, Sidanius, & Levin, 2006). Indeed, group hierarchies are evident not only among humans but also among other primates.

Social dominance theory acknowledges that evolutionary theory may help to explain the initial generation of inequality. According to the theory, it would have been adaptive during the environment of evolutionary adaptedness for humans to evolve in such a way that some people within groups were motivated to control others, resulting in a hierarchical society. Adult control of children aided the survival of offspring. Male control of women, especially women's sexuality—although typically rejected by contemporary standards—was arguably adaptive in a genetic sense because it allowed men to ensure that they devoted resources to genetically related children (by ensuring fidelity from their partners; Trivers, 1972). Also, male control of subordinate men fostered access to resources (food, sexual mates) among dominant men. For these reasons, people have arguably evolved biological and psychological mechanisms that tend to generate a motivation for control and the exercise of power. Some such mechanisms, like testosterone and competitiveness, are more evident among men than women and vary by degree in people of both sexes.

The second observation on which social dominance theory rests is that group hierarchies among humans, once established, are perpetuated by the privileges of dominant groups. Although people at all points on the social ladder can conceivably improve their social status through individual merit, members of dominant groups have advantages that make this easier. For example, with respect to group differences in socioeconomic status, Sidanius, Levin, Federico, and Pratto (2001) pointed out that

> it is perfectly obvious that an upper-class child, with access to outstanding schools, extra tutoring, good nutrition, high-quality health care, and well-connected parents will do substantially better in life than an equally talented and ambitious poor child who lacks such privileges. (p. 308)

This fact does not negate the role of individual merit in individual social mobility but rather exists in addition to it.

Across cultures, privilege hierarchies exist that are organized by age, gender, and a variety of socially constructed groups (e.g., socioeconomic status, ethnicity, religion; Sidanius & Pratto, 1999). Within each of these groups is the control of some by others. Social dominance theory describes the way in which people use ideology to retain these privileges. As social theorists have long noted, people can control one another in quite different ways. Control is sometimes maintained with obvious force or violence as in cases of child abuse, partner abuse, police activity, slavery, war, and genocide. More commonly, control is maintained much more subtly. At the interpersonal level, a parent may tell a child that punishments are "for your own good," and a lover might control his partner's freedoms with claims that he is protecting her virtue (Pratto & Walker, 2001). The young man who calls his girlfriend's cell phone repeatedly when she is out with friends may claim (indeed, he may believe) that he is expressing caring and love. However, the effect is a limitation on her sense of freedom—a form of interpersonal control.

This more subtle type of control also operates at the intergroup level in the perpetuation of inequality. Contemporary social ideologies serve a similar function by providing moral and intellectual justification for inequality. These ideologies—known as *hierarchy-enhancing* myths—help perpetuate inequality by providing seemingly acceptable explanations for the existing social order.

Examples of belief systems that appear to explain (and potentially perpetuate) group hierarchy are "myriad forms of racism, sexism, heterosexism, stereotypes, notions of 'fate,' just world beliefs, nationalism, Confucianism, the doctrine of meritorious karma, classism, the Divine Rights of Kings, Manifest Destiny and internal attributions for poverty" (Pratto et al., 2006, p. 275). Prejudiced beliefs such as stereotypes that imply that subordinate groups deserve their lower status because of lesser competence thus fit among a diverse set of hierarchy-enhancing myths that are at times used to argue that social hierarchy is fair, natural, or even divinely inspired. Consistent with the idea that these ideologies contribute to the perpetuation of inequality, an abundance of research has shown correlations between endorsement of a wide range of hierarchy-enhancing myths and the belief that some groups of people are simply better than others (see Pratto et al., 2006; Sidanius & Pratto, 1999).

One example is the Protestant work ethic, a belief system derived originally from Calvinist theology. The Protestant work ethic promotes the ideas that hard work is intrinsically valuable and that people who work hard and live well will receive rewards from God both in an afterlife and in the here-and-now in the form of a comfortable life (Weber, 1904/1958). The expectation of divine rewards in an afterlife may provide comfort to those working hard for few social rewards. Also, the assumption that rewards in the here-and-now also come from God as a reward for hard work can lead to victim-blaming in situations in which some groups have fewer social rewards than others. Evidence has supported the idea that the ideology of the Protestant work ethic is associated with this form of prejudice. For example, Evangelical Protestants in the United States—whose theology is rooted in Calvinist thinking—are especially inclined to attribute the lower social status of African Americans to lack of motivation rather than to disadvantages (Hinojosa & Park, 2004).

Religiosity can be associated with hierarchy enhancement in other respects as well. For example, the belief upheld in some religions that there is virtue in suffering gives a favorable gloss to disadvantage and can be used to deny help to those who need it. Also, religiosity has been demonstrated to correlate with conservative social values (e.g., tradition, conformity, resistance to change) among followers of many Western monotheistic religions (Roccas, 2005; Schwartz & Huismans, 1995). As such, preserving traditional social structures may be integral to many religious traditions (Hunsberger & Jackson, 2005). In fact, religious fundamentalism is defined, in part, by the ideologically prescribed resistance to change (R. W. Hood, Morris, & Watson, 1986). However, Eastern religions, because they tend not to teach the idea that there is one truth, may generate more openness to variety and change (Roccas, 2005).

In contrast to hierarchy-enhancing myths, *hierarchy-attenuating* myths provide moral and intellectual challenges to inequality. For example, the belief that inequality reflects discrimination and explanations for poverty that focus on factors external to the people who are poor challenge the legitimacy of inequality, as do the politics of socialism and communism as well as philosophies such as humanism and feminism (Pratto et al., 2006). People who endorse these ideologies tend to reject the idea that some groups of people are better than others, and therefore they are more inclined to support social policies that challenge inequality (Pratto et al., 2006; Sidanius & Pratto, 1999).

Just as some religious teachings promote hierarchy-enhancing ideas, others support hierarchy attenuation, such as doctrinal teachings regarding inclusiveness and egalitarianism and the teaching from liberation theology that the Gospels dictate that the poor ought to be given preferential treatment in consideration of physical and spiritual care. Of course, the implications of religious teachings for social hierarchy are often a matter of debate for religious scholars, and religious positions change as social trends prod them to do so. For example, although the Dutch Reformed Church in South Africa legitimized apartheid before the 1990s, in the 1990s the church leadership revised its doctrine to declare apartheid a sin (Kelman, 2001). By a stroke of the pen, a hierarchy-enhancing social structure that was formerly viewed as a reflection of God's will became redefined as a sin, and the church threw its moral authority behind a more progressive hierarchy-attenuating ideal.

Hierarchy-enhancing and hierarchy-attenuating ideologies are both called myths. It is not the point of social dominance theory to suggest that some are correct and others false. Indeed, many of these myths are impossible to put to test (e.g., religious ideas about divine rewards). The point is that as ideologies they have assumptions and consequences. Hierarchy-enhancing myths rest on the assumption that inequality must result from differences among groups in deservingness, and research has shown that people who endorse them tend to agree that some groups are simply better than others. Hierarchy-attenuating myths rest on the assumption that inequality does not result from group differences in deservingness, and research has shown that people who endorse them tend to see groups as inherently equal in deservingness. The consequence of endorsement of hierarchy-enhancing or hierarchy-attenuating myths is support for or rejection of measures that maintain or challenge inequality (Pratto et al., 2006; Sidanius & Pratto, 1999).

Of course, people differ from one another in the types of ideologies they endorse. Why is this? Although the causes are numerous, experiences of privilege and disadvantage play a role. According to social dominance theory, those who—for a variety of reasons—end up at the top of the social heap tend to adapt to these roles by developing ideologies that justify their position. Considerable evidence has shown that members of dominant groups are somewhat more likely to endorse hierarchy-enhancing myths than are members of subordinate groups (Pratto et al., 2006; Sidanius & Pratto, 1999).

People sometimes develop a general ideological approach to understanding society known as *social dominance orientation*. The concept of social dominance orientation refers to "the extent of individuals' desires for group-based dominance and inequality" (Pratto et al., 2006, p. 281; see also Pratto, Sidanius, Stallworth, & Malle, 1994). People considered high in social dominance orientation view group differences in status, power, and wealth as inevitable and desirable. They tend to view the world as a competitive place in which there must be both winners and losers (Esses, Jackson, & Armstrong, 1998) and to agree that it is okay for some groups to dominate others in society even if that means harming members of other groups. People who score highly on a questionnaire measure of social dominance orientation tend to endorse a wide range of hierarchy-enhancing myths, including prejudice. They also tend to be socially conservative in nature, to resist social policies that aid disadvantaged groups (e.g., immigration, social welfare), and to support movements that maintain hierarchy (e.g., the military; Pratto et al., 2006; Sidanius & Pratto, 1999).

In contrast, people who do not end up on the top of the social ladder are more inclined to develop a lower social dominance orientation. People described as low in social dominance orientation see equality as an ideal and tend to agree that societies should strive toward creating equality of living conditions for all groups. Such individuals are more oriented toward achieving connections with others rather than competing for status (Pratto et al., 2006), and they are more inclined to think that win–win situations in which all groups can benefit from greater equality are possible (Esses et al., 1998). They endorse hierarchy-attenuating myths and tend to be comparatively lower in prejudice than others, and they support more liberal policies and institutions that pro-mote equality (Pratto et al., 2006; Sidanius & Pratto, 1999).

What comes first, privilege or a social dominance orientation? Most likely, there is a cycle of influence. Human evolution sculpts people to be more or less oriented toward dominance (Sidanius & Pratto, 1999), and parenting practices that emphasize tough-mindedness and competitiveness reinforce dominant tendencies (Duckitt et al., 2002). Yet, because these differences have led people to create social hierarchies, people at the top of the heap per-petuate their own privileges and legitimize these hierarchies by developing an exaggerated dominance orientation. Two lines of evidence have shown that privilege can lead to the development of a dominance orientation. First, it is clear that people's experiences of privilege and disadvantage vary across differ-ent circumstances. An Aboriginal man may be privileged relative to women within his community, but he is disadvantaged in society at large because of his ethnicity. Consequently, people's social dominance orientation is similarly context dependent. Indeed, evidence has shown that when people focus on their higher status group memberships, they evidence a stronger social domi-nance orientation than when they focus on their lower status group member-ships (Levin, 1996, as cited in Pratto et al., 2006; Schmitt, Branscombe, & Kappen, 2003). Because all people have many group memberships (e.g., gender, age, ethnic, sexual orientation, economic), the varieties of privilege and disadvantage are many. Thus, the unique circumstances of people's lives, including their myriad experiences with privilege and disadvantage, shape their dominance orientation and also their belief systems. Granted that all generali-ties contain exceptions, this logic implies that people who consistently experi-ence greater privilege than disadvantage ought to typically reveal a stronger social dominance orientation than do others, and evidence has supported this proposition (Pratto et al., 2006; Sidanius & Pratto, 1999).

Second, research by Guimond, Dambrun, Michinov, and Duarte (2003) has clearly illustrated how people's experiences shape their social dominance orientation and, as a result, influence prejudice. They examined attitudes and beliefs among upper and lower level university students in law and psychology. These disciplines were chosen because they differ in status and typical income, with law being more of a power profession. The researchers reasoned that stu-dents' experiences with education in these fields would alter their social domi-nance levels and, as a result, influence their prejudice levels. Indeed, they found that although new students in these two fields did not differ from one another in average levels of social dominance orientation or prejudice, senior students differed on both variables, with seasoned law students being both more domi-nance oriented and more prejudiced than senior psychology students. Addi-tional evidence has shown that students in the social sciences become less dominance oriented during the course of their education because this type of education reduces people's belief in the genetic origins of human behavior and personality (Dambrun, Kamiejski, Haddadi, & Duarte, 2009).

Other evidence has confirmed the general point that engagement in roles that emphasize social hierarchy can change social dominance levels. For example, Nicol, Charbonneau, and Boies (2007) found that whereas applicants to a Canadian military school were actually lower in social dominance orientation than were a group of nonapplicants, seasoned students in this context were more dominance oriented than were nonstudents. Because the military is inherently hierarchical with its ranking system, experience with this hierarchy apparently leads people to see it as legitimate.

In conclusion, social dominance theory proposes that inequality and prejudice are pervasive and persistent because social ideologies tend to reinvent social hierarchy. According to the theory, the ability of some people to control others was historically adaptive, and so evolution has shaped some people to have characteristics associated with dominance. Inequality persists in large part not because dominants always force control but because they have the power to shape social thinking by promoting legitimizing ideologies that protect their privilege. Prejudiced beliefs such as stereotypes are one such ideology, although there are many others, such as political and religious beliefs that explain group differences in terms of deservingness. Because many of these ideologies mask their function behind reasonable or ethical-seeming ideals, many people accept them. People who accept these ideologies tend to support social policies that retain inequality and resist policies that alter it. Once social institutions that sustain inequality are stabilized in a society, they tend to reinforce and reinvent the social dominance orientation that gave rise to them in the first place.

Social dominance theory has been criticized for its reliance on evolutionary assumptions to explain inequality. For example, Jost, Burgess, and Mosso (2001) cautioned that approaches to prejudice that rely on evolutionary assumptions risk becoming legitimizing myths themselves because they claim that status differences between groups rest in essential qualities of human nature. Although an important warning to consider, there is a difference between dominance and deservingness, and theorizing that early humans evolved to vary in dominance seeking does not imply that those who now have power deserve it any more (or less) than others do. For example, achieving power through brute force may have aided early human coalitions by placing physically capable people in leadership positions during conflict, but in the modern world effective leadership requires intellectual, emotional, and social effectiveness far more than physical strength or social dominance (see Eagly & Chin, 2010). It is the tendency that some people have to confuse dominance with deservingness—and to elaborate ideologies that justify the former—that shows the essence of a legitimizing myth.

SYSTEM JUSTIFICATION THEORY

In 1939, an African American woman named Mamie Phipps Clark completed a master's degree in psychology at Howard University in which she reported an examination of the self-concepts and attitudes of African American children (Guthrie, 2004). In this now-famous research, Clark asked children to choose between a White doll and a Black doll and to describe the dolls as pretty or ugly, good or bad. A disturbingly large portion of the Black children preferred to play with the White doll, which they saw as pretty and good, rather than the Black doll, which they viewed as ugly and bad (e.g., Clark & Clark, 1939). Apparently, these children had absorbed the negative messages about their own group that were a pervasive part of the culture at the time. As a team, Mamie and her husband, Kenneth Clark, subsequently used this research to challenge school segregation in the United States, which they viewed as detrimental to the self-concepts of African American children.

It is unlikely that similar research findings would emerge today. Most contemporary research has shown that members of minority or disadvantaged groups do not typically devalue their own group. Rather, members of advantaged and disadvantaged groups alike usually show a bias in favor of their own group (see Jost, Banaji, & Nosek, 2004). However, there are important exceptions to this pattern. For example, in a study of the attitudes of African Americans and European Americans, Jost et al. (2004) demonstrated that between 8% and 40% of African American people showed a bias in favor of European Americans, whereas far fewer (5%–9%) of European Americans showed a bias in favor of African Americans. A similar pattern occurred in their parallel study of the attitudes of heterosexual and gay people, with 14% to 38% of gay people but only 9% to 10% of heterosexual people showing an evaluative preference for the other group. Thus, a nontrivial minority of people showed an evaluative bias in favor of the other group rather than their own, and the number who did so were disproportionately among the disadvantaged (see Jost et al., 2004).

Why would members of disadvantaged groups sometimes hold attitudes that seem to conflict with their own interests? System justification theory (Jost & Banaji, 1994) addresses this issue by positing that intergroup attitudes often reflect the interplay of three basic psychological needs. Attitudes sometimes reflect the need people have to feel good about themselves—the need for *ego justification*. Attitudes can also reflect people's need to positively evaluate their own group—the need for *group justification*. Endorsing especially positive stereotypes of one's own group can meet both of these needs because by belonging to a valued group, one can feel good about oneself (Tajfel & Turner, 1986). However, sometimes these needs are trumped by a third need—*system justification*—that is, the need to believe that the society in which one lives is fair, legitimate, and justifiable. As Lerner (1980) described, believing that the world they live in is fair allows people to feel a sense of optimism about their future and to trust that their talents and efforts are worthwhile and will pay off. Indeed, the feeling that one can control outcomes in one's life is a key predictor of psychological well-being (Steptoe, 2000).

According to system justification theory (Jost & Banaji, 2004), the need to believe that life is fair extends to people's understanding of the social realm. The assumption that people are motivated to believe that social arrangements are fair, and feel better if they can be justified, has been substantiated empirically. For example, Haines and Jost (2000) had student research participants participate in an exercise in which other students had power over them. The participants reported that they felt better when an explanation for the power differential was provided, even if it was an unreasonable justification. Moreover, they often later distorted the unreasonable explanation in memory to make it seem legitimate. Apparently, people are indeed motivated to make sense of things even if they are not sensible. By implication, people may derive a sense of fairness and sensibility about the social system by accepting beliefs and attitudes that legitimize inequality. Hierarchy-enhancing myths, such as stereotypes, that imply that advantaged groups are more competent in critical ways than others are system justifying because they purport to explain differences in group status in terms of group deservingness (Jost & Thompson, 2000).

The need for system justification may lead some members of disadvantaged groups to endorse ideologies that legitimize the social system even at the cost of ego and group justification. Jost et al. (2001) analyzed data on the stereotypes that northern and southern Italians endorsed of themselves and one another. The social position of these groups has differed for many years, with northern Italians enjoying higher status and more wealth than southern Italians. Jost et al. showed that northern Italians consistently rated their own group more positively (e.g., more honest and law abiding, less violent and lazy) than they rated southern Italians, yet southern Italians consistently rated their own group more negatively (e.g., less honest and law abiding, more violent and lazy) than they rated northern Italians. This tendency to see the higher status group in a more positive light was especially pronounced for those Italians who described themselves as having a "right-wing" versus a "left-wing" political belief system (Jost et al., 2001; see also Jost et al., 2004). Apparently, for both advantaged and disadvantaged group members, conservative ideology is linked to acceptance of status differences between groups.

Although justifying the social system is presumed to meet a psychological need for a sense of fairness and order, engaging in system justification has quite different implications for members of advantaged and disadvantaged groups. Endorsing beliefs that confirm a sense that life is fair (even if it is not) may be reassuring for those who experience relatively high degrees of privilege. However, system justification is likely to be more troubling to members of disadvantaged groups who are engaging in legitimization of their own lower social status. Women who accept the belief that men are more natural leaders than women are may feel better about the social system, but it is at the expense of their respect for their group and by extension themselves. Members of ethnic minorities may avoid the pain of acknowledging unfair treatment by stereotyping their group as less achievement oriented than others, but this belief can give rise to other more personal hurts associated with self- and group image. It is not surprising, then, that some evidence has shown that although rationalizing inequality tends to make members of higher status groups feel good (e.g., to feel more positive emotions and fewer negative ones such as guilt), it is demoralizing for members of lower status groups and predicts lower self-esteem and more depression (Jost & Thompson, 2000).

In summary, system justification theory begins with the observation that a minority of members of disadvantaged groups show an evaluative preference for the dominant groups rather than their own, at variance with the more common pattern of ingroup preference. To explain this preference, the theory posits that at times the need to perceive the world as orderly and fair leads members of disadvantaged groups to accept negative messages about their group that legitimize inequality. Because engaging in system justification comes at the expense of the need to feel good about the self and one's group for disadvantaged group members, it is associated with costs to personal well-being.

AMBIVALENT PREJUDICE

On March 15, 2008, the *Globe and Mail* (one of Canada's national newspapers) reported a story in which citizens protested at the office of a Toronto politician because of remarks he made about Asian people. In a debate about holiday shopping, the politician argued that there should not be restrictions on holiday shopping, referring to Hong Kong as an example. He is quoted as saying,

> I've been there. You want to see workaholics? These Oriental people work like dogs. They work their hearts out. . . . That's why they're successful in life . . . I'm telling you, Oriental people, they're slowly taking over, because there's no excuses for them. They're hard, hard workers. (Lewington, 2008, p. 12)

In response to the subsequent criticism, he claimed that he did not realize his words were derogatory.

Why did he think it was reasonable to make these claims while others found them quite offensive? On the one hand, there was an apparently positive side of his critique—the reference to the success of Hong Kong residents in the workplace. Yet, he also dehumanized this group with his reference to working "like dogs," and his words suggested a thinly veiled warning, that people from Hong Kong are "slowly taking over." His comments suggest a grudging regard combined with feelings of threat. Although the politician may have perceived his words as complimentary, members of groups targeted by such "compliments" are aware that they are, at best, double-edged swords (e.g., Czopp, 2008). The theory of ambivalent prejudice (Glick & Fiske, 1996, 2001; Glick et al., 2001) and the related stereotype content model (Cuddy et al., 2007; Fiske et al., 2002) describe types of prejudice that have this quality of being double-edged swords that seem to flatter yet also hurt.

According to the theory of ambivalent prejudice, the specific stereotypes that are endorsed about different groups, and the distinct emotional and behavioral responses to groups that are common, reflect two core dimensions of relationships between groups: the relative status of groups and the type of interdependence experienced between that group and the group of the person expressing the attitude (Fiske et al., 2002; Glick & Fiske, 2001). Groups that, on average, enjoy high income levels, education, social power, and prestige are deemed higher in status than those that, on average, have less money, education, power, and prestige. *Interdependence* refers to the fact that outcomes for one group have implications for outcomes for the other group. Cooperative interdependence involves complementary roles that support one another, such as homemakers and breadwinners or employers and employees. Competitive interdependence exists when members of the different groups vie for some of the same resources or when one group is rising in status, provoking a loss of privilege of another. For example, relations between men and women in the workplace or between ethnic majorities and immigrants can be construed as competitively interdependent because these groups have similar interests in accessing and retaining work.

According to Glick and Fiske (2001), the dimensions of status and interdependence are consistently relevant to people's attitudes toward others because they "answer two of the most important questions we seek to answer about other individuals and groups: What is the others' status relative to my own, and is the other likely to be friend or foe?" (p. 281). People are thought to be attuned to such questions because they provide information useful for adaptation and survival. Because people high in status tend to be viewed as competent, answering these questions tells one whether a friend or foe has the capability to enact friendly or hostile intentions (Fiske, Cuddy, & Glick, 2007). People use information about status and interdependence to infer qualities about a group (e.g., stereotypes about competence) and to generate emotional and behavioral responses.

Four distinct types of intergroup attitudes are predicted to follow from the four possible combinations of status (high or low) and interdependence (cooperative or competitive), and evidence has supported these predictions (Fiske et al., 2002). Two types of attitudes are unambivalent. Attitudes toward high-status groups that cooperate with one's own tend to be unambivalently positive and involve admiration. White middle-class Americans view the middle class, Americans (both ingroups), Christians, and Black professionals as fitting this category (Fiske et al., 2007). Admiration involves positive attitudes (e.g., stereotypes that the group is competent, deserving, warm, and likable), emotions (e.g., respect), and behavioral responses (a tendency to help group members and to affiliate with them; Cuddy et al., 2007).

Contemptuous prejudice is also unambivalent, but it is negative in valence. It is directed toward groups that are perceived to be low in status and competitively interdependent because they are economically dependent or use shared resources—for example, welfare recipients (Fiske et al., 2007). This form of prejudice is characterized by stereotypes that a group is neither competent nor warm or likable. Considerable research has shown that low-income people are stereotyped as lazy, uneducated, unintelligent, and socially irresponsible (e.g., inclined to use illegal drugs; Cozzarelli, Wilkinson, & Tagler, 2001). These views are not restricted to North Americans. For example, as Glick and Fiske (2001) noted, "Socioeconomically unsuccessful groups the world over are similarly cast as lazy, animalistic, stupid, and unambitious" (p. 281). Emotional reactions tend to include disrespect, resentment, and hostility (Glick & Fiske, 2001), and people respond to contemptuous prejudice by neglecting the relevant group (e.g., refusing to support programs that aid low-income groups; Cozzarelli et al., 2001) or actively harming or attacking them (e.g., attacks on homeless people).

Two other types of attitudes are ambivalent in that they include both positive and negative elements. *Envious prejudice* arises when a group is perceived to be high or rising in status and in a situation of competitive interdependence. Recall the Toronto politician's remarks about Asian people. He expressed the view that Asian people are rising in status at the potential expense of other groups. Moreover, his tone was envious. Indeed, minority or formerly disadvantaged groups that are perceived to be competing successfully in the marketplace are vulnerable to being the recipients of envious prejudice (e.g., Asians, Jewish people; Fiske et al., 2007). This type of antipathy is characterized by stereotypes that imply that a group is competent and ambitious—as Glick and Fiske (2001) noted, it is "important not to underestimate the abilities of one's competitors" (p. 294)—but also that it is neither warm nor likable. Typical emotional responses involved in envious prejudice include feelings of envy, fear, resentment, and hostility (possibly coupled with admiration). Because envious prejudice is not uniformly negative, under the most hopeful circumstances envious prejudice tends to predict seemingly positive behaviors like tokenism in hiring practices. However, at times—for example, when economic conditions evoke stronger concerns about intergroup competition for jobs or other resources—envious prejudice also predicts active forms of harm such as harassment and bullying (Cuddy et al., 2007).

Paternalistic prejudice is the other type of ambivalent attitude. It arises when a group is perceived to be low in status but in a cooperatively interdependent relationship. In this situation, separate and complementary roles exist for higher and lower status groups. For example, employers may express paternalistic prejudice toward housecleaners or migrant workers, young and middle-aged people may view elderly people in this way, and so on. Stereotypes typical of paternalistic prejudice are sometimes called *benevolent stereotypes* (e.g., Glick & Fiske, 1996) because they involve seemingly positive characteristics (e.g., the stereotype of an elderly woman as sweet), but they are paternalistic because they also include the belief that the group is not especially competent. Emotional reactions typical of paternalistic prejudice involve pity and sympathy. For example, Fiske et al. (2002) reported that these were the primary emotions that people reported feeling in response to disabled, elderly, and intellectually challenged people. Paternalistic prejudice manifests in a tendency to help target groups in direct ways while indirectly being neglectful. For example, minor directly helpful actions such as opening doors for disabled people or women, while failing to help by breaking down barriers to full social participation, represent helping tainted by neglect. Similarly, institutionalization of elderly people can be construed as a helpful yet neglectful response to paternalism (Fiske et al., 2007). Paternalistic prejudice can be difficult to detect because it occurs in the context of affectionate and loving relationships. As Jackman (1994) wrote, "With affection comes the ability of those in command to shape the needs and aspirations of subordinates and to portray discriminatory arrangements as being in the best interests of all concerned" (p. 15).

Paternalistic prejudice also serves to perpetuate inequality through the way in which it shapes interpersonal behavior by prescribing stereotypes to which people are encouraged to conform. For example, people sometimes behave in a way that rewards women for acting in line with benevolent stereotypes yet punishes them for violating these stereotypic expectations. Hebl, King, Glick, Singletary, and Kazama (2007) reported the results of a field experiment in which people tended to treat a woman who appeared to be pregnant in a benevolent manner (e.g., touching, showing kindness) when she was shopping but to treat her in a more hostile manner (e.g., being rude) when she violated a role expectation by applying for a job, especially in a masculine field. According to Glick and Fiske (2001), benevolent stereotypes and old-fashioned hostile sexism are "complementary tools of control" (p. 290), with benevolent stereotypes serving as the carrot that leads women to accept inequality (because in a sense it is flattering to accept stereotypes involving one's own positive qualities) and more traditional hostile sexism being the stick that ensures that women do not challenge it.

These tools may be especially effective when they are used within ideological systems with broad acceptance and legitimacy, such as religions. Some contemporary teachings about gender in the Catholic Church, for example, appear to reflect benevolently sexist beliefs in that they suggest that distinct traits and roles for women are divinely inspired (Glick et al., 2002). In a letter to women written by Pope John Paul II in 1995 in conjunction with the Fourth World Conference on Women in Beijing, the Pope upheld the Virgin Mary as the "highest expression of the feminine genius" (Pope John Paul II, 1995, para. 30) for her service to God and family. Although his words were intended to express praise, they also prescribed a set of roles for women that communicated women's place in supportive roles. Do such messages shape benevolent sexism? It appears that they do. For example, Glick et al. (2002) found that practicing Catholics in Spain were more accepting of benevolent sexism than were nonpracticing Catholics, who, in turn, were more accepting of benevolent sexism than were nonbelievers.

In summary, the theory of ambivalent prejudice distinguishes between nonambivalent intergroup attitudes (admiration and contemptuous prejudice) and ambivalent forms of prejudice (envious, paternalistic). The latter two forms of prejudice mix positive and negative judgments, but by so doing they increase their negative impact through their greater appeal and acceptance. Envious prejudice leads people to engage in backlash against groups that are moving toward greater equality, and paternalistic prejudice serves to keep disadvantaged groups in their place. These forms of prejudice thus function as ideologies that serve to perpetuate the status quo.

Approaches to understanding prejudice that emphasize ideology show how society's institutions (e.g., politics, religion) generate belief systems that have wide appeal yet that also serve to maintain inequality. Core to all of the theories discussed in this chapter is the view that many forms of prejudice are difficult to detect because they include seemingly positive or benign beliefs. However, as Jackman (2001) powerfully argued, ordinary experiences and beliefs that are viewed as justifiable by many are responsible for powerful oppression. For example, she reported that the number of deaths of African American people in recent years that were the result of common forms of discrimination (e.g., inequalities in access to health care, education, and employment) is "infinitely higher" (p. 454) than the number of tragic deaths that occurred by lynching between 1882 and the 1950s. However, people may be less horrified by these more numerous deaths than by the more striking ones because the former are justified by common beliefs—specifically, popular ideas like meritocratic ideology that function as a velvet glove that hides an iron fist by which dominant groups maintain their advantages (Jackman, 1994).

5

DEVELOPMENT OF PREJUDICE IN CHILDREN

In 1997, in British Columbia, Canada, 14-year-old Reena Virk was attacked by a group of peers (seven girls, one boy) and subsequently murdered by two of them. Reena was different from many of her peers in a variety of ways. Her family had immigrated from south Asia, and thus in her majority-White neighborhood, Reena was an ethnic minority. Her parents were Jehovah's Witnesses, and so she was part of a religious minority even within her ethnic community. Also, Reena was a heavy girl who did not fit conventional standards of feminine beauty. However, the courts denied that prejudice played a role in the murders. Instead, the motivation for the murder was said to involve relatively trivial interpersonal conflicts (e.g., Reena apparently stole another girl's phone book and showed interest in a boy who was coveted by one of Reena's murderers). Yet, such common adolescent conflicts do not typically end in murder, and some people involved in the case felt that prejudice played a role. As lawyer Brenna Bhandar (2000, "Exploring the Missing Pieces," para. 1, para. 2) wrote,

> Reena did not fit into the dominant norm of white, middle-class (heterosexual) femininity. Her mere existence as a brown female, with facial hair, and with a large body, represented deviance from this dominant

norm. . . . The alleged act that led to her murder, that of stealing a phonebook from a girl, and calling boys and spreading rumours was perceived by her peers as yet another, more unforgivable transgression; the brown, large female (who was supposed to remain de-sexualized or a-sexual) was asserting her sexuality, thereby infringing on the territory of the white girl whose address book she allegedly took.

According to Bhandar's (2000) analysis, this crime occurred in part because of a pervasive climate of ethnocentrism and sexism. Inherent in this critique is the assumption that prejudice in children and adolescents is powerful, and research has confirmed that this is, sadly, often true. Therefore, understanding how and when prejudice arises in youth is a critical task, and it may aid in the prevention of growing problems of bullying and violence faced by youth. Fortunately, in most cases stigmatized children do not face the ultimate consequence experienced by Reena Virk. However, prejudice in children is hardly benign. In their work, Wessler and DeAndrade (2006) found that children and teenagers who were the targets of prejudice from their age peers frequently reported negative impacts such as pervasive anxiety, wanting to hide their identity (when possible), and self-destructiveness (truancy, drug use).

The following words are from an anonymous high school student who experienced considerable prejudice after immigrating to the United States from Africa:

> Every day I feel like I'm getting closer to going insanely psycho. This is mostly because of how racist, prejudiced, and homophobic my school is. I get so mad when I hear people say words like "nigger," "gay," "fag," and "retard" or when people come up to me and say "can I pat your hair?" I'm just hoping that I don't snap one day and do something I'll regret forever. (Wessler & DeAndrade, 2006, p. 523)

As this quote suggests, prejudice among school-age children and adolescents exists, and it hurts. After conducting focus groups with 7,000 students across 11 states in the United States, Wessler and DeAndrade (2006) concluded that most high school students hear degrading language (slurs, offensive jokes) directed at girls and racial, religious, and sexual minorities daily or several times each week. Examples provided by students were "highly degrading, often violent, and deeply disturbing" (Wessler & DeAndrade, 2006, p. 516).

It is not only adolescents who are capable of prejudice. Evidence has shown that by the age of 5, many children already show signs of prejudice on the basis of race, gender, age, physical ability, body weight, and attractiveness (Bigler & Liben, 2006). Researcher Phyllis Katz and her colleagues followed 200 families with infants for about 6 years in an effort to understand the development of prejudice. When the children were about 3 years old, to determine whether they would evaluate people differently on the basis of ethnicity, Katz (2003) showed White children pictures depicting other children, some of whom were Black and some of whom were White, in ambiguous school contexts. Children viewing the slides were asked questions about which child had initiated positive or negative events, such as "Which child will do something naughty?" or "Which child will win a game?" Katz (2003) reported that a surprising number of very young children showed signs of prejudice. For example, one 3-year-old White girl, "Elizabeth," answered every interview question in a biased way, saying for example that a Black child would do naughty things and get in trouble and so on "because he [or she] is Black," whereas a White child would win a prize or win a game of checkers "because he [or she] is White" (p. 897). By 6 years of age, White children in this research showed bias in favor of White children and against Black children. It does not appear that this was a unique sample of children. For example, research in Canada has similarly shown high levels of prejudice among young children, with even higher proportions of 5- to 6-year-olds showing prejudice in some studies (e.g., Doyle & Aboud, 1995).

If the goal is to reduce levels of prejudice in society, it is probably desirable to focus some energy on preventing the development of prejudice in children. Many forms of prejudice that are notable among adults begin to develop early, at a time in children's lives when their personalities, core values, and life goals are being formed. Although attitudes can change during the life span, even adults who embrace egalitarianism and nonprejudice often show some signs of subtle, unconscious biases that were formed during childhood (e.g., Devine, 1989; Rudman, 2004). Understanding how these attitudes originally develop is critical to the goal of attitude change.

DEVELOPMENTAL TRENDS IN THE EXPRESSION OF PREJUDICE

An infant cries when picked up by a stranger. A toddler stares wide eyed the first time she sees a person with a physical disability. A White preschool child does not want to play with a Black doll. Schoolchildren repeat sexist jokes and avoid a child whose minority status is visible. As these examples show, young children notice differences and at times express things that sound like prejudice. Even babies sometimes show signs of distress when exposed to unfamiliar people, and young children do often show fear, suspicion, or disapproval of different others (e.g., Aboud, 2005; Aboud & Amoto, 2001). At times, the negativity is striking. For example, Bar-Tal (1996) reported results of research with preschool Israeli children in which a large majority of very young children (as young as 2.5 years of age) described Arabs in negative ways (e.g., saying that they are aggressive, dirty).

A majority of the children in Bar-Tal's (1996) research did not really know what *Arab* meant; most showed considerable difficulty identifying Arab people from photographs. Children who do not understand what a group is do not seem to hold prejudice in the same form as do adults. Probably the children in Bar-Tal's research learned a verbal association between the word *Arab* and negative terms from listening to parents and the media and simply repeated what they heard without understanding the reference. Their own verbal behavior likely did not correspond to negative attitudes toward actual Arab people. Nevertheless, their evaluations of Arabs are not inconsequential. As these children developed the capability to accurately categorize people as Arab, the negative associations with the word *Arab* they learned may have generalized to the real group. Thus, early forms of bias may develop into genuine prejudice, and prejudice in older children may build on very early foundations.

For these reasons, analyzing young children's responses to different others may help in understanding the bases of prejudice. In what follows, I use the term *prejudice* to refer to evaluative responses to people on the basis of their group membership regardless of the age or cognitive ability of the children studied. However, it should be understood that this is a descriptive term, not a moral judgment, and the nature of prejudice (and its ethical implications) clearly differ at different points in the life span.

Research With Infants: Detecting Differences

Research with infants is generally geared toward understanding the age at which babies notice differences, what differences they notice, and how they respond to them. The ability to recognize categories is necessary to people's functioning, and much of infants' early learning involves differentiating different types of things (e.g., things to put in the mouth or not, things that are soft and things that are hard, familiar things and novel things). Children also categorize people (e.g., caregivers vs. strangers) and learn many types of differences between people as they develop. Because young children are faced with an amazing amount of new information, the development of categories serves an important function (Narter, 2006). Categorization is also a prerequisite of prejudice; without categories, prejudice would not be possible. With categorization comes the potential for prejudice. For example, categorization has the effect of highlighting differences between and similarities within categories (Brown, 2000) and can therefore lead to stereotyping.

A research technique often referred to as the *habituation paradigm* tests for preverbal children's categorization tendency by tracking the stimuli they attend to. It has infants view photographs of people who vary on some relevant dimension such as gender while the child's eye movements are carefully recorded. If a baby becomes inattentive after viewing photographs of several women (e.g., looks away) but then shows renewed interest in the task when a photograph of a man is shown, it suggests that he or she had noticed this distinction. Studies using this technique show that infants of about 6 months of age typically differentiate people on the basis of gender (Ramsey, Langlois, & Marti, 2005), age, and physical attractiveness (babies prefer to look at attractive than unattractive faces; see Narter, 2006). This shows that children notice differences related to some group distinctions earlier than they are able to articulate or understand them (Aboud & Amato, 2001).

Evidence is more mixed with respect to infants' tendency to notice racial cues. Some work has shown that babies do not seem to differentiate people by race (e.g., Fagan & Singer, 1979), whereas other research has shown that infants as young as 6 months of age do differentiate between people on the basis of racial cues (e.g., Katz, 2003). These mixed findings may reflect the fact that racial distinctions are especially socially constructed on the basis of a variable and complex set of physical characteristics. Thus, infants may notice and respond to some of the most evident cues (e.g., differentiate between very dark and light skin) but learn some of the more subtle cues used by adults to categorize by race at an older age. Consistent with this possibility is the fact that it takes longer for children to learn to label people by color than by gender. By age 3, the majority of children can label people correctly on the basis of gender, but only a minority can label people on the basis of skin color. The latter distinction seems to emerge around age 4 or 5; however, children often do not label people according to ethnicity until a few years later (see Narter, 2006).

Research With Young Children: The Emergence of Prejudice

An implication of categorizing people is that children may tend to see members of a group as especially similar to one another. Relevant research has tested children's tendency to use social categories by showing children photographs of people and asking who is similar and who is different. This methodology has revealed age-based trends (Aboud & Amato, 2001). Children about 4 years of age tend to focus on idiosyncratic individuating information and do not lump people together as similar on the basis of ethnicity. However, at between 5 and 6 years of age children typically start to show a tendency to view members of the same color as alike.

As well, children about this age often associate value with the categories they tend to use (Aboud, 2003). For example, Aboud (2003) measured attitudes toward White, Black, and native people among White children ages 4 to 7 in a large Canadian city. She gave the children three boxes, each of which showed one child (one White, one Black, one native). She asked the children a series of questions about the characteristics these children might have. For example, one question was "Some children are naughty. They often do things like drawing on the wall with crayons. Who is naughty?" (p. 50). Questions addressed 10 negative characteristics and 10 positive characteristics. Children were given three cards and told they could place a card into the box of the person they thought was described by the attribute. For any characteristic, the child could place a card in all three, two, only one, or none of the boxes. Ingroup favoritism was inferred from relatively high numbers of positive attributes in the White child's box, and outgroup prejudice was measured by relatively high numbers of negative attributes in the other boxes. Four-year-old children showed only a weak trend toward ingroup favoritism, whereas 70% of children 5 and older showed clear ingroup favoritism. Furthermore, children who attended an ethnically homogeneous school and therefore had little exposure to diversity often also showed outgroup prejudice.

Among minority children, attitudes are more mixed during early childhood (e.g., ages 3–6), with some studies showing the development of ingroup favoritism, some research showing outgroup preference, and some work showing an absence of ethnic bias among minority children. It is not clear why minority children's attitudes appear to be mixed, but there is some suggestion that group status, group norms, parental attitudes, and the type of prejudice being tapped by researchers play a role in the discrepant findings. For example, Katz (2003) reported that in a longitudinal study of White and Black children in the United States, at age 3 both White and Black children showed some ingroup preference. However, when these children reached ages 5 and 6, attitudes were quite different for White and Black children. Ingroup preference increased between ages 3 and 6 among White children, but it dropped among Black children. Moreover, when asked to select a friend from photographs, 86% of White children chose a White friend, whereas only 32% of Black children chose a Black friend. Katz suggested that this reflects status differences between European Americans and African Americans in the United States and that Black children begin to show signs of recognizing and responding to such status differences between groups by age 3. However, minority children who are taught to identify with their ethnic group are more likely to show ingroup favoritism than those who do not (Doyle & Aboud, 1995), and most research has shown that the majority of 7- to 10-year-old minority children no longer show preference for the outgroup (Aboud & Amato, 2001).

EXPLANATIONS OF THE DEVELOPMENT OF PREJUDICE

Why do children show prejudice, and why does it follow the developmental patterns that it does? Most current approaches to answering these questions emphasize either socialization processes or the social–cognitive development of children. A third approach considers the effect of intergroup relations on how children learn about social groups.

Socialization Perspective

It seems self-evident that children learn prejudice from the people in their environment, and there is certainly good reason to think that they do. Social learning theory (Bandura, 1977) describes how people learn from those in their environment. With respect to prejudice, Bandura (1973) wrote that "parents and other influential people, through precept, example, and their approving reactions, teach children whom they should hate and for what reasons, and how they should express their aggression toward the stigmatized targets" (p. 36). In other words, children learn prejudice through direct instruction (e.g., when racist parents share their beliefs with their children), by observing role models (when children hear stereotypes expressed on television), and by experiencing the rewards or punishments of their own early expressions of prejudice (e.g., when parents or peers laugh or frown at a prejudiced joke told by a child).

Parental Influence

The premise that children learn prejudice from their parents is so often claimed as to seem a truism. Recall Elizabeth, the 3-year old White girl in Phyllis Katz's (2003) research who answered all interview questions in a prejudiced manner, for example, claiming that it would be Black child who would get in trouble and a White child who would win at games. When reading about Elizabeth, did you assume that she must be a product of her family environment and visualize her parents as racists who taught her such ideas? According to Katz, Elizabeth's mother watched the interview with Elizabeth in horror because unlike Elizabeth she held clearly egalitarian attitudes and values. It turns out that Elizabeth's mother is not alone; the relation between parents' and children's attitudes is not entirely straightforward. For example, some research has shown that the correlation between parents' and young children's attitudes toward other groups is weak because many parents simply do not share their intergroup attitudes—positive or negative—with their young children (Aboud & Amato, 2001; Katz, 2003). However, where parents' attitudes are strongly prejudiced, the correspondence with children's attitudes tends to be stronger (e.g., Altemeyer, 1988; Altemeyer & Hunsberger, 2005). Also, adolescents' intergroup attitudes and experiences do parallel their perceptions of their parents' attitudes (Edmonds & Killen, 2009).

In more typical cases, the correspondence between children's attitudes and those of their parents may be weaker because parents do not directly address issues of difference with their children. As a consequence, children may pick up on subtle biases that parents communicate unintentionally. In the longitudinal study by Katz and colleagues (see Katz, 2003) in which children were followed from infancy to 6 years of age, the researchers observed parent–child interactions when the children were about 1.5 years of age. During the interaction, parents looked through a picture book with the child. The book contained pictures of people of different colors, ages, and sexes. The researchers noted that the parents almost never mentioned racial differences to the children, although they did mention gender frequently. However, they also found that some parents tended to focus especially on photographs of people of their own color and to ignore the others. It was the children of the parents who did this who, at age 5 or 6, showed higher levels of prejudice. This suggests one subtle form of learning that occurs. Some parents send a mixed message to children, implying the importance of color in their behavior but failing to address issues of difference explicitly to their children. It is as though some parents think that talking about race will "cause their children to see racial differences they hadn't noticed before" (Katz, 2003, p. 907). However, the reality seems to be that children hear silence as well as words.

In many cases, children may learn prejudice from adults who do not realize that they are communicating it. A variety of research programs have shown that White American and Canadian adults show nonverbal signs of discomfort when interacting with members of ethnic minorities. Even people who are committed to egalitarian ideals and generally seem non-prejudiced sometimes show nonverbal indicators of subtle prejudice such as avoiding eye contact, showing nervous tics, and so on when interacting with members of other groups (e.g., Dovidio & Gaertner, 2008; Dovidio, Hebl, Richeson, & Shelton, 2006). Children who observe adults repeatedly showing signs of discomfort around certain people are likely to learn similar feelings of discomfort.

Although parental influence may in many respects be subtle, parents do have strong influences in some ways that one might not ordinarily consider socialization. For example, parents determine where their children will grow up. Children who grow up in ethnically diverse areas show much lower prejudice than do children who grow up in homogeneous areas (Katz, 2003). Parents also influence how much television and of what sort their children watch, who their peers are likely to be, and so on, and as discussed next these are additional important socialization influences.

Media and Cultural Influences

When asked to explain prejudice, people typically point first to parents and second to the media. Certainly media attention (or lack thereof) to minority or disadvantaged groups can shape attitudes by reinforcing stereotypes and modeling prejudice. It can also communicate that people are likely to be rewarded or punished for expressing prejudice by showing this happening to television or movie characters.

Stereotypic representations of many other groups, such as ethnic, religious, and sexual minorities, are less overt than they were in previous decades. One exception may be depictions of Middle Eastern people within North America that have been, since September 11, 2001, noticeably negative. For example, after September 11, then President George W. Bush consistently used rhetoric in his speeches that depicted people of Arab or Middle Eastern background as hostile outsiders by using terms such as *us versus them, these people, evil,* and so on (Merskin, 2004). Images in motion pictures are not more realistic. Shaheen (2009) reviewed more than 1,000 Hollywood movies depicting people of Arab background and found that Arabs were consistently depicted as "brute murderers, sleazy rapists, religious fanatics, oil-rich dimwits, and abusers of women" (p. 8). In contrast, Shaheen described real Arabs as an ethnically diverse group of people, the majority of whom are young, are peaceful, and have no connections to the oil industry and whose ancestors "gave the world three major religions, a language, and an alphabet" (p. 9).

Research that examines the content of television programming has shown that typically, stereotyping persists in subtle form. For example, cartoon superheros have recently been found to be represented as primarily masculine (Baker & Raney, 2007), reinforcing the stereotype of male invulnerability and doing nothing to expand perceptions of women to include heroism. In addition, ethnic minorities continue to be depicted in subtly stereotypic ways (Rodgers, Kenix, & Thorson, 2007). For example, Rodgers et al. (2007) found that African Americans were often depicted in television programming as relatively excitable, consistent with stereotypes of aggressiveness, and Asians tended to be depicted as calm, consistent with stereotypes of studiousness. Even news media can inadvertently promote stereotypes because the news tends to focus on rare and problematic events rather than common and positive or neutral events. For example, the fact that the North American media focus on terrorism perpetrated by a comparatively small number of people of Muslim faith arguably supports the belief that Muslims are aggressive or threatening and increases perceptions of the threat of terror (e.g., Breckenridge & Zimbardo, 2007).

Stereotypes are also reflected in the media in less obvious ways, such as in the language used when discussing different groups. After Hurricane Katrina in the southern United States, news images circulated widely on the Internet were revealing. Compare the photograph of a Black man walking through water carrying a case of soft drinks that had the caption "A young man walks through chest deep flood water after looting a grocery store" to a photograph of a White couple similarly walking through water carrying food and drink that had the caption "Two residents wade through chest deep water after finding bread and soda from a local grocery store" (Sommers, Apfelbaum, Dukes, Toosi, & Wand, 2006). Clearly, looting does not have the same connotation as does finding food and drink, and only the former reflects a negative stereotype of criminality. Research has confirmed that people often use less flattering language to describe behavior when it is performed by members of other groups than when the same behavior is performed by a member of their own group (Maass, Ceccarelli, & Rudin, 1996). In this way, stereotyping may shape people's responses to others in ways they may not always even detect.

Another way that prejudice may be socialized in the media is by communicating that people are likely to be rewarded with social acceptance or punished by disapproval for expressing prejudice. If comedians are rewarded with laughter when they make prejudiced jokes, people conceivably learn that this type of commentary is valued. In some cases, characters in the media are punished for having a stigma, whereas those who devalue them are rewarded with acceptance or laughter. Consider the movie *The Nutty Professor*, in which the size of the professor is a constant joke. Not only is he named in a derogatory way (Dr. Klump), but explicit references to his weight occur throughout the movie (e.g., in one scene a colleague of his calls him a "fat tub of goo"; Himes & Thompson, 2007, p. 712). This simultaneously communicates that there are social sanctions for being a heavy person and also that one can be funny (hence liked and accepted) by expressing prejudice against overweight people.

The devaluation of overweight people in the media appears to be more severe for women than for men. Not only are heavy women underrepresented in the media relative to unusually thin women, but thin female characters receive more social rewards (praise, dates) and fewer social punishments (criticism, isolation) than do heavier female characters (Fouts & Burggraf, 1999; Fouts & Vaughan, 2002). Heavier women are depicted as receiving much more negative feedback than are heavier men (Fouts & Burggraf, 2000; B. S. Greenberg, Eastin, Hofschire, Lachlan, & Brownell, 2003). Much of the critique of heavy women occurs in a very direct manner, suggesting that this type of prejudice is more socially accepted than some others. For example, in the movie *Erin Brockovich*, one female character says to another, "Bite me, Krispy Kreme" (Himes & Thompson, 2007, p. 714). Not only do such portrayals play a role in shaping girls' body images, but they also communicate devaluation of overweight people and suggest that this form of prejudice is socially accepted.

When discussion turns to these types of influences in the media and popular culture, a debate typically emerges between those who assume that such depictions shape people's attitudes and those who think that people are able to separate reality from fiction and so remain uninfluenced. Yet others might point out that many messages in the media are positive; for example, many newer television shows embrace diversity. So what does research tell us about the effects of exposure to the media on prejudice levels? The general trend seems to be that among elementary school children, higher levels of television watching tend to be linked with more prejudice, whereas among preschool children the reverse is true; for them, television watching is associated with more positive attitudes. Younger children tend to watch more educational programming, such as *Sesame Street*, which depicts diversity in a positive way, whereas older children watch more problematic material (Katz, 2003). Of course, correlational data like these cannot demonstrate whether television watching causes school-age children to be prejudiced or whether more prejudiced children are for some reason more inclined to watch television. However, research with adults has shown that media coverage of diversity issues shapes people's attitudes (Esses, Jackson, Nolan, & Armstrong, 1999), and so it is likely that media exposure functions as a socialization agent with children as well.

Peer Influence

It is commonly assumed that peers play a strong role in shaping the attitudes of adolescents in particular, and there seems to be good reason for this assumption. Certainly with respect to attitudes other than prejudice, evidence is clear that peers shape their friends' attitudes, especially during adolescence (Rubin, Bukowski, & Parker, 2006). During the teen years, peer relations are becoming more complex, and peer groups are especially relevant in the formation and perpetuation of norms. However, with respect to the socialization of prejudice among adolescent peer groups, the evidence is mixed. Some work has shown a lack of peer influence (e.g., Ritchey & Fishbein, 2001), whereas other research has shown that peers play a strong role in shaping attitudes (e.g., Poteat, 2007). Part of the reason for the mixed findings may be that the importance of peers in shaping attitudes depends on the target group at issue. Peer influence may be especially relevant in shaping attitudes toward strongly stigmatized groups because teens may be most inclined to discuss these groups and generate group norms (Kiesner, Maass, Cadinu, & Vallese, 2003).

In many adolescent circles, gay men and lesbians are especially stigmatized. Male teens in particular report that their peers display a lot of homophobic behavior (Plummer, 2001), although reports of harassment by girls suspected of being lesbian have shown that the problem is not limited to boys (Wessler & DeAdrade, 2006). Although in general there is a trend toward more open attitudes toward gay men and lesbians among younger generations (e.g., Herek, 2000), prejudice has sometimes been found to temporarily increase during early adolescence (Fishbein, 2002), and homophobia in particular may do so. Adolescents who are experiencing puberty are especially receptive to social messages about their emerging sexuality, and so they are likely candidates for peer influence on their attitudes about sexual minorities.

Longitudinal research with adolescents has shown that peers do play a clear role in shaping these attitudes (Poteat, 2007; Poteat, Espelage, & Green, 2007). Poteat et al. (2007) surveyed a large group of high school students ages 12 to 18 at two points in time, 8 months apart. In addition to measuring homophobic attitudes at both points in time, they also asked the teens to report whom they considered friends. In this way, the researchers were able to identify peer groups (clusters of students who considered themselves friends) and assess whether students' attitudes changed over the 8-month period and whether they became more similar to friends or not. Initially, they found considerable similarity in attitudes toward gay men and lesbians within peer groups and substantial differences between groups. Thus, peer groups appeared to have norms regarding appropriate attitudes. Moreover, they found that over the 8-month period the students changed their attitudes in the direction of the group norm such that attitudes became even more similar within peer groups and even more different between groups. Thus, among teens, peers play a clear role in socializing prejudice and shaping adolescents' attitudes toward social groups.

In summary, the socialization perspective suggests that children learn prejudice from parents, the media and popular culture, and peers. Children learn when they are directly or indirectly taught attitudes, when they observe the actions of role models, and when they see which attitudes and behaviors lead to social rewards and which are met with punishments. The socialization perspective leaves some questions unanswered, however. It does not address why parents or peers are prejudiced or why prejudice shows up in the media. Furthermore, the socialization perspective does a poor job of explaining the developmental trajectory of prejudice. In particular, it fails to explain research findings that prejudice tends to peak in children around age 5 or 6 before declining again in about half of children after age 7 (Aboud & Amato, 2001). Understanding this pattern requires consideration of the social–cognitive developmental perspective.

Social–Cognitive Developmental Perspective

When my friend's daughter was about 3 years old she declared to me one day, "When I grow up, I'm going to be a banana head!" Her tone was as serious and proud as though she had proclaimed her intention to be an astronaut or cardiologist. Part of the reason that this is so amusing is that clearly she had generated this imaginative idea herself; no adult had suggested to her directly through instruction or modeling that one occupation she might choose in the future is that of banana head. Rather, based on bits of information in her environment—for example, information suggesting that people grow up to "be something" and perhaps an expression she heard somewhere involving the phrase *banana head*—she determined herself that the role of banana head is an option for adults. The broader point is that child development is not a passive process in which children inertly learn from adults. Children are not simply sponges who absorb information fed to them. Rather, they actively construct meaning from information in the environment given the constraints of the limits on their experiences and their stage of cognitive development.

This is true in the development of prejudice as well, and so understanding the development of prejudice requires analysis of children's cognitive development. The social–cognitive developmental theory (Aboud, 2008) is inspired by the work of Jean Piaget, whose theory of the stages of cognitive development in children has shaped several decades of work in developmental psychology. It considers how the skills and interests of children at different ages shape how they process the information available from parents, the media, and so on. The theory has four key propositions reviewed by Aboud (2008). First, prejudice in children does not increase gradually but rather emerges in a stepwise fashion with a sharp increase around age 5 and declines around age 7. Second, parental influence on children's prejudice is minimal, but where it occurs it involves children's active attempts to understand parental behavior. Third, age-based trends in prejudice are partially the result of changes in children's focus of attention from the self, to groups, to individuals. Fourth, age-based trends in prejudice are also the result of developmental shifts in the primary basis of children's judgments, from emotion to perception to cognition. I discuss these propositions next.

The first proposition is that prejudice in children peaks at about age 5 or 6. Proponents of the social–cognitive perspective point out that if prejudice were learned as the socialization perspective suggests, it would form gradually as children are exposed to more and more messages about social groups. However, the evidence has contradicted this. Rather, it has shown that prejudice is acquired very rapidly among children ages 4 to 6, and then after age 7 it tends to decline in many children (Aboud, 2008). Children in the 4-to-6 age range often view people as all good or all bad, and they tend to view distinctions between groups of people as absolute and rigid, whereas older children are capable of more nuanced judgments. Prejudiced thinking during the early years (ages 4–6) does not seem to predict later prejudice at older ages. Doyle and Aboud (1995) found that between the ages of 5 and 9, children's prejudice declined, and attitudes at age 9 were unrelated to attitudes at age 5. This finding is consistent with the perspective that constraints on children's cognitive abilities in the early years, rather than personality or some other stable factor, give rise to the early spike in prejudice. There is also some evidence that some types of prejudice may rise again during adolescence (some forms of ethnic prejudice and homophobia; Aboud, 2008; Plummer, 2001), but this is likely due not to cognitive factors but rather to other dynamics specific to adolescence, such as the motivation to articulate a unique identity or the need to achieve peer acceptance.

The second proposition is that parental influence on children's prejudice is minimal, but where it occurs it involves children's active attempts to understand parental behavior. Children who are seeking to understand their social world are attentive to parental behavior and make inferences based on it. The inferences they make will be shaped by their cognitive abilities. Children in the 4-to-6 age range are in the process of learning about social groups, and their thinking is notably concrete and rule bound. They are likely to make assumptions that seem prejudiced because of their need to create order in how they understand the world. For example, a young child who observes his or her mother and father engage in separate recreational activities may conclude that men and women have different interests and skills, regardless of the parents' gender attitudes, because this child is in the process of learning about social categories and social regularities. An adolescent who observes the same parental behavior is more likely to understand that it could reflect many things, such as their individual preferences and their relationship style, as well as gender differences. As Aboud (2008) concluded,

> Parents and peers are important aspects of the social environment, but their input is sought and interpreted by the child in line with an age-related mindset that may look for attributes to use when categorizing or for rules to be followed. (p. 58)

Third, the theory states that age-based trends in prejudice are partially the result of developmental changes in children's focus of attention from the self, to groups, to individuals. Very young children, around 2 to 4 years of age, tend to be egocentric in that they are unable to understand other people's perspectives. For example, a 3-year-old girl who helps to wrap a gift may think, on presenting the package, that the recipient, like her, knows what is inside. Between ages 4 and 6, when prejudice levels tend to peak, children become less egocentric than toddlers and have achieved an ability to understand that people differ. However, they also become much more inclined to view people in terms of group membership than they previously were. When my former neighbor, Mitchell, was about 4 years old, he came charging out his back door one day and ran up to the fence where I was working in the yard. He excitedly asked me, "Lynne, are you a *girl?*" Having learned about the differences between boys and girls, he was very interested in placing people into the appropriate box. At the same time, children are learning about good and bad things (e.g., naughty and nice behavior) and are motivated to label things as *good* and *bad*. As a result, they are inclined to see their own groups as good (Aboud, 2008). Although older children and adults can understand that people from different groups might understandably have especially favorable attitudes toward their own group, children in this age range tend to think that only their own ingroup bias is justifiable (Aboud, 2008). When older children become less focused on understanding and evaluating groups and more inclined to view people in individual terms, prejudice declines.

The fourth proposition is that age-based trends in prejudice are also the result of developmental shifts in the primary basis of children's judgments, from emotion to perception to cognition. Among very young children, responses to others tend to be rooted in emotion. Children's primary response to others may involve emotional responses of comfort or discomfort, liking or disliking, and trust or fear. A form of early prejudice can be seen in these children, but it takes the form of preference for familiar others, wariness of unfamiliar people, or both. In the early school years, children's thinking becomes increasingly based on perception. Children become attuned to physical attributes that differentiate people and tend to base their understanding of differences between people on visible attributes. They may become rigid in their thinking about group differences, for example, being very concerned with wearing gender-appropriate clothing. At this stage, children often tend to think that people who look similar in some way must be similar in other ways. Thus, they are inclined to view members of a group as "all alike." To the extent that social messages convey more favorable information about some groups than others, these exaggerations can take the form of prejudice. As children begin to develop the ability to think in more complex, differentiated ways (generally after about age 7), it becomes possible for them to understand that group boundaries can be fluid, that group depictions (e.g., stereotypes) can be inaccurate, and so on.

Prejudice in children is shaped by other aspects of cognitive development as well. If you were to take a soft candy, such as a caramel, and squeeze it so that it became elongated, place it beside another caramel that was not altered, and offer one of the candies to a 4- or 5-year-old child, he or she would most likely choose the elongated piece, thinking it was bigger. If she or he did, this would suggest that she or he had yet to achieve conservation ability, the ability to understand that properties of entities (e.g., amount of caramel) do not necessarily correspond to physical appearances (e.g., length). Underlying the lack of conservation in young children is a tendency to focus on one dimension of an entity (e.g., length) at a time and to ignore others (e.g., height). This is also related to children's classification ability. If you showed the same child a bunch of large and small red and blue toys and asked him or her to sort the toys by color, she or he would probably do so accurately. But if you asked this child to separate the toys by size and color at the same time, she or he would likely have more difficulty. Typically, multiple classification ability (the ability to categorize things along multiple dimensions at one time) is achieved around age 7. The absence of both conservation and multiple classification ability before age 7 has been implicated in prejudice (e.g., Aboud, 2008; Katz, 2003) because conservation ability allows one to see that physical appearances do not necessarily correspond to inner attributes, and multiple classification ability allows one to appreciate that one can be simultaneously female, tall, an athlete, a doctor, and so on. Encouragingly, helping children to develop the ability to classify objects in multiple ways (e.g., to group toys by color and size) also helps to reduce their prejudice because it encourages flexible thinking (Aboud & Levy, 2000).

Developmental Intergroup Approach

Developmental intergroup theory (Bigler & Liben, 2006, 2007) is a recently developed theory of the development of prejudice in children that attempts to address the question of why children develop prejudice on the basis of particular group markers, such as gender and ethnicity. Like social–cognitive theory, this approach acknowledges the importance of children's efforts to understand their world and the constraints of their cognitive developments. To this is added the observation that the form that children's prejudice takes is shaped by the nature of relations between groups among adults (e.g., occupational role segregation between men and women, economic differences between ethnic groups).

According to the theory, the development of prejudice involves four processes. First, there is the establishment of psychological salience of certain dimensions of difference. Children come to identify some differences, such as age, sex, and race, as important indicators of difference, and they come to view other differences (handedness, hair color) as less meaningful. Second, children develop a tendency to categorize individuals along those dimensions deemed important (e.g., to "see" and think of people as men and women or young and old rather than as lefties and righties, brunettes and blondes). Third, children develop stereotypes and prejudices regarding the group markers deemed important. Finally, children come to use stereotypes as a filter for their perceptions of others. The bulk of the theory describes the first and third processes (the establishment of psychological salience of certain markers of difference and the development of stereotypes and prejudices regarding these differences, and so it is to a discussion of these dynamics that I now turn.

Establishment of Psychological Salience

Children come to focus on certain dimensions of difference, such as gender, ethnicity, and age, and not on many of the other ways in which people differ (e.g., hair color, food preferences, being a day or night person, being a dog or cat person). As discussed in Chapter 2, the differences that become markers for prejudice in a given social context are those that have socially meaningful consequences for people (e.g., because in North America people of African descent were once enslaved, skin color is a salient marker of difference). Developmental intergroup theory adds to this observation the assumption that children come to the world equipped to survey their surroundings and to extract information regarding which bases of classification are important in a given environmental context. That is, children are not biologically wired to respond to certain differences such as race or sex but rather are wired to figure out what differences in their world matter. This makes sense from an evolutionary perspective because it allows for flexibility in how people respond to their varied environments. In the words of Bigler and Liben (2006), "Survival is likely to have been promoted by the evolution of a highly flexible cognitive system that—rather than providing 'hardwired' biases for categorization—instead leads children to construct hypotheses about which bases of classification are appropriate within a given context" (p. 56). Along similar lines, Hirshfeld (2001) theorized that the human brain contains an innate "theory like knowledge structure" or "acquisition device" (p. 108) that sensitizes children to information about aggregates. This aids in learning because it leads children to be attentive to the categories that are used in their community to make sense of the world and to function practically.

Children do tend to notice perceptually salient attributes of others (Bigler & Liben, 2007), and so they especially notice visible markers of difference. However, this does not imply that it is inevitable that children will attend to certain types of difference because those differences that are meaningful in a given social context tend to be made even more salient than they naturally are. For example, men and women wear different clothes and hairstyles, often occupy different roles, are identified by sex in many languages, have their sex (but not other biologically determined attributes) noted on their birth certificates, and so on. These social dynamics make gender much more salient than it would otherwise be to children. Indeed, some evidence has shown that children as old as 7 years cannot readily differentiate male and female faces when typical social cues associated with gender (e.g., make-up) are lacking (Wild et al., 2000). Skin color, too, is made more salient by social trends. In many places, people who have different skin colors live in different neighborhoods and occupy different social and occupational roles. This segregation highlights skin color as a basis for categorization. Even invisible differences are often made visible in certain social contexts, as for example when people display religious symbolism on their jewelry.

Language is a powerful tool in shaping the salience of certain differences. People often label children *boys* and *girls*, for example, although they do not label children *redheads* and *blondes*. Research by Katz and Seavey (1973) illustrates the role of labels in shaping 4-year-old children's tendency to categorize. They had preschool children observe pictures of faces colored either purple or green and showing either a smile or a frown. Labels were used that in some cases differentiated the faces by color (one label for green smiling and green frowning faces and another label for purple smiling and purple frowning faces), whereas in others the labels differentiated facial expressions (one label for green and purple smiles and another label for green and purple frowns). Children were asked how similar the faces were. Children's responses corresponded to the labels provided: Those who were given color labels saw the similarly colored faces as similar to one another, and those who were provided with expression labels saw the faces with the same expression as similar. Thus, the children did not naturally respond to physical attributes in their categorization but rather responded to the verbal labels provided to describe the differences they viewed.

The use of particular types of language can further solidify perceptions that groups differ. When differences are expressed in terms of nouns or noun phrases (with labels such as *boys* and *girls* or *Black girl, native boy,* and so on), children are likely to infer that differences run deeper than when they are expressed differently. For example, Gelman and Heyman (1999) found that when 5- to 7-year-old children were told stories about other children, the language used to describe the children influenced perceptions about them. Children were told identical stories with one variant—half of the children were told stories about other children using nouns (a story about a "carrot eater" and a "guinea pig lover"), whereas the other half were told the same story using verb–predicate phrases (a girl who "ate carrots whenever she could" and a girl who "loved guinea pigs"). The children who heard the noun form of the stories believed that the children would have these characteristics (carrot and guinea pig loving) for a longer time, and they thought they were more likely to retain the characteristics even under family opposition or other different life circumstances than did children who heard the verb–predicate versions of the stories. It seems that children inferred that these characteristics were lasting aspects of personality when a noun—but not a verb phrase—was used to describe them. This type of research has suggested that differences routinely described by nouns or noun phrases are likely to be viewed as especially meaningful to children. Referring to "Christians" or "Jews" rather than "people who are Christian" or "people who are Jewish" misleads children into assuming that differences are more profound than they are.

Associating Stereotypes and Prejudice With Categories

Once children come to focus on certain differences as meaningful distinctions among people, some of the groups identified become associated with negative beliefs and stereotypes. A variety of factors influence the development of prejudice against such groups. One factor not addressed by the other perspectives is essentialism. The term *essentialism* is derived from a philosophical position that all categories, by their essence, have characteristics that all members of the category share (e.g., all trees have branches). Psychologically speaking, essentialism is the tendency to view groups as defined by core features that apply to all members of the social category and to see group differences as discrete. Some children are more likely than others to engage in essentialist thinking, and this tendency is presumed to contribute to stereotyping and prejudice.

Some research has shown that essentialism is shaped by the status of one's group and that members of higher status groups are particularly likely to think in essentialist terms about lower status groups. This may be especially true among older children and adults whose thinking has been influenced by social factors such as inequality. Mahalingham (2007) studied Brahmins (the highest status caste in India) and Dalits (the lowest status caste in India, formerly called "Untouchables"). To a degree, adolescents' and adults' thinking about caste differed depending on their own group membership. Brahmin adolescents and adults were inclined to think in essentialist terms, especially about Dalits, attributing caste to inherent qualities. In contrast, Dalit adolescents and adults tended to view their caste as an acquired aspect of identity. Mahalingham concluded that essentialism may be a cognitive tool for children who are learning about categories in that it simplifies the task of thinking about social groups, but it is a social tool for older children and adults who have a stake in justifying inequality.

As suggested by work described earlier, prejudice in children also builds on *ingroup bias*, the tendency to especially favor one's own group. Children, like adults, are inclined to favor their own groups. For example, although boys and girls have some tendency to endorse traditional gender stereotypes (e.g., "Girls cry more than boys"), they sometimes show an even stronger tendency to associate positive traits with their own gender regardless of their association with gender stereotypes. For example, Powlishta (1995) reported that in a large group of 8- to 10-year-olds, both boys and girls tended to report that positive traits (intelligence, dependability, independence, bravery) were especially descriptive of their own gender group. Bigler and Liben (2006) gave the example of a young girl who on seeing apparently yucky oysters for the first time proclaimed that "only boys eat oysters." Although this is cute because it seems harmless, it also shows how the tendency to associate something negative with an outgroup (and to view the ingroup more favorably) emerges early in life and does not necessarily reflect social learning (no adult taught the young girl that only boys eat oysters).

Developmental intergroup theory observes that children also learn stereotypes by observing covariations between groups and social roles or attributes. For example, Canadian children may observe that all prime ministers have been White and that most kindergarten teachers are women. On the basis of such observations, children may infer stereotypes, for example, that White people are capable, that women like children, and so on (see Eagly & Steffen, 1984). It is noteworthy, however, that children form stereotypes that correspond to particular group-attribute covariations. For example, they often form a belief that women like children but do not tend to believe that buck-toothed people like children. Why is this? Is it true that women like children but not true that buck-toothed people have any special affinity for children? Or is it possible that if one was to survey dental records and attitudes toward children, one might find a correspondence never before noticed? In other words, do children observe all the ways in which people differ and accurately detect covariations between attributes? Alternatively, do they observe only those covariations to which their attention is drawn by adults? This is an important question because it speaks to the accuracy of stereotypes.

Although it is conceivable that children observe all the variables in the world and calculate which attributes actually do correspond with one another, this seems highly implausible given the vast number of human attributes and even vaster number of possible correlations among them. As Bigler and Liben (2007) noted, is seems unlikely that

> children calculate the relation between a person's height and the likelihood of being a nurse, between hair color and the likelihood of being gentle, or between religion and the likelihood of using an ironing board. Yet, most children detect the correlation between gender and each of these characteristics. (p. 165)

Thus, the process of stereotype formation is not simply a process of observing covariations between group markers and behaviors or attributes. Rather, children seem to have their attention drawn to some group distinctions and to the markers of those distinctions that are deemed to be meaningful in a given social context.

Bigler, Jones, and Lobliner (1997) demonstrated this in a study of the development of prejudice in White middle-class children ages 6 to 9 in a Midwestern American summer school program. They had children wear special T-shirts to class every day for several weeks. Half of the children in each class were given a yellow T-shirt, and half were given a blue T-shirt. In some of the classes, the teachers were asked to make functional use of the color distinction by referring to it in daily tasks, analogous to how teachers often refer to boys and girls (e.g., having children line up by T-shirt color, referring to children by T-shirt color). In other classes, the teachers did not refer to the T-shirts. After several weeks, the children's attitudes were assessed. The researchers found that only among students in the classes in which the teacher drew attention to the T-shirt color distinction did children develop prejudice against the other T-shirt color group. In these classes, children were more likely to associate negative characteristics, and less likely to associate positive characteristics, with the other group than with their own. Moreover, 80% of the children said they would not want to change T-shirt color if given the chance. Young children, who are in the process of learning about regularities and variations in the world, may be especially attuned to notice differences that are visually obvious and to be attentive to information in their environment that suggests that the difference is meaningful (e.g., adults' use of the information). These tendencies combine with the relatively natural tendency to favor one's own group to create prejudice against those who appear different.

In summary, developmental intergroup theory describes the development of prejudice in children as resulting from the interaction between children's desire and need to create a sense of coherence in their world and the messages—both subtle and overt—they receive from the environment about what distinctions between people matter and what attributes ought to be attended to. Children's cognitive development interacts with socialization influences in a context in which group differences in roles and status are entrenched. The prejudices that children form reflect these aspects of social reality. As a whole, the literature on children and prejudice has shown that children come to the world with a host of potentials and age-based limitations, that they are flexible in terms of how they use the abilities they have at different ages, and that they are very attentive to their social environments. Although many children do pick up on the prejudices that surround them, many instead develop progressive attitudes, and this latter tendency is encouraged when children are given sufficient support to develop the ability to think critically about the world around them.

6

INTERGROUP RELATIONS
AND PREJUDICE

In Chapter 1, I used the example of Canadian Prime Minister Stephen Harper's June 2008 apology to Canada's First Nations people for forced residential schooling to illustrate societal change toward equality and respect. Despite this positive move, problems remain to be solved. For example, First Nations people have considerably lower incomes, on average, than do non–First Nations people (Maxim et al., 2001), as well as lower average levels of education (Morrison et al., 2008). Evidence has pointed toward a clear role of discrimination against First Nations people in these domains and in others, such as the health care system (for a review, see Morrison et al., 2008). Reviews of the criminal justice system in Canada have consistently revealed inequality in the application of the legal system and in ways ranging from rates of arrest to parole decisions (e.g., Correctional Services Canada, 1998; La Prairie, 2002; Welsh & Ogloff, 2000). Prejudice persists, too. Some non-native Canadian citizens admit to holding attitudes toward First Nations people that are overtly negative (Esses et al., 1993; Morrison et al., 2008), and many people persist in holding ambivalent attitudes toward native peoples that include both positive and negative elements (Bell & Esses, 2002; Bell, Esses, & Maio, 1996).

According to the intergroup perspective on prejudice, the persistence of these problems exists in large part because relations between First Nations people and non-native people involve competition over land and other resources and also because group differences exist on important aspects of people's identity such as religion and culture and groups strive to assert a positive and distinct identity. In the sections that follow, I describe two main intergroup approaches to prejudice: the group conflict perspective as typified by realistic group conflict theory (LeVine & Campbell, 1972; Sherif & Sherif, 1953/1966) and the social identity perspective as illustrated by social identity theory (Tajfel & Turner, 1979, 1986; J. C. Turner & Reynolds, 2001). After this review, I present the unified instrumental model of group conflict (Esses, Jackson, Dovidio, & Hodson, 2005). This model integrates and extends key intergroup perspectives on prejudice and helps to explain prejudice against First Nations people in Canada. As distinct from the approaches to prejudice reviewed in earlier chapters, these theories address proximal influences on prejudice because they describe the circumstances that give rise to specific types of prejudice in particular circumstances, although to varying degrees they acknowledge more distal influences as well.

GROUP CONFLICT PERSPECTIVE

In summer 1949, Muzafer and Carolyn Sherif, along with several colleagues, conducted some now-famous experiments with a group of 24 twelve-year-old boys at a summer camp in northern Connecticut (Sherif & Sherif, 1953/1966). In the first phase of the research, spanning 18 days, the 24 boys interacted together as one large group participating in camping activities, such as hiking, softball, and swimming. During this baseline period, camp counselors took notes about which friendships emerged and how the boys interacted together. During Phase 2, which lasted 5 days, the experimenters divided the boys into two groups, ensuring that close friendships were split up. Boys participated in all activities with their new group; even mealtime and sleeping arrangements were organized by group.

During this second phase, Sherif and Sherif (1953/1966) noted that the boys developed their own group hierarchies and leaders, and group structure emerged. The groups developed a sense of solidarity, for example, giving their groups names ("Red Devils" and "Bull Dogs") without prompting from camp counselors and making a norm of ingroup commitment (e.g., in one case, a boy was labeled a traitor for retaining a cross-group friendship). Contact between the groups remained friendly, but within their groups boys used *we* and *they* language and showed favoritism toward the ingroup. Moreover, the majority of boys now reported that their best friends were from within their own group. This phase of the research showed that social bonds and friendship were strongly shaped by the social arrangements of the groups. More important, the groups were determined not by the boys themselves but rather by the researchers, and so social bonds were not based on factors such as shared interests or personality. It also showed that simply being in a group facilitated the beginnings of preference for the ingroup.

During Phase 3 of the research, which also lasted 5 days, Sherif and Sherif (1953/1966) implemented a series of competitive activities, giving groups points for success in athletic games and for demonstrating cabin cleanliness. A much-coveted prize of a camping knife for each boy in the high-point team was offered. During this competitive phase, the boys became especially oriented toward their own group and its norms. Also, the goodwill that had existed between the groups changed to animosity. The boys used verbal insults when referring to other group (e.g., calling them "cheats") and engaged in mean-spirited actions such as changing a cheer from "2-4-6-8, who do we appreciate" to "2-4-6-8, who do we appreci-hate" (Sherif & Sherif, 1953/1966, p. 279). Tensions rose between the groups until a food fight erupted in which the boys threw knives and saucers at one another. At this point, the researchers stopped the competitive phase of the research and attempted to reestablish friendly relations through instruction and joint cooperative activities. Apparently, this was somewhat successful; although many of the boys continued to interact primarily with members of their group, the overt animosity was noticeably reduced, particularly with the use of cooperative games.

Sherif and Sherif (1953/1966) concluded that the effect of intergroup competition was twofold. First, it served to "solidify the in-group belongingness and solidarity, to enhance in-group democracy, and to strengthen in-group friendships" (p. 284). Second, the effect was to "generate and increase out-group hostility, to produce derogatory *name calling* which came close to standardizing of negative stereotypes in relation to the out-group (*rudiments of prejudice*)" (p. 284). In other words, the competition generated both ingroup favoritism and outgroup prejudice.

Social scientists have long since noted that competition in the form of the relative ability of groups to access desired resources or outcomes is an important influence on prejudice (e.g., Blumer, 1958). The findings of Sherif and Sherif (1953/1966) substantiated this point and, considered along with subsequent research and the writings of several other social scientists, contributed to the formulation of realistic group conflict theory (LeVine & Campbell, 1972). LeVine and Campbell (1972) used the term *realistic conflict* to describe the perspective that "group conflicts are rational in the sense that groups do have incompatible goals and are in competition for scarce resources" (p. 29). Competition over scarce resources appears ubiquitous. Community groups compete for limited public funding, environmentalists and loggers compete for access to trees, ethnic and national groups compete for ownership of land, nations compete for access to fishing rights and oil reserves, and so on. Sometimes competition arises over less tangible yet equally consequential resources such as power, as when groups vie for political representation or military groups take turns bolstering their resources in an escalating power play.

Competition between groups is thought to cause a variety of intergroup responses ranging from mild ingroup favoritism to severe hostility toward the outgroup (Sherif, Harvey, White, Hood, & Sherif, 1961). Consistent with this view, several decades of research have supported the position that perceived competition over resources generates prejudice against many groups in many contexts (Riek, Mania, & Gaertner, 2006). For example, in various countries, perceptions of conflict of interest between immigrants and members of the host population have been found to predict prejudice against immigrant groups (e.g., Esses et al., 1999; Stephan, Ybarra, & Bachman, 1999). Using national surveys in 12 countries, Quillian (1995) found that attitudes toward immigrants became more negative when economic conditions were poor and when immigrant groups were relatively large, presumably evoking greater perceptions of economic threat or competition for jobs. Transient events that generate competition vis-à-vis incompatible goals between groups can also evoke animosity. For example, Brown, Maras, Masser, Vivian, and Hewstone (2001) found that when French fishermen prevented British people from entering France via ferry by demonstrating about fish prices at a ferry port, attitudes toward the French became temporarily hostile among British travelers.

Perceived competition also can lead to discrimination. For example, Canadian research has shown that men who view working women as a source of competition for jobs are not only more inclined to express sexism but also more likely to discriminate against women in employment settings and to oppose affirmative action programs that benefit women (Beaton & Tougas, 2001; Tougas, Brown, Beaton, & Joly, 1995). In the United States, perceptions of group conflicts of interest between African Americans and European Americans have led to opposition to school busing (Bobo, 1983). Research in East Germany showed that people who viewed some foreigners as a source of threat were more likely than others to endorse politically antagonistic actions against them (Watts, 1996). In many countries, the belief that immigrants are a source of competition for economic resources predicts not only prejudice but also resistance to immigration policy (e.g., Esses et al., 1999; E. Green, 2009; McLaren, 2003).

Perceived competition from another group can even lead to genocide. For example, Esses and Jackson (2008) described how competition between northern and southern Sudanese people over scarce and valuable natural resources (water, arable land, oil) contributes to the ongoing strife in Sudan that has escalated to genocide in recent years. The strength of prejudice that arises in response to competition—be it mild attitude changes or overt hatred coupled with aggression—corresponds to a number of factors, such as the scarcity and value of the resource over which groups compete, the importance of acquiring it, the size and proximity of the competitor group, and the degree to which the competitor is interfering with the goal of acquiring the resource (Allport, 1954/1979; LeVine & Campbell, 1972).

According to realistic group conflict theory, competition generates feelings of threat and prejudice against the perceived source of threat—the competitor—because the potential success of the competitor group threatens the well-being of the ingroup (LeVine & Campbell, 1972). These feelings of threat to the well-being of one's group can persist within a group, becoming part of the culture, even when overt competition no longer exists. For example, in Jamaica, where gang violence makes the country one of the world's most dangerous places, conflict between the gangs is historically rooted in political differences—and associated competition for power and influence—that peaked when Jamaica achieved independence in 1962. However, violence between warring gangs is now maintained with ongoing feelings of generalized threat resulting from eruptions of violence over a host of matters, many of which are unrelated to the original political differences (see Gunst, 1995).

An important point that distinguishes realistic group conflict theory from some other perspectives on prejudice is that prejudice is thought to arise from real social conditions. It is not merely a psychological phenomenon. For example, the way in which land claims made by native groups are resolved has real consequences for the availability of natural resources to native and non-native groups. However, psychological factors do shape people's perceptions that others are a source of competition. In fact, in many situations it is unclear whether the perceptions of competition that generate prejudice are accurate or not. For example, as reviewed earlier, when people view immigrants as a source of competition for jobs or other economic resources, prejudice tends to result. This belief that immigrants are a source of competition for jobs is common despite the many ways in which immigrants may improve the general economic situation in their host country (e.g., opening businesses, paying taxes, investing), hence potentially increasing opportunities for the host population. In fact, research has shown that immigration creates economic opportunities for the host population (Economic Council of Canada, 1991), and so the interests of immigrants and residents are compatible. Nevertheless, these economic benefits of immigration are complex, and it may be easier, if not accurate, to assume that immigrants "take our jobs." Thus, in some cases competition is a real part of group relations, and in other cases it is an inaccurate perception; in both cases the perceived competition creates prejudice (Allport, 1954/1979; Sherif & Sherif, 1953/1966).

Competition over material resources like jobs, money, or access to valued institutions is an important influence on prejudice, but so too are other kinds of threats. In particular, symbolic or value-based threats also generate prejudice (e.g., Esses et al., 1993; Stephan & Stephan, 2000). Symbolic threats arise when people believe that another group threatens their values in some way. For example, some people express concern that immigrants threaten national cultural values. People with such concerns tend to be prejudiced against immigrants (Stephan et al., 2005). Symbolic threats have also been shown to generate prejudice against overweight people (Crandall, 1994), gay men and lesbians, and a variety of ethnic minority groups (Esses et al., 1993).

Symbolic threats sometimes arise from people's religious views. For example, people with a fundamentalist approach to religion, who think that there is one and only one true religion (Altemeyer & Hunsberger, 2005), tend to view others in terms of whether they support or threaten their values. This can lead to prejudice and discrimination. For example, fundamentalist Christians tend to view gay men and lesbians, as well as single mothers, as a threat to their values, and this belief has been found to lead them to endorse discrimination against these groups by denying them help in gaining employment (Jackson & Esses, 1997). The sense of threat from some groups that at times arises from religious beliefs may involve a concern that groups are in competition for representation of their values in the community, politics, and schools. The recent debates in several countries regarding what religious symbols students may wear to school (e.g., the hijab worn by some Muslim girls, the kirpan worn by baptized Sikhs) probably involve an element of competitive concern regarding what religions may dominate in their representation.

In brief, realistic group conflict theory proposes that an important source of prejudice is competition between groups for valued resources such as food, land, money, and power or for representation of values. Groups perceived to be in competition with one's own group tend to be the targets of prejudice, and such negativity is stronger to the extent that the resource at issue is valued and the competitor group is likely to usurp it. This perspective on prejudice is important because it illustrates the power of people's group interests and it shows that the availability and distribution of resources within a society can shape intergroup attitudes by making competition more or less likely.

SOCIAL IDENTITY PERSPECTIVE

Recall from the opening discussion of the group competition perspective that during the early stages of Sherif and Sherif's (1953/1966) famous research with boys at camp, boys were assigned to groups in such a way that boys with close friendships were placed in different groups. Soon, these same boys developed friendship preferences for those children within their newly assigned group. This preference suggested that simply belonging to a group may lead people to prefer others within their own group. The preference the boys at camp showed for members of their own group set the stage for the later development of overt prejudice and hostility when the researchers introduced competitions between the groups of boys. This research showed that given a situation in which people identified with others within their group, the introduction of intergroup competition to the environment led to the eruption of prejudice and tension between groups.

Not long after this research was conducted, Henri Tajfel of Bristol University in England undertook a series of experiments with his colleagues (Tajfel & Turner, 1986) that similarly showed that mere membership in a group can be an important factor in the development of prejudice and discrimination. However, Tajfel's experiments unexpectedly revealed that even in the absence of competition between groups, some intergroup biases can emerge from simple group identification. In the typical experiment, participants were assigned to be part of one of two distinct groups. Assignment to groups was random, but participants were told that the groups were assigned on the basis of some trivial criterion (e.g., whether the participant tended to underestimate or overestimate when doing a dot-estimation task). Participants then engaged in an exercise in which they allocated rewards, such as money, to other participants. In such studies, people reliably discriminated against members of the other group in favor of members of their own (Tajfel & Turner, 1986).

These *minimal group experiments*—so called because there was minimal basis for people to feel any connection to their group nor were people's interests tied to the interests of their group—suggested that people will discriminate in favor of their own group even in the absence of any obvious benefit to themselves or competition between groups. This observation stimulated the development of social identity theory (Tajfel & Turner, 1979, 1986), which was subsequently elaborated to explain a variety of intergroup phenomena including prejudice. Key to the theory is the idea that prejudice can arise in the absence of group competition because people tend to develop preferences for the groups to which they belong as a means to establish and maintain a positive sense of identity. Next, I discuss key principles of the theory as they are relevant to prejudice.

Answer the question "Who am I?" and you will likely think of personal attributes or traits that highlight how you are distinct from others, such as sense of humor, athleticism, and so on. You may also think of connections you share with some others along dimensions that are important in society, such as your ethnicity, age, religion, gender, sexual orientation, or occupation. According to social identity theory (Tajfel & Turner, 1979, 1986), *personal identity* encompasses those traits or characteristics that emphasize how one is unique as an individual (e.g., "I am outdoorsy"), whereas *collective identity* consists of associations with groups of people (e.g., "I am a Canadian"). Moreover, people's sense of their own value—their self-esteem—is rooted in both personal and collective elements (Tajfel & Turner, 1986). One feels good about him- or herself not only if one values one's personal attributes but also because one positively values one's groups. The term *social identity* refers to the content and evaluation of one's collective identity. It is "that *part* of an individual's self-concept which derives from his knowledge of his memberships in a social group (or groups) together with the value and emotional significance attached to that membership" (Tajfel, 1978, p. 63). According to social identity theory, people's social identity is an important part of who they are, how they understand and evaluate themselves, and how they respond to others.

Social identity theory posits that because people like to feel good about themselves and because social identity is part of the self-concept, people are motivated to hold favorable evaluations of the groups to which they belong. A variety of strategies can be used to achieve this end. One primary way in which people achieve a positive social identity is by endorsing beliefs that one's group is distinct from other groups on dimensions that are deemed valuable. For example, Canadians often describe the Canadian identity as including tolerance or respect for differences. People sometimes attempt to support this view by pointing to Canada's multiculturalism policy. This policy, originally established in the 1970s, endeavored to improve relations between ethnic groups in Canada by providing support for ethnic group community development and interaction, with the hope that this would foster group confidence, openness, and respect for diversity (Berry, 1984). In 1988, a formal Canadian Multiculturalism Act with the same goals was passed by Parliament. By focusing on one way in which Canada is somewhat unique, Canadians can achieve a sense of *positive distinctiveness*—that is, the belief that Canadians are distinct on a positive dimension of identity.

More important, one need only to believe that one's group is positively distinct for it to contribute to a positive identity; positive distinctiveness is not necessarily a state of reality, it is a form of belief. For example, Canada is not the only country to have a multiculturalism policy. In addition, there is ample evidence that some Canadians do not value diversity and also plenty of evidence that many non-Canadians do. Yet, Canadians continue to define themselves along this dimension. According to social identity theory, this is likely because so doing allows Canadians to maintain a positive social identity.

The cultivation of a belief in positive distinctiveness can generate prejudice in a variety of ways. The *outgroup homogeneity effect* refers to a tendency to view members of other groups as especially similar to one another ("They are all alike"; Ostrom & Sedikides, 1992). Outgroup homogeneity is especially likely to occur on negative characteristics (Brown, 2000). For example, Canadians who stereotype members of other nations as "generally nontolerant" are showing the outgroup homogeneity effect. People are also inclined to view negative characteristics as less descriptive of their own group than of other groups (Reynolds, Turner, & Haslam, 2000) and also to express *ingroup homogeneity*—that is, the view that members of one's own group are especially similar to one another on positive traits (Bernd & Pettigrew, 1990; Brown, 2000). For example, Canadians may overestimate how similar Canadians are to one another in terms of endorsing fairness, respect for diversity, and so on.

A number of other routes to prejudice and discrimination that involve efforts to protect social identity are possible. When members of relatively privileged groups sense that their advantage may be challenged by capable members of less privileged groups, they may react with hostile backlash efforts that sabotage the efforts of the less advantaged (Rudman & Fairchild, 2004). Consistent with social identity theory, Rudman and Fairchild (2004) showed that engaging in backlash can have the effect of enhancing people's self-esteem. Presumably, protecting privilege serves to maintain a positive social identity, as well as more material advantages. Another route to prejudice vis-à-vis social identity occurs among members of minority groups who value their unique identity. These people may show prejudice toward other similar but more mainstream minorities to clarify their unique social identity. Because religion can be an important aspect of social identity (Burris & Jackson, 2000), this occurs, for example, when conservative religious group members negatively evaluate more liberal members of the same religion (J. B. White & Langer, 1999). It has also been demonstrated among strict vegans who negatively judge the more flexible vegetarians (J. B. White, Schmitt, & Langer, 2006). At times, people may even appear to show prejudice against atypical members of their own group when they ostracize those who do not fit within the group norms. The tradition of some conservative religions of shunning people who violate religious teachings is an extreme example of this dynamic; more common would be a tendency of teenagers to reject socially awkward children who do not reflect well on the peer group. This *black sheep effect* (Marques, Yzerbyt, & Leyens, 1988) presumably serves a social identity function because rejecting an atypical or nonconforming group member serves to maintain the positive social value of the group.

People also make creative use of their own and others' dual identities (e.g., French Canadian, African American) to reflect well on their own group. For example, Stelzl, Janes, and Seligman (2007) observed that Canadians tended to refer to Jamaican Canadian Olympic athlete Ben Johnson as Canadian after he won gold at the 1988 Olympics but as Jamaican after he was subsequently disqualified for steroid use. The researchers subsequently tested and confirmed the prediction that when a person with a dual identity engages in favorable behavior, people tend to want to bask in the reflected glory by referring to the shared identity, but when someone with a dual identity does something negative, people are inclined to cut off the reflected failure by referring to the nonshared identity.

In summary, social identity theory posits that people's group affiliations are an important part of their identity and self-esteem. Consequently, people often exaggerate differences between ingroups and outgroups to place the former in a favorable light. This can lead to prejudice in a variety of ways: Outgroups may be viewed as homogeneous on negative traits, or ingroups may be viewed as homogeneous on positive traits; privileged groups may show backlash against groups rising in status who threaten their own group's advantage and positive social identity; members of disadvantaged groups may denigrate other disadvantaged groups in an effort to elevate their own social identity; people may selectively include or exclude others in their social identity, and so on. Of course, not all people show these effects. Because these strategies bolster social identity, it is people who are most highly identified with their group—those for whom the group is an especially important part of their identity and thus those who have most at stake with respect to their evaluation of their group—who are most likely to show these effects (Brown, 2000). For example, in a meta-analysis of 55 empirical studies linking measures of religiosity with intergroup attitudes, Hall, Matz, and Wood (2010) found that people who placed more importance on their identification with their religious group showed more racial prejudice than did others, which they interpreted as suggesting that because religion is often practiced within ethnic–racial groups, religious and ethnic–racial identities may become combined.

The clearest theme that has emerged from the empirical literature on this theory is that people tend to highly prize their own groups relative to others even when the groups are formed on a trivial basis. Although the fact that people tend to prefer members of their own groups is not a startling observation, it is important to note that this tendency to favor group members may provide the precondition necessary for the development of more virulent forms of prejudice that emerge when other influences on prejudice become evident (e.g., Moghaddam, 2005). Preference for the ingroup can function like hot coals—left alone they are not dramatic, but add some fuel, and flames can erupt. The fuel often involves social conditions such as competition over a scarce and valued resource. For example, biases toward ingroup favoritism among native and non-native groups are often quiet, if unpleasant, aspects of social reality until something happens—such as initiation of developments by non-natives on land claimed in legal battles by natives—at which point hostility erupts. For this reason, the trend among psychologists taking an intergroup approach to studying prejudice is toward viewing the dynamics described by the group competition and social identity perspectives as complementary and additive contributors to prejudice. This is the case with the unified instrumental model of group conflict (Esses, Jackson, et al., 2005), to which I now turn.

AN INTEGRATIVE APPROACH: THE UNIFIED INSTRUMENTAL MODEL OF GROUP CONFLICT

The unified instrumental model of group conflict (Esses, Jackson, et al., 2005) was developed to explain how a variety of situational and psychological factors combine to generate prejudice and discrimination. According to the model, psychological factors and situational factors together lead people to see other groups as competitors for something valuable because some situations enhance perceptions of competition and some people are especially sensitive to threats to their resources or status. The model also describes how responses to competition are utilitarian. When people think that their group must compete for something, they become motivated to reduce the ability of the other group to compete effectively. According to the model, prejudice is one of several means by which this goal can be achieved. The model is described as instrumental because it conceptualizes prejudice as a tool people use to achieve the reduction or elimination of competition from another group. This model has been used to explain various problems, such as prejudice against immigrants (Esses, Dovidio, Semenya, & Jackson, 2005; Jackson & Esses, 2000), ethnic prejudice (Esses, Dovidio, Jackson, & Armstrong, 2001), and conflict and genocide (Esses & Jackson, 2008). Next, I explore its application to understanding prejudice against First Nations people among colonists in North America and their contemporary descendents.

According to the model, some ideologies lead people to see other people and groups as competitors for resources. This is the case for social dominance orientation (see Chapter 4, this volume), for example, because people who endorse this ideology believe that the world is a competitive place in which gains for one group necessarily come at the expense of another (Sidanius, Pratto, & Bobo, 1994). The ideology of *anthropocentrism* may be particularly relevant to attitudes toward First Nations people. Anthropocentrism involves the belief that humans are intrinsically more valuable than nonhuman animals or nature (Chandler & Dreger, 1993). People with an anthropocentric worldview tend to hold negative attitudes toward nonhuman animals (Bizumic & Duckitt, 2007) and to believe that humans have a right to exploit the natural environment (Chandler & Dreger, 1993). This ideology may be relevant to attitudes toward First Nations people for a couple of reasons. First, because native forms of spirituality promote respect for the animal world, people with an anthropocentric worldview may see their values as at odds with those of First Nations people. Second, because anthropocentric people tend to feel entitled to expropriate natural resources, they may be especially likely to perceive conflicts of interest with First Nations people over resources such as land, hunting and fishing rights, and so on.

Even among people who do not endorse ideologies that sensitize people to intergroup rivalry, situational factors can generate perceptions of competition. Social upheaval, war, unemployment, population changes (through immigration), and collective action by disadvantaged groups in the service of greater equality can all cause people to perceive competition from other groups (Esses & Jackson, 2008). Although prejudice against native people is an ongoing blemish in many countries, it erupts strongly when disputes over land interfere with the interests of non-natives. For example, prejudice against First Nations people in Canada increased notably in 1990 when Mohawk protestors slowed the expansion of a golf course because it encroached on disputed land deemed sacred to them (Esses et al., 1993). In the United States, controversies over Native Americans' treaty rights have led to eruptions of conflict and overt prejudice. For example, in recent decades tensions between the Chippewa and other residents of Wisconsin heightened when some Chippewa individuals claimed their rights to fish, hunt, and trap on nonreservation land (Bobo & Tuan, 2006). Although rights to do so were established when the land was ceded to the American government in the 1800s, a sense of entitlement among non-natives to the area's natural resources has given rise to challenges to these rights.

People tend to see some particular groups as competitors, and although people may assume that these perceptions are logical, they may not always be (Esses, Jackson, et al., 2005). Things that make a group salient or noticeable can lead people to see the group as a relevant competitor, whereas groups that do not stand out may be overlooked. People are especially likely to see a group as a potential competitor if that group stands out by looking different, having different cultural traditions, speaking a different language, holding a different social status than the ingroup, being of a different political persuasion, or increasing in size (Esses & Jackson, 2008). First Nations people likely stand out to non-natives as distinct for a variety of reasons, including their partial segregation on reservations, unique cultural and religious traditions, their lower-than-average socioeconomic standing, and occasional visible use of traditional ceremonies and clothing.

When people view members of another group as competitors for something valuable, they tend to feel threatened, anxious, or fearful (Stephan & Stephan, 2000) and to think in zero-sum terms (e.g., if "they" get the goods, "we" will lose out; Esses et al., 1998). Competition is disconcerting because it means that one has something valuable to lose. The unified instrumental model of group conflict posits that for this reason, competition motivates people to act in a way to reduce or eliminate the competition from the other group. For example, perpetuating negative stereotypes of a competitor group could lessen their competitiveness by making them seem less worthy of desirable outcomes. Early American stereotypes of Native Americans as innocent and spiritual encouraged early explorers and settlers to come to America. However, this positive stereotype later changed to a much more negative depiction of Native Americans as savage and bloodthirsty, which justified the expropriation of land and resources from them. In Bobo and Tuan's (2006) words,

> Benign early images of Indians as trading partners eventually gave way to starkly opposed images of savages and barbarians standing in the path of permanent white settlement and expansion. The former imagery suited a goal of peaceful trading relations, whereas the latter was conducive to violent domination whenever Indians resisted white encroachment. (pp. 72–73)

Contemporary surveys by psychologists show that the attitudes of non–First Nations people toward First Nations people are very much shaped by feelings of threat and beliefs about competition over land as well as by values (Corenblum & Stephan, 2001; Islam & Jahjah, 2001), and they arguably serve goals of reducing competition over both land and social identity value.

Competition can also be minimized by ensuring that the voices of competitor groups are silenced so they are less able to rock the boat. During summer 2006, police arrested 25 citizens for attempting to stop the expansion of a highway into a unique natural area in British Columbia, Canada. Those protestors who were not First Nations people were given fines or community service, whereas an elderly and ill First Nations protestor, Harriet Nahanee, was sent to a jail known to have poor living conditions. She died not long after (Mair, 2007). In 1995, a First Nations man named Dudley George was shot and killed by a police officer. George was unarmed and was protesting the government's use of contested land at Ipperwash Provincial Park in Ontario. The events prompted an inquiry that resulted in a negative critique of actions of the provincial government and police of the time and in numerous recommendations for change (Bonoguore, 2007). Actions such as putting people in jail and killing them clearly reduce people's voice and so limit their competitiveness. Even the existence of the residential school system for which the Canadian prime minister recently apologized can be viewed as a competition-reducing tool because it was designed to strip First Nations people of their culture. Indeed, it has been cited as a cause of a loss of a positive group identity and collective self-esteem among First Nations people (e.g., D. M. Taylor, 1997).

In this chapter, I have described how intergroup dynamics can create and exaggerate prejudice and discrimination between groups. The group conflict perspective explains how competition over material or symbolic resources generates animosity, and the social identity perspective adds that people use intergroup comparisons to bolster their own social identity, sometimes at the expense of others. The unified instrumental model of group conflict (Esses, Jackson, et al., 2005) describes how these factors work together, as occurs when the ideologies that bolster people's social identity exacerbate perceptions of competition between groups and these perceptions in turn lead to efforts to reduce both the material power and the social value of competitor groups. Together, these perspectives show how attitudes toward and treatment of other groups can be shaped by ongoing social relationships between groups involving often unequal access to resources.

7

COGNITIVE, AFFECTIVE, AND
INTERACTIVE PROCESSES
OF PREJUDICE

In February 1999, 22-year-old Amadou Diallo was shot at 41 times by four police officers. Nineteen of the shots hit and killed him. Diallo was unarmed, was no threat to the police, and had done no wrong. When the officers approached him standing at the door of his New York apartment building, they ordered him not to move because he apparently resembled a rape suspect they were seeking in the area. When Diallo reached into his pants pocket to retrieve his wallet, the officers shot and killed him, thinking he was retrieving a gun. The police officers were acquitted of all charges of wrongdoing (Correll, Park, Wittenbrink, & Judd, 2002). Diallo was a West African immigrant.

A similar case occurred in November 2006, when 23-year-old Sean Bell was killed by police officers on his wedding day in Queens, New York. As he and his friends left his bachelor party in the early morning hours, a group of officers shot 50 bullets at them, killing Sean and seriously wounding two of his friends because one of the men made a move that police thought implied that he had a gun. All officers were acquitted of all charges ("Sean Bell," 2008). Sean was a man of color, as were his friends.

Tragedies such as these raise a host of serious questions about the nature and consequences of prejudice. Did prejudice play a role in the shootings, or were police officers responding to the situations and the men's actions alone? Would police officers have shot at Diallo and Bell if they were White or in upscale neighborhoods? To be sure, police officers are often in situations of real danger, and in these cases the officers thought that their lives were at risk and so acted out of their perceived need for self-defense. However, it warrants asking whether the way in which the officers interpreted what they saw was shaped by stereotypes that link men of color to violence. Given that such stereotypes have existed in American culture for some time (Devine & Elliot, 1995), might anyone who has been exposed to them have done the same thing in a similar situation?

This latter issue raises a question about the relationship between this type of tragedy and the subtle and common manifestations of prejudice that occur every day. One can imagine that on the days when Diallo and Bell were killed, as on all others, subtle prejudice was expressed by many people in their homes, in the workplace, and in public through nervous laughter, uncomfortable gestures, inappropriate jokes, and cultural insensitivity. Do these kinds of common manifestations of prejudice perpetuate cultural stereotypes in a way that makes tragedies like the shooting deaths somehow more likely to occur? In this chapter, I address some of the basic cognitive and affective processes (i.e., how people think and feel) that can help to answer such questions.

The dynamics discussed in this chapter often function to maintain the stereotypic beliefs, uncomfortable intergroup relations, or discriminatory actions that have already become prevalent in a society. To begin to understand such issues, I address some basic processes by which people perceive and interpret information about others in social situations, in particular, how stereotyping can occur in subtle ways yet lead to devastating consequences; how emotional responses to others can be shaped in unremarkable, even unconscious ways; and how the basic functioning of the brain can at times lead to the perpetuation of prejudice.

STEREOTYPING

Why is it that "a regular teenage girl can swathe her head in a scarf . . . and be instantly transformed into a humorless, vaguely threatening fanatic who prays all day long, censors everything she says, [and] has no interest in boys or fashion" (George, 2007, p. 58) when the reality suggests that she is likely to be a typical teen? Stereotypes tend to shape how people are perceived. Stereotyping occurs when an individual is viewed through the lens of stereotypes, for example, when a Muslim girl's quiet behavior is interpreted as humorlessness rather than something unrelated to the stereotype, such as emotional or intellectual depth. Stereotypes often shape what people notice about others, how they interpret it, and whether they remember it (Fiske & Taylor, 1991). In places such as North America in which the dominant religion is Christianity, markers of other religions, such as the hijab, are likely to be readily noticed and to lead people to focus on things that may be relevant to the stereotype (e.g., quiet behavior), interpret them in light of the stereotype, and remember those things more than things that are unrelated to the stereotype. So stereotypes perpetuate themselves because people selectively view others in a way that confirms stereotypes and fail to recognize or recall contradictory information.

Stereotypes also shape how people understand what they see. Many experiments have shown that people interpret the same behavior differently depending on the identity of the actor. In one early, often-cited experiment (Duncan, 1976), researchers asked White European American university students to watch a video that they thought was taping people in real time in an adjacent room but was in fact scripted. In the tape, two students had a discussion that gradually built to an argument. At a given point in the argument, one student shoved the other. There were four versions of the film: one that showed a White man shoving a Black man, one that showed a Black man shoving a White man, one that showed a Black man shoving a Black man, and one that showed a White man shoving a White man. Otherwise, the videos were identical. Students who observed the video were asked to describe the parties depicted in it. Their responses revealed the influence of stereotypes. The White participants were much more likely to describe the behavior as violent if the person doing the shoving was Black, especially when the person who was shoved was White. For example, among those who observed a White man shove a Black man, 17% described the behavior as violent, whereas 75% of those who observed a Black man shove a White man described it as violent. Moreover, when the actor who pushed the other person was White, research participants tended to suggest that he did so because the situation prompted him to (i.e., it was not his fault), whereas when the actor who pushed the other was Black, they were more inclined to suggest that the situation occurred because he was a violent sort of a person (i.e., it was his fault). More important, the videotaped interactions were scripted and identical aside from the color of the people engaged in the interaction. Thus, skin color alone led people to alter what they saw.

What is especially distressing about this type of effect is that people may be unaware of how stereotypes shape their judgments. Those who saw the shove as violent could, after all, point to evidence in the film of aggressive behavior. The fact that most social situations are characterized by a degree of ambiguity opens the door for stereotypes to shape how people perceive what they see. Recall the shooting deaths mentioned at the opening of the chapter. Amadou Diallo and Sean Bell were ethnic minority men who were shot and killed by police despite being innocent of a crime and no threat to police. Yet, the officers involved thought that they were in danger of being shot themselves, and they used their weapons in self-protection. They "saw" men reaching for guns.

Is it possible that stereotypes linking ethnic minority men to attributes associated with aggression can lead well-meaning people to interpret innocent behavior by minority men as threatening? Psychologist Joshua Correll and his colleagues (2002) examined this issue in a series of studies on a phenomenon that has come to be known as the *weapons effect*. In their research, Correll et al. had participants play a video game that involved making quick decisions about whether a person shown in a photo was armed or not. A series of photographs were displayed on a computer screen that depicted a man holding an object, either a gun or another small object such as a cell phone or wallet, in a complex background such as a train station, a city street, or a park. Some of the photographs were of Black men, and some were of White men. Otherwise they were identical. Participants were to decide quickly whether the object was a gun or not. If they thought it was a gun, they were to press a "shoot" button. If they thought it was not a gun, they were to press a "don't shoot" button. The computer registered both what decision was made and how quickly the decision was made. In the real-life situations that prompted the research, speed mattered. As Correll et al. noted, had the officers involved in the Diallo and Bell cases taken the time to repeat the order to freeze or paused for a second or two, they might have realized that the victims were unarmed. Participants in the research also completed questionnaires that assessed their prejudice level, their personal belief in stereotypes of African Americans, and their knowledge of the cultural stereotype of African Americans (regardless of whether they believed it to be true).

Results of the research showed that participants were faster to make the correct decision to shoot when the target holding a gun was Black versus White and were faster to make the correct decision to not shoot when the target holding a different object was White versus Black. Furthermore, when participants were encouraged to make decisions very quickly, they made more errors: They were more likely to wrongly shoot when the man in the photograph was Black and more likely to wrongly not shoot when he was White. The tendency for participants to make fast decisions to shoot when the target was Black was related to participants' knowledge of the cultural stereotype of African American men but not to their own endorsement of the stereotype or their prejudice level. That is, the more aware they were of the content of the cultural stereotype, whether they believed it or not, the more likely they were to wrongly shoot the man. In fact, even African American participants showed this bias, suggesting that the effect was not the result of general anti–outgroup prejudice but rather of the way in which the cultural stereotype of African American men shaped what people "saw."

Follow-up research has confirmed and extended these findings. For example, Correll, Park, Judd, and Wittenbrink (2007) reported that people who were exposed to stories linking Black people to crime showed a stronger shooting bias against Black men in the video game task than did those who were not exposed to this information. This research points to an important but disturbing conclusion: Even nonprejudiced people who are exposed to cultural stereotypes may at times—especially in the heat of the moment when fast decisions are necessary—act on those stereotypes.

Findings such as these seem to imply that people may stereotype others in the absence of awareness that they are doing so. In fact, considerable evidence has shown that impressions of others can be influenced by stereotypes and prejudice in ways that are not recognized by the person forming the impression (Banaji & Greenwald, 1994). *Implicit stereotyping* occurs when people form impressions of others that they think are based on the facts (the person's behavior or characteristics) when in fact the interpretation of these facts is influenced by stereotypes (Greenwald & Banaji, 1995). The term *implicit* suggests that people are unaware of the way in which stereotypes shape their social judgments; the biasing effect of stereotypes occurs outside of conscious awareness. This process is in contrast to *explicit stereotyping*, which occurs when people are aware of the factors that guide their impressions (e.g., when people believe that stereotypes are accurate and relevant to interpretations of individuals).

Payne (2001) showed how serious mistakes in social perception, such as confusing an innocuous object for a gun, can be implicit, operating outside of awareness. Payne had research participants, none of whom was Black, observe a computer screen and make a series of decisions about images they saw flashed on the screen. Repeatedly, they saw a face, which had either Black or White skin, followed by an object that was either a tool or a weapon. Each face and object was presented very quickly, for only 200 ms each, and the object was shown immediately after the face. The participants were instructed to ignore the face and to indicate whether the item shown next was a tool or a weapon by pressing a key on the keyboard. Because the faces and objects were flashed very rapidly and participants responded quickly, there was no opportunity for introspection and little chance for people to exert control over their responses. Payne found that participants showed evidence of implicit stereotyping: They were faster to classify weapons when the preceding face was Black than when it was White. Also, when participants were encouraged to respond as quickly as possible, they made stereotypic errors, misclassifying a tool as a gun more often when the preceding face was Black than when it was White. This research showed that when non-Black people simply detected—for a fraction of a second—a Black face, the cultural stereotype associating people of color with violence shaped their interpretation of what they saw.

This type of research shows that stereotyping can occur at a very subtle level. The fact that implicit stereotyping is a real phenomenon, despite being difficult to detect, has been substantiated with neurological evidence. For example, in one study of the brain processes underlying stereotyping (Osterhout, Bersick, & McLaughlin, 1997), participants read sentences, some of which implied an exception to a stereotype. For example, the sentence "Our aerobics instructor gave himself a break" contradicts the occupational stereotype that aerobics instructors are female. Participants who read the sentences were monitored with an electroencephalograph, a set of electrodes that are attached to the scalp and measure electrical activity associated with the firing of neurons in the brain. Osterhout et al. (1997) found that when people read sentences that contradicted a stereotype, there was increased activity in the electroencephalograph, suggesting that such information caused increased attentiveness or surprise. This is important because it confirms, with neurological evidence, that stereotyping can occur extremely rapidly and without conscious intent. On encountering the term *aerobics instructor*, people must have immediately anticipated that the instructor was female and were surprised— at the level of brain activity—to then read that the instructor was male.

Various models of prejudice distinguish between processes of social perception that are implicit and explicit (Greenwald & Banaji, 1995). Other terms, such as *automatic* versus *controlled* stereotyping, are often used to describe similar processes (e.g., Devine, 1989). Some aspects of stereotyping may occur relatively automatically, when, for example, stereotypes seem to pop into mind without any warning when one encounters a member of a different group. Controlled processes are those that are more subject to conscious manipulation. For example, although stereotypes may pop into one's mind when he or she encounters different others, people who are nonprejudiced in their more conscious beliefs and feelings are often able to dismiss those stereotypes as not relevant and instead attend to people as distinct individuals (Devine, 1989).

Nevertheless, it is clear that people who are generally nonprejudiced do not always avoid implicit stereotyping because implicit and explicit measures of stereotyping are only weakly related to one another (Hofmann, Gawronski, Gschwendner, Le, & Schmitt, 2005). That is, people who seem to be nonprejudiced and score low on measures of conventional explicit stereotyping are only somewhat less likely than people who appear to be prejudiced to engage in implicit stereotyping. Avoiding the effects of implicit stereotypes requires not only that people consciously reject stereotypes but also that they be aware of the possibility of being vulnerable to implicit stereotyping and able and motivated to use more controlled processes to avoid it (Fazio, 1990). Situations in which people react reflectively or are distracted, tired, or unmotivated are more vulnerable to the effects of stereotyping. For example, a good deal of early research showed that people who are distracted by trying to do two things at once are often more inclined to stereotype others, provided they are not so distracted that they do not detect the person's group membership at all (e.g., Gilbert & Hixon, 1991).

More recently, attention has turned to the biological factors that might influence whether people are able to avoid engaging in stereotyping. This research has shown that, in a variety of ways, when people's physical and cognitive resources are taxed, they are more inclined to stereotype others, presumably because they lack the resources to detect and inhibit implicit stereotyping processes. For example, people are more likely to stereotype others when they have consumed alcohol (Bartholow, Dickter, & Sestir, 2006) and when their levels of cortisol—the stress hormone—are high (Amodio, 2009). Furthermore, people are less likely to stereotype others when they have consumed a sugar drink, adding glucose to the body and brain (Gailliot, Peruche, Plant, & Baumeister, 2009). Taken together, such findings suggest that stereotyping is a sort of lazy process that emerges when people lack the resources to process information carefully.

The ability to inhibit stereotyping corresponds to specific patterns of activity in the brain (Bartholow et al., 2006; Stanley et al., 2008), a fact that confirms the assumption that people often need to exert deliberate intention to avoid stereotyping. An area of the brain known as the anterior cingulate cortex tends to be active when people are attentive to the need to monitor their actions for potential conflicts between a relatively automatic response and an alternative (Amodio, Devine, & Harmon-Jones, 2007). For example, if you were asked to read out loud a Stroop test—a list of color words in which the ink color does not match the word (e.g., the word *green* written in red ink)—you would experience a conflict because you would have to check the automatic tendency to say red and say green instead, and your anterior cingulate cortex would tend to be active when you experienced this. However, if the ink color and written word were congruent, there would be no conflict, and your anterior cingulate cortex would be less active. Similarly, when people engage in tasks that require them to control stereotypic responses, their anterior cingulate cortex tends to be active, and this tendency is strongest among people who are intrinsically motivated to avoid stereotyping others (Amodio et al., 2007).

To summarize, stereotyping can occur in subtle and insidious ways, and people are not always aware of the ways in which the impressions they form of others are shaped by stereotypes. However, it is possible for people to avoid stereotyping by directing deliberate intention to engage in more careful impression formation. This ability tends to be hampered when people's physical or cognitive resources are taxed, and so sometimes stereotypes slip out even though people may be generally nonprejudiced and well intentioned.

The effects, however, can be extremely serious, including death, as the cases of the shooting deaths of Diallo and Bell suggest.

AFFECTIVE PROCESSES

Have you ever had the experience of meeting a person who is different from you in some way and feeling awkward, nervous, or a bit uneasy, even though you reject prejudice and want to be open and respectful? People find themselves occasionally experiencing a conflict between their beliefs and their emotions (also known as *affect*). For example, people who value equality and diversity may nevertheless feel some discomfort, unease, self-consciousness, or nervousness when interacting with people of different backgrounds. Although such feelings are common and often contradicted by people's beliefs and conscious attitudes, prejudice researchers are interested in them for two reasons. First, they may lead people to behave differently than they would in the absence of these feelings. Second, feelings people have in reaction to other groups may lead to different outcomes than do stereotypes (Jackson et al., 2001).

In an early examination of emotional prejudice, Gaertner and Dovidio (1986) described the subtle negative feelings aroused by different others that can linger in people who embrace egalitarian ideals, which they called *aversive racism*. It is an apt phrase because the type of bias that exists in some people involves feelings of mild aversion and also because for many people who are genuine in their desire to be nonprejudiced, uncomfortable feelings of any sort around people who are different are themselves aversive.

In an active program of research, Dovidio, Gaertner, and their colleagues have demonstrated a number of ways people who embrace egalitarianism sometimes show indications of aversive racism (Dovidio & Gaertner, 2004). People may try to avoid encounters with others who arouse uncomfortable feelings, not because they dislike the people but because they dislike the feelings they have. At times, people may be scrupulous in their intergroup encounters, or they may bend over backward to treat others well, out of a concern not to be seen as biased. However, this does not advantage the targets of prejudice. Many studies of aversive racism have shown that aversive racists will tend to be egalitarian only when providing some kind of negative evaluation of a member of a disadvantaged group would clearly suggest prejudice or discrimination. For example, if a member of a minority group is clearly the best applicant for a job, most people will tend to be fair, and aversive racists may be especially supportive of the minority. However, in common situations in which things are more ambiguous, such as when a group of people of different backgrounds all have mixed qualifications for a job, aversive racism will tend to lead people to discriminate against the minority. Such situations are characterized by attributional ambiguity; it is difficult to know to what preference for a candidate should be attributed. Therefore, people can discriminate yet point to the mixed qualifications as evidence of objectivity (see also Son Hing et al., 2008).

Recently, aversive racism has been described as involving high implicit prejudice but low explicit prejudice (Son Hing et al., 2008). Just as stereotypes can function implicitly, so too can more emotional kinds of evaluative responses to people. *Implicit prejudice* refers to negative emotional responses to people that may go unrecognized (Greenwald & Banaji, 1995). People may not be aware that their emotions change subtly when they encounter a different other, or they may feel the change but not be aware of the cause of the change. Research has consistently shown that this kind of implicit prejudice has a variety of negative implications (Greenwald, Poehlman, Uhlmann, & Banaji, 2009). For example, a study by Dovidio, Kawakami, and Gaertner (2002) demonstrated that implicit prejudice leads people to behave in a less friendly manner with members of other groups.

In their research, Dovidio et al. (2002) had White research participants interact with a Black research assistant (who they were led to believe was another participant). They were subsequently asked about their impressions of the interaction and how they thought they came across. In addition, trained observers rated the behavior of the participants in terms of verbal and nonverbal friendliness. Measures of both implicit and explicit prejudice were also taken. Research participants who admitted being prejudiced on the explicit measure thought they were less friendly with the Black interaction partner than did those who did not report prejudice, and observers agreed. People who showed prejudice on the implicit measure also acted in a less friendly manner with the Black partner than did people who showed less implicit prejudice. However, they were not aware of doing so. This research suggests that in encounters between people of different backgrounds, implicit prejudice may shape behaviors, such as eye contact or nervous gestures, over which people do not have full awareness. Such behaviors are likely to be detected by the interaction partner, however.

How do implicit, emotional forms of prejudice develop? Childhood experiences may be particularly relevant here (Rudman, 2004; Rudman, Phelan, & Heppen, 2007), especially if they involve basic evaluative conditioning. Visualize a woman with long fingernails raising her hand to a chalkboard and dragging her nails down its surface. Did you cringe or feel even the slightest tightening of your shoulders? Does the music of the classic movie *Jaws* give you the creeps? If you answered yes to either of these questions, you have experienced a particular form of conditioning known as *classical conditioning*. Classical conditioning is a simple form of learning that occurs when some type of response changes as a function of repeated pairings between sets of stimuli. The *Jaws* music repeatedly predicted—was paired with—a shark attack, and so many people spontaneously feel fear, or some kind of muscle tension or twinge in the tummy, as soon as they hear the music. Classical conditioning often, but not always, involves learned changes to simple, reflective physical responses (Passer, Smith, Atkinson, Mitchell, & Muir, 2008). For example, people being treated with chemotherapy for cancer often develop anticipatory nausea and vomiting, becoming ill before receiving therapy, when their bodies learn that the stimuli that precede treatment (e.g., entering the hospital) reliably predict the administration of a drug that naturally creates nausea (Passer et al., 2008).

In a similar way, conditioning can also shape preferences, what people like and do not like, a process known as *evaluative* or *affective conditioning*. Evaluative conditioning occurs when a person's attitude toward something is altered after being paired with something positive or negative. I love the smell of mothballs and feel happy on the rare occasion that I smell them because when I was a child, I smelled them when I entered my much-loved grandparents' home. Evaluative conditioning has been shown to shape attitudes in many domains, such as liking for visual, kinesthetic, and gustatory stimuli (De Houwer, Thomas, & Baeyens, 2001).

Attitudes toward people can also be conditioned, for example, through exposure to media images depicting minority groups with negative stimuli such as devalued social roles or through observing subtle negative behaviors by people interacting with different others. Such processes can shape implicit attitudes toward others, even when people are unaware that conditioning is occurring (M. A. Olson & Fazio, 2001, 2002). Olsson, Ebert, Banaji, and Phelps (2005) conditioned the attitudes of African American and European American participants by having them observe photographs of faces of Black and White people on a computer while receiving a mild electric shock when they observed either the Black or the White faces. They found that both European American and African American participants developed more negative attitudes toward the group that was paired with a shock (whether it was the ingroup or the outgroup), but when the shocks were discontinued, people's newly formed prejudice against their own group diminished, but the conditioned prejudice against the outgroup persisted. They also found that people who had greater familiarity with members of the other groups through interethnic dating experiences were less susceptible to developing conditioned prejudice. This type of research suggests that affective conditioning may perpetuate prejudices that exist in a society by creating negative or wary responses to members of other groups, but also that the cycle can be broken when people seek out experiences that increase their familiarity with different others. In fact, affective conditioning can work in the positive direction as well, when a social group is repeatedly associated with positive stimuli or experiences (Kawakami, Phills, Dovidio, & Steele, 2007; M. A. Olson & Fazio, 2006).

Specific neurological mechanisms are involved in emotional forms of prejudice. Understanding these mechanisms can shed light on the nature of implicit prejudice. Brain-imaging techniques allow researchers to look inside the brain using X-rays and scans that detect blood flow to, and glucose metabolism of, the neurons of the brain (processes that occur immediately after activity of the neurons). One such technique, functional magnetic resonance imaging (fMRI), uses magnetic fields to detect structures and functions of the brain. Using fMRI, researchers can watch as people engage in activities (e.g., look at words or images on a computer) to see how much activity occurs in different regions of the brain. A benefit of this technique is that it allows researchers to look beyond the surface of the brain to the central regions where much emotional processing initially occurs.

Several lines of research using fMRI to study implicit prejudice have pointed to a particular role for the amygdala (Stanley et al., 2008), a small set of nuclei in the limbic system of the brains of complex vertebrates (including humans) that is related to the experience of emotional responses such as fear, aggression, surprise, arousal, and interest. It is associated with the experience of vigilance and has therefore been referred to as "the brain's burglar alarm" (Fiske, 2005, p. 48). It tends to be active in situations that would be expected to involve the fight–flight system (Amodio, 2008), and it is thought to generate rapid, nonconscious responses such as muscle tension or sweating. When someone unexpectedly taps you on the shoulder from behind and you jump in surprise, your amygdala has been involved.

The amygdala has been implicated as being relevant to the development of conditioned fears (LeDoux, 2000). Through conditioning, the amygdala can become activated when someone is in the presence of something or someone he or she has previously had reason to fear. Thus, the kinds of things that may lead to the development of conditioned emotional prejudices (e.g., behavior of parents around different others, media depictions of minorities) may do so in part because the amygdala becomes conditioned to respond to certain other people. Consistent with this logic, the amygdala tends to become active when people view pictures of strangers from different ethnic backgrounds (e.g., Hart et al., 2000). This occurs especially among people who score high on measures of implicit prejudice when they look at faces of unfamiliar, rather than familiar, members of an outgroup (Phelps et al., 2000). Moreover, the amygdala is more likely to become active when such stimuli are presented very rapidly and people do not have the opportunity to monitor or control their responses (Cunningham et al., 2004), and it is less likely to become active when people are encouraged to focus on individual characteristics of others than on group markers (Wheeler & Fiske, 2005).

Whether the amygdala becomes active when people are exposed to different others depends on many factors, such as prejudice level, ability to monitor responses, and what people attend to. This shows that just because a brain mechanism corresponds to a psychological phenomenon, it does not necessarily cause it. People may wrongly assume that if prejudice is linked to amygdala activity, the amygdala causes it. Not so. Everyone has an amygdala, yet people vary tremendously in prejudice level. Also, the link between brain and experience involves a chicken-and-egg problem (i.e., Which comes first?). Amygdala activity can indeed lead people to feel wary of others, but negative expectations about others can also cause the amygdala to become active.

Nevertheless, the fact that the amygdala tends to be involved in responses to others is not unimportant. Because it is associated with emotions such as fear, its activity can shape how people are likely to respond to others. If people feel fear, caution, or even mild discomfort around others, they may be inclined to avoid them or to justify their feelings. This is likely to prevent people from learning about others and becoming familiar with them, which would have the effect of preventing future amygdala reactivity. As Öhman (2005) wrote,

> Once we feel fear, we focus on escaping the situation rather than on in depth evaluation of the real danger . . . avoidance precludes learning about a feared individual, making that person a blank slate for projections that serve to justify the fear. (p. 711)

However, when people do become more familiar with different others, their amygdala is likely to cease its reactivity. The fact that prejudice coincides with brain activity does not mean that it is inevitable (Wheeler & Fiske, 2005). However, the fact that an ancient brain system that orients people to danger is involved in prejudice does help to understand its persistence.

Overall, it is clear that hidden forms of prejudice exist, that they correspond to distinct neurological processes, and that they are consequential. Because stereotyping and emotional prejudice can operate implicitly, and because they do not necessarily coexist with conventional explicit prejudice, people are probably often unaware that their behavior reflects bias. Thus, they are unlikely to engage in the critical self-examination that might reduce their biases. Fortunately, some evidence is emerging that it is possible to reduce implicit prejudice with direct instructions that have people practice behaviors that symbolize approaching members of a targeted group (Kawakami et al., 2007). Nevertheless, because many people are often oblivious to their own biases, it is quite likely that implicit cognitive and affective processes, and their neurological underpinnings, are part of the problem of the perpetuation of prejudice, discrimination, and inequality.

INTERACTIVE PROCESSES

In the earlier sections, I considered ways in which prejudice can be perpetuated because of the subtle ways that it can exist. When prejudice is difficult to detect, it is hard to eliminate. In the sections that follow, I consider a related issue: how prejudice can be perpetuated by the way that the kinds of subtle biases discussed earlier can shape social encounters between members of more and less advantaged groups. In a variety of ways, members of less advantaged groups pick up on the biases of others, and this shapes how they respond to social interactions. Furthermore, members of more advantaged groups sometimes worry that members of less advantaged groups will suspect them of being prejudiced, and this shapes how they respond to encounters. Together, these factors can negatively shape how people feel and act when they interact with someone from another group, and at times this contributes to the perpetuation of prejudice.

Self-Fulfilling Prophecies

In the 1960s, Robert Rosenthal and Lenore Jacobson conducted a study in an elementary school classroom that would become famous for showing that the expectations that teachers have about their students' abilities can mold the students' performance. They administered a test of nonverbal intelligence to all children in the school from kindergarten to Grade 5. Although it was an intelligence test, the researchers told the teachers that it was a test of "inflected acquisition" (Rosenthal & Jacobson, 1968, p. 65) that would identify students who had the potential to bloom in terms of their abilities. They then chose 20% of students in the class and told the teachers that these students were likely to show such blossoming in the near future. In reality, the 20% of students identified to the teachers were selected at random. Thus, the researchers created an expectation among teachers that some students would excel when, in reality, these students were no more or less likely to do so than the other students. Then, the researchers returned to the classrooms 1 and 2 years later and administered the intelligence test again. Comparing changes over time in intelligence scores showed that teacher expectations made a difference to students in the early years of school: Students who had been identified as bloomers in Grades 1 and 2 showed greater increases in intelligence than did those who were not identified, even though these students were selected at random. Moreover, these differences tended to remain for the 2 years of the study. Apparently, when the teachers expected certain students to bloom, they altered their treatment of the students in such a way that those students did, in fact, bloom.

The self-fulfilling prophecy occurs when people think that something is true even though it may not be, but because they think it is true they act in such a way that they make that thing come true (Merton, 1948). Merton (1948) described how the self-fulfilling prophecy functions in social trends, yet it operates psychologically as well. For example, in the context of education, when teachers believe that their students have a certain ability level, they sometimes treat students in such a way that they confirm those expectations, even if they were initially false (Rosenthal & Jacobson, 1968). Although teachers expecting their students to excel can be a good thing, the concern is that negative expectations that some students are not capable can be harmful to students and lead them to underperform. This is especially of concern given that stereotypes of some groups imply lack of capability in some domains (e.g., stereotypes that girls cannot do math or that children from low-income groups lack initiative or ability).

The self-fulfilling prophecy may contribute to the perpetuation of prejudice and inequality if stereotypes function as expectations that can shape people's behavior. If Person A (say a teacher or employer) believes that people from Group B are not competent, does he or she then treat members of Group B in a way that leads them to become disinterested, annoyed, discouraged, or otherwise negatively influenced? If so, then their behavior may appear to Person A to confirm the stereotype, even though it was initially false. In a review of research looking at the self-fulfilling prophecy in the schools, Jussim and Harber (2005) concluded that this dynamic does occur in the classroom, but much more often it does not (they estimated that about 5% to 10% of students showed changes in performance that can be attributed to teachers' expectations). However, they also found that teachers' expectations about stigmatized groups in particular (e.g., low achievers, people from low social classes, ethnic minorities) are much more likely to be influential.

The self-fulfilling prophecy can alter the experience and behavior of members of minority ethnic groups in other interpersonal encounters, such as job interviews. Word, Zanna, and Cooper (1974) provided a good illustration of how the self-fulfilling prophecy can operate. In their research, White university students were asked to interview applicants to be a member of a team that would work together on a marketing project. Unknown to the participants, interviewees had been trained by the researchers to behave similarly and give similar answers to the interview questions. Participants interviewed both Black and White applicants. Observers found that the White interviewers behaved differently toward Black and White interviewees. When interviewing a Black applicant, participants showed less immediacy (e.g., they sat further away and used less eye contact), made more speech errors (e.g., stuttering), and ended the interview sooner than when the interviewee was White. A second phase of the research tested whether this kind of awkward behavior would alter the experience and behavior of interviewees. The researchers trained White interviewers to act in a manner comparable to how interviewers behaved when speaking with a Black inter-viewee and then had them interview other students (who were White). They found that when interviewers behaved in this manner (e.g., showing low immediacy, stuttering), people being interviewed behaved in a less compe-tent manner, acted more nervously, and were themselves less immediate than were people who were treated in a more friendly and direct manner. Together, the two phases of the research showed that the kinds of discomfort shown by people interacting with a member of a different group—which have been shown to persist in contemporary research (e.g., Dovidio et al., 2002)—can alter the interpersonal encounter in such a way that negative beliefs or expec-tations end up being confirmed and members of stereotyped groups may underperform relative to their ability.

This type of research suggests that when members of disadvantaged groups are exposed to the kinds of behavior that emerge from subtle prejudice, their response can, ironically, lead members of advantaged groups to think that their negative expectations were warranted. Thus, they remain oblivious to the role they played in shaping the other's behavior, and so their prejudice seems to them to be justified. This self-fulfilling prophecy has been shown to occur in a variety of contexts and to affect a variety of groups. For example, recent research has shown that when older adults are exposed to negative stereotypes associ-ated with aging (e.g., stereotypes about cognitive and physical declines), they perform more poorly in these domains than when they are exposed to more pos-itive beliefs about aging (Levy & Leifheit-Limson, 2009). Challenging and changing prejudice and inequality thus seems to require that members of advan-taged groups reflect on the way that their own expectations and behavior may play a role in shaping the behavior and experience of others.

Stereotype Threat

The self-fulfilling prophecy involves interactional dynamics that occur during encounters between members of different groups. Members of dis-advantaged groups can be negatively influenced by stereotypes in other ways as well. For example, when people are aware of stereotypes of their own group, they may be motivated to prove, through their behavior, that the stereotype is false. Women may sometimes want to show that they are good at math, men may wish to prove that they can be capable with young children, and so on. Although people are often successful in these efforts, there are instances in which the very awareness of the stereotype and the motivation to disprove it can interfere with people's performance and ironically lead to the stereotyping being confirmed. This process is known as *stereotype threat*.

The phenomenon of stereotype threat was first described and demon-strated by Steele and Aronson (1995). They reasoned that people sometimes underperform, relative to their ability, in academic settings because they are aware of stereotypes of their group, and this awareness hampers their performance. They demonstrated this to be true in a convincing set of experiments. Initially, they had African American and European American participants take tests using different sets of instructions. In one condition, they said that the test was diagnostic of people's verbal abilities and would point to people's potential strengths and weaknesses. They reasoned that by so doing, African American people would be reminded of the stereotypes that imply their lesser ability in this domain, and this awareness of the stereotype would hamper their performance. In contrast, they reasoned that if the test was described differently, this would not occur. They tested this by comparing performance of people who took the test said to be diagnostic of verbal ability with a control group who took the same test described simply as an exercise in problem solving, a domain less directly linked to stereotypes of African American people. Results showed that in the control condition, African American and European American participants performed at the same level. However, when the test was described as being diagnostic of verbal ability, the performance of African American participants was reduced. In follow-up research, Steele and Aronson (1995) found that merely asking people to indicate their race on a test before taking the test hampered performance on the test among African American people. When not asked to provide racial information, European Americans and African Americans performed equivalently on the test. However, when asked to provide this information, the performance of African Americans declined. Apparently, anything that reminds people of the stereotype of one's group can interfere with performance on a test that is relevant to that stereotype.

Subsequent research has confirmed the stereotype threat phenomenon for many groups in many domains. When people perform in a domain for which there are stereotypes about their group's ability, performance is hampered by things that make that stereotype salient to people. Stereotype threat has been shown to influence the performance of women, other ethnic minorities, people low in socioeconomic status, gay men and lesbians, and elderly people (Maass & Cadinu, 2003) because there are stereotypes about the abilities, strengths, and weaknesses of all of these groups. It can even emerge among members of traditionally advantaged groups in domains in which they are negatively stereotyped. For example, if men and women take the same test, men will tend to outperform women if it is described as a test of logical ability (a stereotype that favors men), but women will tend to outperform men if it is described as a test of interpersonal ability (a stereotype that favors women; see Maass & Cadinu, 2003). It is important that it is not the test that differs, only the label. The label reminds people of the stereotype of their group, and that is sufficient to influence performance on the test.

Apparently, when people are evaluated in a domain in which the stereotype says they are not fully capable, they become distracted. They may feel anxious or determined to disprove the stereotype. They may become less creative or unwilling to take risks because of this determination. The ironic effect is that the distracting thoughts and feelings end up hampering performance (Maass & Cadinu, 2003). A further irony is that some evidence has suggested that it may actually be people who think that stereotypes of their group are not widely endorsed any longer who are most susceptible to the effect because they are especially motivated to uphold what they view as the relatively positive emerging view of their group (Ho & Sidanius, 2010). The consequences can be considerable. Steele and Aronson (1995) argued that stereotype threat has damaged the scholastic performance of some ethnic groups. Moreover, it may contribute to a tendency of negatively stereotyped groups to disengage or withdraw from domains that become unnecessarily frustrating for them. The ultimate effect is the perpetuation of the inequality and prejudice that caused the performance gap in the first place.

Fortunately, the negative effects of stereotype threat ought to be mitigated by altering the contexts that evoke it. For example, tests can be relabeled or group markers can be deemphasized to decrease the likelihood that stereotypes will be salient to people, and counterstereotypic information and role models can be provided to alter the nature of the connections people make between groups and their performance abilities (Maass & Cadinu, 2003). Additionally, making alternative, more positive stereotypes accessible (e.g., university students are good at math) can undermine the harmful effects of negative stereotypes (e.g., women are not good at math) on test performance (Rydell, McConnell, & Beilock, 2009). One particularly successful intervention reduced the impact of stereotype threat significantly by using a simple exercise in class in which African American and European American students had an opportunity to affirm their identity and values at the beginning of the school term by identifying and writing about their most important values (Cohen, Garcia, Apfel, & Master, 2006). This simple exercise had dramatic effects. At the end of the term, African American students who had affirmed their own values performed on average about one third of a grade point higher than did African American students in a control group. Moreover, the intervention reduced the racial achievement gap between African American and European American students by 40%, apparently by interrupting a downward trend in grades that otherwise tends to occur among African American students over the course of the term. Cohen et al. (2006) suggested that the simple act of affirming their identity and values reduced the impact of stereotype threat among African American students early on in the term and so strengthened their performance throughout the school year.

Stereotype Lift

Researchers Danso and Esses (2001) demonstrated an important flip side to the phenomenon of stereotype threat. They found that when White undergraduate university students were given a test of intellectual ability by a Black researcher, they performed better than did White students who were given the very same test by a White researcher, and this was especially true among people who were high in social dominance orientation (see Chapter 4). The researchers reasoned that when people who are part of an advantaged group feel entitled to their privilege (as people high in social dominance orientation tend to) and when they are confronted with a successful member of the less advantaged group (e.g., a Black person administering a test of intellectual ability), they may feel a sense of competitive threat that motivates them to achieve. The implication is that the same conditions that may hinder the test performance of stereotyped groups—such as tests taken in a context that makes awareness of social stereotypes salient—may enhance the performance of advantaged groups if such contexts evoke a sense of competitive entitlement.

Subsequent to this discovery, researchers Walton and Cohen (2003) coined the term *stereotype lift* to describe the phenomenon whereby members of advantaged groups experience a boost in their performance because of their awareness of a negative stereotype of an outgroup. These researchers reviewed previous research on stereotype threat in which members of advantaged and less advantaged groups were given tests under conditions that did and did not evoke stereotype threat. In a meta-analysis of these studies, they found that the conditions that tend to create stereotype threat (performance decrements among members of disadvantaged groups) also create stereotype lift (performance enhancement among members of the advantaged group) and that this effect is especially pronounced among people who tend to identify strongly with achievement in the ability being tested. This is an important discovery because it shows that testing situations can not only disadvantage some people, they can also unfairly advantage others. By implication, stereotype threat and stereotype lift can serve to perpetuate inequality even in the absence of any overt prejudice or discrimination.

Metastereotypes

If you are White, heterosexual, able bodied, or of middle or upper income level, think about how you may be viewed by people who are of color, gay, disabled, or of lower economic standing. Do they hold negative stereotypes about you or the groups to which you belong? Vorauer, Main, and O'Connell (1998) showed that many people hold *metastereotypes*, that is, beliefs regarding the stereotype that out-group members hold about [one's] own group . . . a White Canadian hetereosexual may expect to be seen as submissive and polite by Americans; as arrogant, selfish, and materialistic by Aboriginal persons; and as uptight and conservative by homosexual individuals. (p. 917)

In fact, Vorauer et al. found that White Canadians held metastereotypes about First Nations Canadians' views of them. They reported thinking that First Nations people viewed White Canadians as holding many negative traits, such as being self-centered, unfeeling, prejudiced, ambitious, wealthy, and phony. People who were less prejudiced were more likely to assume that their group was viewed in this way.

When people interact with someone from another group, feeling stereotyped by that person has negative effects on the encounter, and this is true of metastereotypes as well. For example, members of advantaged groups may feel robbed of their sense of individuality and control if they feel that they are unfairly labeled as prejudiced by members of less advantaged groups (Vorauer et al., 1998). Indeed, Vorauer et al. (1998) found that White Canadians who felt that they were stereotyped during an interaction with a First Nations person experienced more negative feelings about the encounter than did people who did not assume that they were stereotyped. This kind of experience may lead people to avoid intergroup encounters, to respond to them in an unnecessarily defensive manner, or to fail to engage in behaviors that facilitate positive interactions. For example, Vorauer and Turpie (2004) showed that among White Canadians who scored low on a measure of prejudice against First Nations people, being concerned about how one would be evaluated by a First Nations person led to "choking effects" (p. 395) whereby these individuals engaged in fewer behaviors that tend to foster friendship development, such as self-disclosure and eye contact. Ironically, some individuals' concerns that they might be viewed as prejudiced led them to behave in a manner that is likely to come across as prejudiced to their interaction partner. Other evidence has shown that, at times, people who tend to score low on measures of prejudice overestimate how likely members of disadvantaged groups will be to see them as distinct from other, more prejudiced members of their group. As a consequence, they may become complacent and fail to make efforts to generate positive interactions (Vorauer, Martens, & Sasaki, 2009).

Metastereotypes held by members of minority groups can also erode the quality of intergroup relations. This was demonstrated in a study of metastereotypes among Dutch Moroccan teenagers in the Netherlands (Kamans, Gordijn, Oldenhuis, & Otten, 2009). The researchers showed that this minority group was aware of the prevalent negative stereotypes held by the Dutch majority about their group, which include characteristics such as criminality and aggression. Moreover, they found that among those Dutch Moroccan teenagers who tended to be prejudiced against the Dutch majority, personalized metastereotypes—that is, the belief that Dutch people stereotyped them personally—led them to legitimize the negative stereotype of their group, for example, by endorsing the view that aggression by their group against the majority is warranted.

Taken together, the material covered in this chapter shows how a variety of subtle yet pervasive aspects of the way in which people process information and respond emotionally to social situations can lead to the perpetuation of prejudice and inequality. It also shows quite clearly that for people who wish to be nonprejudiced, endorsing positive values is not enough. It is also necessary to recognize that the best of intentions can coexist with unfair treatment of others or uncomfortable interpersonal encounters. Fortunately, on the basis of these discoveries a number of ways that prejudice and its effects can be reduced have been developed, topics that are discussed in the final chapter. Before addressing those techniques, though, in Chapter 8, I take a step back to look at prejudice in broader perspective.

8

TOWARD A WIDER LENS: PREJUDICE AND THE NATURAL WORLD

At the Aamjiwaang First Nations reserve near Sarnia, Ontario, Canada, residents suffer from unusually high levels of diabetes, thyroid problems, asthma, skin rashes, miscarriage, and chronic headaches (Dubinski, 2007). Beside a creek where children used to play and deer and birds and other animals continue to drink stands a sign with a skull and crossbones followed by the warning that the creek contains toxins known to be linked to serious health risks. Surrounding the reservation on three sides are 52 industrial plants, primarily linked to the petrochemical industry. Soil and sediment tests in the area have revealed heavy contamination by numerous pollutants known to cause health risks, and epidemiological research has shown altered reproductive patterns in both humans and animals that are likely linked to the environmental toxicity (E. Hood, 2005). On the other side of the country in Alberta, in the areas surrounding the Athabasca oil sands (an area in the northern part of the province where oil is extracted from deposits of sand, clay, and water), First Nations communities suffer from high rates of thyroid diseases and rare cancers. Some in these communities are employed at the oil sands "raking in the carcasses of ducks floating on vast pools of rotten water, the by-product of the sands' oil-extraction methods" (Kohler, 2007, p. 20).

At Aamjiwaang, band member Ron Plain reportedly claimed that it seems that "[Europeans] took our land from us and said, 'Thanks for the land, now here's cancer'" (Dubinski, 2007, p. A3).

Although on the surface environmental issues, prejudice, and discrimination seem to have little connection, the reality revealed by the foregoing examples is that they are part of a web of problems related to inequality. Other links exist as well. Prejudiced attitudes toward groups and attitudes about environmentalism are connected; people who are more prejudiced seem to be less concerned about the environment (Chandler & Dreger, 1993). In addition, environmental crises increase the risk of prejudice and conflict between groups as groups compete over access to increasingly scarce natural resources (Homer-Dixon, Boutwell, & Rathjens, 1993). Moreover, many of these dynamics affect the animals that are part of the natural environment. For example, the development of industries near First Nations reserves causes death and health damage to animals that live in and eat from the damaged land and water (e.g., Kohler, 2007). Prejudice against human groups and the lack of moral concern for the environment and the well-being of the animals that are a part of it appear to share common themes of domination and control (Plous, 2003). In fact, people who devalue nature and animals are more likely than others to be ethnically prejudiced as well (Bizumic & Duckitt, 2007; Chandler & Dreger, 1993).

In this chapter, I examine the myriad connections among prejudice, environmental issues, and attitudes toward and treatment of animals in more depth. Connections between environmental and intergroup issues have received serious attention within the field of sociology (e.g., Mohai & Saha, 2007) and among those with interests in international relations (e.g., Intergovernmental Panel on Climate Change [IPCC], 2007). Within psychology, researchers have examined belief systems relevant to both environmental and intergroup attitudes (e.g., Chandler & Dreger, 1993). Recently, Esses and Jackson (2008) described how competition over environmental resources can foster intergroup conflict, and some emerging research has shown that feelings of entitlement to environmental resources may fuel discriminatory intergroup decision making (e.g., Bitacola, Jackson, Esses, & Janes, 2010; Janes, Jackson, & Esses, 2010). Thus, this is an area of practical importance that is established in other disciplines and is emerging as a research interest among psychologists.

Connections between prejudice and attitudes toward animals have similarly been given more serious attention outside the discipline of psychology than within in. In philosophy, questions of whether animals have rights as "people," whether humans are meaningfully distinct from other animals, and whether attitudes toward animals reflect prejudice akin to human-to-human prejudice have been subjects of significant discussion among philosophers for some time (e.g., Midgley, 2005; Singer, 2002). These issues are also addressed by some in the natural sciences, such as evolutionary biologist Richard Dawkins (2003). Within psychology, at least one serious analysis of prejudice against animals has been introduced (Plous, 2003), and theories of justice have been explored in relation to people's views about animals (Opotow, 1993). In addition, empirical research is demonstrating psychological influences on people's tendency to construe themselves as distinct from the animal world (Goldenberg et al., 2001). Moreover, recognition of the devaluation of animals relative to humans is implicit in an active and growing area of research in psychology that examines the phenomena of dehumanization and infrahumanization of human groups (Castano & Kofta, 2009)—that is, prejudice that manifests in animal-like depictions of disrespected human groups (Haslam, 2006) or the denial to others of uniquely human qualities (Leyens et al., 2003). This work looks at one side of the dehumanization coin: the devaluation of humans through associations with animals. In the latter part of this chapter, I explore the possibility that furthering that line of work to critique the other side of the coin—people's evaluations of animals per se— may deepen people's understanding of the human propensity to misunderstand, denigrate, and exploit the other.

ENVIRONMENTAL INEQUALITY

As this chapter's opening example showed, across North America minority groups are disproportionately exposed to environmental contaminants, a problem known as *environmental inequality* (e.g., Mohai & Saha, 2007) or *environmental racism* (e.g., Santiago-Rivera, Talka, & Tully, 2006). In Canada, the problem exists for First Nations people and a variety of other groups. Immigrant and refugee groups as well as low-income people are also exposed to more environmental burdens than are more privileged groups because of the proximity between industries that generate pollution and communities in which underprivileged groups often live (Jafri, 2008). In the United States, race and ethnicity are among the best predictors of exposure to environmental pollution; roughly 60% of communities in the United States that are dominated by people of color contain one or more toxic waste sites within their boundary (Kovel, 2003). In 1990, minority groups made up about 25% of the U.S. population, yet 40% of people who lived within 1 mile of hazardous waste sites at that time were people of color (Mohai & Saha, 2007). Environmental inequality is also associated with the development of intensive animal agriculture. For example, in North Carolina, the pork industry, which is responsible for numerous environmental pollutants and health risks, is growing in rural areas that are disproportionately African American and Latino (Wilson, 2007).

A number of causes of environmental inequality have been theorized (see Mohai & Saha, 2007). One possibility is that economic factors are responsible. Because real estate is less costly in areas close to industries that produce environmental toxins and hazardous waste sites, members of groups that have, on average, lower incomes will tend to become overrepresented in such areas. Another possibility is that groups that have less power in society have a weaker voice when it comes to opposing undesirable developments in their communities. For example, minorities may have less access to legal representation than do majorities. Therefore, they may be less likely to succeed in efforts to oppose placement of problem activities such as hazardous waste sites in their communities. Over time, such activities may become disproportionately represented in more marginalized communities. A third explanation is that prejudiced attitudes lead decision makers and business owners to place hazardous sites near minorities and away from areas dominated by more privileged groups.

Mohai and Saha (2007) conducted a national-level study in the United States to compare these types of explanations for environmental inequality. They found that although economic factors played a role in creating environmental inequality (the idea that income differences between ethnic groups shape where people can live), more explicitly racial considerations involving prejudice also played a role. Activities such as racial targeting in the placement of problem industries and housing discrimination also appeared to contribute to the problem.

This position assumes that prejudiced attitudes lead people to be more willing to accept practices that produce environmental toxins if the people most directly exposed to the pollutants are members of another group. In other words, as long as the environmental damage occurs primarily "over there" or hurts "them" but not "us," people may be willing to accept or support environmentally degrading activity. This may be especially true if one's own group has something to gain from the industry that creates the environmental problems.

To test this position directly, Janes et al. (2010) conducted an experiment in which Canadian students were asked to make judgments about the appropriateness of a business activity that created environmental damage. Specifically, people read an article about the practice of mining for bauxite, a natural resource used in the home building industry. The mining was described as creating significant environmental damage, including air and water pollution and scarring of the earth's surface. The mining was said to occur in another part of the world (in Romania, Vietnam, or Jamaica). Half the participants read that the resource would be used in the country where it was mined, and the other half read that the resource would be used in Canada. Participants indicated how much they supported the industry, and they also completed a measure of social dominance orientation (the ideology that some groups are simply better than others; Pratto et al., 1994; see Chapter 4, this volume).

The results indicated that people with a high social dominance orientation were more accepting of the mining practice if Canada, rather than the country where the mining occurred, stood to benefit. In contrast, people with a low social dominance orientation supported the practice more if the country that did the mining benefited from it. These findings suggest that prejudice does shape environmental decision making for some people. People who tend to be prejudiced and to protect their own groups' interests (those people who have a high social dominance orientation) are willing to support environmental damage for their own benefit as long as the harm occurs elsewhere. The negative environmental impact of industrial and agricultural development ultimately hurts everyone given that all people live in one world, but many people appear willing to look the other way when it is members of other groups who suffer the most severe consequences (Janes et al., 2010).

PREJUDICE AND ENVIRONMENTAL ATTITUDES

This "not-in-my-backyard" phenomenon (Janes, Jackson, Esses, & Sibanda, 2009) implies a connection between prejudice and lack of regard for the environment. Some other evidence has suggested that this is true. Bitacola et al. (2010) showed that people with a high social dominance orientation—who by definition tend to view some human groups as superior to others—tended to be more supportive of an environmentally damaging industry, and more likely to justify the environmental costs of natural resource extraction, than were people lower in social dominance orientation. Moreover, social dominance orientation tended to predict a tendency to minimize the costs of environmental damage when members of another group would bear the burden of that damage.

Other studies that have spoken to the relation between prejudice and environmental attitudes involve measures of *anthropocentrism* and *ethnocentrism*. The ideology of anthropocentrism involves people's orientation toward the environment and environmental issues. People who endorse anthropocentrism view humans as the most important species on Earth and inherently separate from and more important than nature and other animals. They also tend to view the natural environment as valuable primarily in its usefulness to people (rather than inherently valuable), and they are generally unconcerned with the rights or interests of animals and nature (Chandler & Dreger, 1993). The more familiar concept of ethnocentrism refers to a kind of ethnic group self-centeredness (Bizumic & Duckitt, 2007). Ethnocentric people tend to prefer their own ethnic group to others, to view their own culture as superior to others, and to be prejudiced against other groups.

At least two lines of evidence have shown that people who are more anthropocentric (who devalue nature and nonhuman animals) are also more ethnocentric (they also devalue other cultures; Bizumic & Duckitt, 2007; Chandler & Dreger, 1993). Moreover, they show more negative attitudes than others toward ethnic minority groups (Bizumic & Duckitt, 2007). It is not entirely clear why people who devalue nature are also more prejudiced, but possibly it is because both anthropocentrism and ethnocentrism involve a general tendency to prefer one's own group, whether that be between humans and nonhumans or between one ethnicity and others (Bizumic & Duckitt, 2007). Both anthropocentrism and ethnocentrism also involve a group-based hierarchical worldview in which some entities are deemed inherently better than others (Chandler & Dreger, 1993). They also both seem to involve a sense of group-based entitlement. Anthropocentric people view humans as entitled to use nature and other animals for their benefit, whereas ethnocentric people see their own ethnic group as entitled to more privileges than other groups. Hierarchical worldviews and feelings of entitlement may give rise to both prejudice and negative environmental attitudes.

ENVIRONMENTAL CHANGES, PREJUDICE, AND GROUP CONFLICT

A third point of connection between prejudice and environmental issues is that ongoing environmental damage has the potential to increase existing prejudices or create new ones. Combinations of population growth around the world and industrial development have led to many environmental changes, including reductions in the quantity and quality of agricultural land, forest, water, and fish. The increasing scarcity of these natural resources can generate social changes that foster conflict and prejudice between groups, including direct competition for increasingly scarce resources, decreased economic productivity, and migration, as people move to seek more productive areas (Homer-Dixon et al., 1993). For example, according to the IPCC (2007), which is responsible for summarizing scientific literature related to climate change for the United Nations, global warming is likely to create large-scale increases in migration as people leave dry, hot climates to seek agriculturally productive areas.

The result will be not only increased diversity in host countries but also increased concerns about competition over increasingly scarce natural resources. One way this may manifest is in increases in prejudice against immigrants, who may be viewed as taking natural resources. For example, the group Immigrant Watch Canada opposes immigration because of a concern about the environmental impact of population increases. Yet, it describes immigration in disparaging terms (calling it a "flood" and a "tsunami"), and it suggests that immigration and the resulting multiculturalism comes at a social cost (Immigration Watch Canada, 2009). Although such stances may or may not reflect prejudice against immigrants, such descriptions of immigrants may serve to promote it by engendering feelings of threat in those exposed to the alarmist messages (see Esses et al., 1999).

At worst, competition over scarce natural resources can increase violent conflict. For example, recent years have witnessed genocide in the Darfur region of Sudan. Long-term conflicts between the northern Arab population, which forms the government, and the southern, less powerful Black African population erupted violently in recent years. The national army and the allied militias murdered hundreds of thousands of people from the south, and millions more were displaced from their homes as a result of violent and destructive attacks on villages (Associated Press, 2007). Competition over natural resources, including water and land, contributed to the violence and genocide (Esses & Jackson, 2008). In an area already strained by poverty, significant long-term declines in precipitation reduced crop yields and food production, increasing competition between groups over increasingly scarce water and arable land (United Nations Environment Programme, 2007). These problems were exacerbated by overgrazing of the available land as well as a controversial plan by the northern government to divert water from the south of the region to support crop growth in the north (Esses & Jackson, 2008). These problems increased conflict between the northern and southern Sudanese and energized ongoing violence.

Some of the violence, ironically, harmed the environment as well as people, a fact that only perpetuated the cycle of damage. For example, scorched-earth tactics were used in which militia groups cut and burned trees to deny cover to resistance groups; targeted rural water sources and pastures; and looted lumber, charcoal, ivory, and animals sold for bushmeat (United Nations Environment Programme, 2007). People whose villages were flattened had little option but to use the few remaining trees to build new shelters, further devastating the area (Marlow, 2006). These tactics fuel hatred and further conflict, and they hurt the environment that sustains those who live in it.

It has been shown that human activities—in particular, the production of fossil fuels, deforestation, and factory farming of ruminant animals such as cattle and sheep (which contributes significantly to environmental methane)—contribute to global warming (IPCC, 2007). In turn, environmental damage has contributed to conflicts between groups around the world for many years, and such conflicts are likely to escalate in the future, especially in poorer parts of the world in which shortages of water, trees, and land are coupled with population growth (Homer-Dixon et al., 1993). Because of the myriad connections between prejudice and environmental damage, understanding and responding to prejudice requires a broad lens in which related problems, like the environmental crisis, are considered.

The idea that human conflict can be deeply intertwined with environmental damage is a problem that social psychologists are just beginning to examine. Further ahead in the vanguard is the concept of *speciesism*, the idea that human attitudes toward and treatment of nonhuman animals constitutes a form of prejudice not unlike human-to-human prejudice (Plous, 2003; Ryder, 2006; Singer, 2002). General public awareness about the treatment of nonhuman animals in North America's industrialized food system is emerging, although so far the main media focus has been on the food industry's effects on the environment, human health, economics, and workers' rights (e.g., Pollan, 2006). Within academic circles, parallels between prejudice and speciesism are also being explored (e.g., Midgley, 2005; Plous, 2003; Singer, 200). I examine this issue in the next section, beginning with discussion of a relevant form of human-to-human prejudice, dehumanization.

DEHUMANIZATION

This chapter opened with an example of the health problems faced by a First Nations group resulting from the environmentally damaging effects of nearby industrial development. This is among the latest in a series of problems resulting from colonization. Despite its many negative effects, colonization of First Nations people in North America was rationalized historically by stereotypic images of them, such as the characterization of native people as savages (e.g., Ellingson, 2001) who needed cultural development and refinement. Today, such negative imagery persists. For example, Morrison et al. (2008) found that non–First Nations Canadians currently associate First Nations people with stereotypes such as being physically dirty, aggressive, sexually easy, and undisciplined. It is not a coincidence that these characteristics are notably animal-like in the imagery they evoke. Many groups that have suffered from atrocities such as colonization, holocausts, and genocide have been depicted in distinctly dehumanizing animal-like terms, a phenomenon known as *dehumanization* (Haslam, 2006).

Although colonized groups have been historically represented as savages with excessive violent and sexual impulses, other ethnic groups that have been subjected to ongoing exploitation, extreme aggression, or genocide have been depicted as inhuman vermin, demons, or monsters (Bar-Tal & Teichman, 2005) as part of the justification for their treatment (Staub, 1989; Opotow, 1990). For example, during the Holocaust, Jews were often depicted with rat or serpent imagery, seemingly to justify efforts to exterminate the supposed threat. Today, similarly dehumanizing imagery emerges at times in Israeli Jewish society in representations of Arab people (Bar-Tal &Teichman, 2005). In many places, including North America, immigrants are similarly sometimes dehumanized by being portrayed as animal-like carriers of disease (Esses & Lawson, 2008). After the acquittal of the police officers involved in the Rodney King beating case, media reports emerged that it was routine among public officials in the Los Angeles legal system to use the abbreviation NHI—standing for "no humans involved"—to refer to cases in which the rights of young, poor Black men were violated (Wynter, 1992, p. 13). Women have been referenced as animals by being depicted as meat as part of a process whereby their humanity is denigrated (Adams, 2000).

Dehumanization has often been linked to situations of intergroup exploitation or violence because imagery that denies people their humanity apparently serves to justify doing harm (e.g., Staub, 1989). Opotow (1990) proposed that dehumanizing groups is one strategy by which people can place others outside the scope of justice—the circle within which moral rules are thought to apply. When dehumanized beings are deemed to be outside the sphere of moral consideration, exploitation or violence is deemed justified (Opotow, 2005). Consistent with this view, Goff, Eberhardt, Williams, and Jackson (2008) found that African Americans who had been convicted of capital crimes and were described in dehumanizing apelike terms (e.g., using terms such as *beast, brute, wild,* and *barbaric*) in the *Philadelphia Inquirer* between 1979 and 1999 were more likely to have been executed than those who were not described in this way.

Although explicit dehumanization has often occurred in relation to intergroup aggression, recent research has shown that subtle forms of it are relatively common aspects of intergroup attitudes and relations. Leyens et al. (2003) proposed that intergroup attitudes are often characterized by *infrahumanization*, the tendency to view other groups as less human than one's own by attributing to these groups fewer distinctly human qualities. They found that people tend to view the secondary emotions (complex emotions like love, hope, contempt, and resentment) as distinctly human, that people view these emotions as especially characteristic of their own group and less characteristic of other groups, and that infrahumanization has consequences for things such as willingness to cooperate with members of other groups. Haslam (2006) described how some groups are subtly dehumanized in another way—by being denied valued qualities such as interpersonal warmth and creativity and thus viewed as "soulless machines" (p. 258), resulting in indifference toward and a lack of empathy for these groups.

In addition to prompting neglect or mistreatment of other groups, infrahumanization has been shown to result from awareness of maltreatment of others. Both being exposed to information or images about how one's group has harmed other groups and merely being exposed to images involving human violence increase infrahumanization (Castano & Giner-Sorolla, 2006; Delgado, Rodriguez-Peréz, Vaes, Leyens, & Betancor, 2009). Castano and Giner-Sorolla (2006) proposed that infrahumanization may be one strategy that people use to restore psychological equanimity when awareness of injustice challenges it.

Regardless of its source, it is clear that dehumanizing imagery has negative implications for intergroup attitudes and behavior because viewing others as being like animals or as less distinctly human psychologically lowers the bar of ethical responsibility to these others. Implicit in this observation is the existence of a pervasive negative evaluation of animals—that is, people who are dehumanized are degraded because animals are not valued the way humans are.

SPECIESISM

It appears self-evident that associations between humans and animals degrade humans because animals are not typically endowed with the same regard that humans are. Why is this? Does devaluation of animals arise from similar psychological and social dynamics that human-to-human prejudice does? Analysis of this question may deepen understanding of the ways in which people situate themselves relative to the other.

Some writers have argued that prejudice against animals exists on the basis of their observations of cruel treatment of nonhuman animals in research, farming, and other animal industries (Ryder, 2006; Singer, 2002). Ryder (2006) reportedly first used the term *speciesism* in the 1970s to describe what he viewed as cruel practices in psychological research using animals and later argued that speciesism is analogous to "similar forms of irrational discrimination such as racism, sexism, and ageism" (p. 89). In a philosophical analysis of the topic, Singer (2002) defined speciesism as "a prejudice or attitude of bias in favor of the interests of members of one's own species and against those of members of other species" (p. 6). Key to this definition is the observation that this attitude of bias is based on species demarcation alone. From this point of view, when the harm done to other animals for human benefit (e.g., laboratory research and food production with nonhuman animals) is viewed as justified solely because of species membership—the view that it is appropriate to harm animals to benefit humans because they are animals and we are humans—the thought process is said to involve speciesism.

Although Singer (2002) emphasized the logic of thought process in defining speciesism, psychologists tend to define *prejudice* in terms of evaluative attitudes and examine these attitudes in the context of related problems such as discrimination and exploitation of other groups. In Chapter 1, prejudice was defined as a disrespectful attitude or negative evaluative response toward groups as a whole or toward individuals on the basis of their group membership. Subsequent chapters demonstrated that in relation to human-to-human prejudice, the focus on respect allows for the coexistence of seemingly positive yet also problematic attitudes. Such ambivalence appears to characterize people's attitudes toward nonhuman animals as well.

On the one hand, positive attitudes toward domesticated and familiar animals are apparent. A large-scale poll of Canadian adults showed that of the 53% of the sample who owned a cat, dog, or both, 98% talked to the pet, 83% considered the animal a family member, 53% said they would go into debt to treat an illness suffered by the animal, and 26% considered the pet the baby in the family (Ipsos Reid, 2001). Similar trends exist in the United States (Anderson, 2008). In addition, a majority of both youths and older adults reported that they would try to save an injured mouse or bird brought to them by a cat (Fidler, Coleman, & Roberts, 2000). Also, when asked to rate their attitudes toward animals on scales with end points such as *good* or *bad* or *valuable* or *worthless*, most people give generally positive ratings (Beatson & Halloran, 2007).

On the other hand, when people face more significant moral dilemmas, such as whether to kill 1,000 dogs to allow one human to live or kill one person to allow 1,000 dogs to live, a majority of people sacrifice the dogs (Petrinovich, O'Neill, & Jorgensen, 1993). This finding shows that people value nonhuman life less than human life. In addition, cruelty toward nonhuman animals is a fact of life, evidenced for example by the existence of anti-cruelty laws and humane societies in many countries that deal with cases of neglect and abuse of animals. The Humane Society of the United States estimates that 6 million to 8 million animals enter shelters annually as a result of neglect, abuse, or abandonment (Anderson, 2008). Moreover, abuse exists in a variety of institutions, such as puppy mills (which breed high numbers of animals in crowded and often unsanitary conditions), dog-fighting rings (which may be linked with drug trafficking and gambling), the international fur trade, and so on (Anderson, 2008).

Humans also cause other animals to suffer through institutions and practices that the majority of people support economically, such as animal agriculture. In a review of common practices in the production of animals for food, Mason and Finelli (2006) identified the following, among many others. In chicken hatcheries, male chicks that are unwanted because of their inability to lay eggs and poor quality flesh are routinely thrown into plastic bags to be suffocated or ground up alive and used for dog food. The ends of chickens' beaks (which contain nerve endings) are cut or burned off to prevent damage from fighting, causing acute and long-term pain and difficulty eating. Laying hens are confined, several to a tiny cage, in such a way that they cannot move. Breeding sows are housed in stalls that are so tiny they can only stand

and lie down; they cannot turn around. Male piglets are castrated, and both sexes have their teeth clipped, tails cut off, and ears notched with no use of anesthesia. Many calves are taken from their mothers at birth and confined to dog house–sized crates where they spend their lives before being slaughtered for veal. In crowded feedlots, cattle kept for beef routinely suffer painful liver and kidney failure because of the unnatural grain diet and unsanitary conditions. Ducks raised for foie gras ("fatty liver," a French dish) spend the first several months of life in a dark waterless building with the tips of their beaks burned off, only to then be immobilized in small cages for 2 to 3 weeks, during which time "up to two pounds of a corn/fat mixture [is] forced down their throat through a 12- to 16-inch pipe attached to a motorized pump," causing throat injury and ruptured livers (Mason & Finelli, 2006, p. 110). Farmed fish are housed in shallow crowded tanks where they show abnormal behavior, suffer high rates of infection, and are often starved for days before slaughter or left alive on bins of ice to suffocate.

The fact that most people give human interests greater weight than other animals' interests (Petrinovich et al., 1993) and tolerate pervasive cruelty against nonhuman animals in animal industries (Mason & Finelli, 2006) suggests that nonhuman animals are not generally valued intrinsically, although their usefulness to humans may be valued. Individual attitudes toward various animal species are no doubt varied and complex, yet the general pattern whereby nonhuman animals seem to be viewed as less worthy of moral consideration than are humans implies the existence of an evaluative bias in favor of humans relative to other species and possibly also an evaluative bias against other animals. The degree of bias probably parallels degrees of difference and familiarity. The well-established finding that people like and respond with empathy toward similar human others (Hoffman, 1981; Newcomb, 1961) also applies to responses to animals. Plous (2003) reported data showing that people showed less evidence of physical arousal (using a measure of skin conductance) when observing a video of the abuse of a dissimilar animal (e.g., a bullfrog) than a more similar animal (e.g., a monkey).

In parallel with the definition of prejudice used in this book, speciesism can be understood as a disrespectful attitude or negative evaluative response toward nonhuman animals that is based on species designation alone. As with human-to-human prejudice, speciesism may lead people to misconstrue information about the other species and support or tolerate practices that do harm to the other (Plous, 2003). One fundamental way it may manifest is in terms of the way in which people categorize humans versus animals.

In Chapter 2, I reviewed the tendency people have to highlight particular categories of human difference and to single out some groups for special (or problematic) treatment. The analysis made it clear that the boundaries people draw between human groups are not always logical but more often functional: They serve to protect some groups' interests at the expense of others. For example, despite the flawed nature of the concept of race from a genetic point of view, in North America social constructions of race persist because ideas of race historically became embedded in legal and social institutions in a way that protected the interests of slave owners at the expense of the slaves. A similar misrepresentation of biological reality is true of the way in which people categorize humans and animals.

Social Construction of *Animal*

What is an animal? Although people recognize degrees of similarity between humans and other animals (Marcu, Lyons, & Hegarty, 2007), the term *animal,* as used in popular discourse, typically refers to all members of the animal kingdom except humans (Dawkins, 2003). The tendency to view humans and other animals as making up two distinct categories of beings has a long history in Western philosophy and religion (Waldau, 2006), and the tendency to draw a sharp line between categories of us (humans) and them (animals) persists despite widely accepted scientific evidence that humans are animals. *Homo sapiens* is one group of bipedal primates, who fall under the family *Hominidae* in the kingdom *Animalia.* Specifically, in biological taxonomy, humans are categorized as one of the African apes, along with gorillas and chimpanzees (Dawkins, 2003). This scientific construction is contradicted by what Dawkins (2003) called the "unquestioned yawning gulf" (p. 537) that people mistakenly perceive between humans and other animals. The fact that people typically use the term *animal* to refer to all animals except *Homo sapiens* reflects this unquestioned yawning gulf. To approach accuracy, the terms *nonhuman animal* and *other animals* are used in the remainder of this book to refer to species other than humans, but even these terms are suspect from a taxonomic point of view because they lump together an enormously diverse array of species.

People often view humans as distinct from other animals on specific attributes, such as intelligence, language ability, emotionality, and morality (Haslam, Kashima, Loughan, Shi, & Suiter, 2008; Leyens et al., 2003) and use such perspectives to support a view of humans as unique or special within the animal kingdom. Despite these common perceptions, the similarities among the great apes, and even among other species, are well documented. Approximately 95% of the human and chimpanzee genome is comparable, and many nonhuman animals have attributes often thought to be uniquely human, such as language. For example, chimpanzees, bonobos, and gorillas are able to communicate using American Sign Language (ASL) and other novel symbol systems and have been observed using these languages to communicate novel ideas with unique combinations of symbols (e.g., Gardner &

Gardner, 1969; Patterson, 1978; Savage-Rumbaugh, Shanker, & Taylor, 1998). To name just a few examples of cognitive abilities in other species, dolphins have been shown to recognize themselves in mirrors (Reiss & Marino, 2001), indicating conscious self-awareness. Parrots can add, recognize sets, have a zerolike concept, and can express these understandings in English words (Pepperberg, 2006; Pepperberg & Brezinsky, 1991). Even seemingly simple animals, like rodents, have long since been shown to think, for example, through their ability to generate mental maps of mazes (Tolman, 1948).

In addition to commonalities between humans and other animals in various cognitive skills, parallels exist in the capacity to experience emotion as well. Neurobiological evidence has shown that the limbic system of the mammalian brain, which is central to the production of emotion, is notably similar across species, humans included (e.g., Panksepp, 1998). This fact, combined with the observation that the brain circuits that give rise to emotions probably evolved to regulate adaptive behavior (e.g., fear elicits avoidance of predators; affection motivates caregiving), led leading neuroscientist Jaak Panksepp (1998) to conclude that "the 'raw feels' of emotions are a shared mammalian experience" (p. 33). His work has identified core mammalian brain areas that regulate basic emotions such as pleasure and fear, motivational experiences such as anticipation, and social emotions such as love, loneliness, and play. Other scientists have come to the same conclusion and demonstrated evidence for emotions in many nonhuman animals such as dogs, birds, chimpanzees, elephants, and dolphins (e.g., Bekoff, 2002; Grandin, 2005, 2009; Pepperberg, 2008); even seemingly simpler animals such as the iguana reveal biochemistry suggestive of emotion (Bekoff, 2002).

Evidence exists as well that speaks to speculations about other dimensions on which humans might be unique—ethics, for example. Stanley Milgram's (1974) classic work showed that when told to do so by a researcher—and for no other reason—the majority of normal, healthy human adults would do what they thought involved administering potentially lethal shocks to another person. Curiously enough, using a similar paradigm in which hungry rhesus monkeys could choose to either receive food while simultaneously causing another monkey to receive a shock or go hungry, a majority of them opted to self-starve (Masserman, Wechkin, & Terris, 1964). Whether such findings suggest morality in nonhumans is debatable; however, they do, at minimum, suggest that the idea of human ethical superiority is also debatable.

Several decades of laboratory and field research have demonstrated that nonhuman animals reveal intellectual and other capacities that exist on a continuum with humans (Pepperberg, 2008). Reflecting on the meaning of this evidence, noted scholar Irene Pepperberg (2008) has said that "the idea of humans' separateness from the rest of nature is no longer tenable" (p. 222). Just as stereotypes of human groups can be associated with mistreatment of them, understandings of the nature of nonhuman animals are consequential. For example, people who are uninformed about the nature of animals' varying abilities tend to be less cautious about how humans use animals in research than are people who are more informed (Knight, Vrij, Bard, & Brandon, 2009), and perceptions of wild animals' intelligence (or lack thereof) influences the tendency to exclude their interests in ethical environmental decision making (Opotow, 1994). Yet, representations of animals that are contradicted by scientific findings are pervasive. Arguably, this is true for a reason similar to why erroneous conceptions of human differences persist—they are functional. Indeed, some evidence has suggested that people may construct understandings of human–animal differences and similarities in a way that justifies the human use of animals for food, research, companionship, and so on (Marcu et al., 2007). The tendency to incorrectly categorize humans as qualitatively distinct from other animals creates the division on which the devaluation of animals rests. The causes of this devaluation are examined more fully in the next section.

Causes of Speciesism

As previous chapters have shown, attitudes toward other human groups are determined by a host of factors that can be characterized as distal (e.g., evolutionary and psychodynamic influences), midrange (e.g., ideology and socialization processes), or proximal (e.g., intergroup relations) in terms of their impact. Some evidence has indicated that a similar characterization of influences on beliefs about and attitudes toward nonhuman animals may be appropriate.

Distal (Psychodynamic) Influence: Emotional Threat

The cultural anthropologist Ernest Becker (1973) described a paradox faced by humans. Being cognitively sophisticated animals, humans have the capacity to comprehend their own animal nature and hence their mortality, a fact that has the potential to cause considerable existential anxiety. Freud (1939/1955) claimed that belief systems that promote ideas about human uniqueness (e.g., religion) calm people's anxiety by allowing them to believe that humans are separate from the rest of the animal kingdom, with more pure and admirable qualities as well as immortality. Drawing on such ideas, terror management theory (Pyszczynski et al., 2004) proposes that because cultural meaning systems such as religion provide an existential buffer against the terror of death, when people are reminded of their mortality, they tend to engage in efforts to defend their worldviews, including expressing prejudice against those who are deemed to threaten them, such as members of other religions (see Chapter 3, this volume). Endorsing beliefs in human uniqueness may serve a similar purpose. Denial of human animal nature and concomitant devaluation of animals relative to humans may reduce existential anxiety by holding at bay thoughts of human creatureliness and mortality (Goldenberg et al., 2001).

In an experiment designed to test the position that people tend to separate themselves from other animals to allay existential terror, Goldenberg et al. (2001) manipulated whether or not people would be likely to feel anxious about death by having some participants answer questions dealing with death (what thinking about death caused them to think and feel, and what they thought would happen to them when they die). Subsequently, they assessed participants' feelings toward nonhuman animals and also their evaluation of essays that argued for or against human uniqueness. Those who were led to consider death subsequently reported feeling more disgust toward animals, and they also preferred the essay that argued in favor of human uniqueness. Goldenberg et al. concluded that these findings showed the human tendency to "protest against that which reminds us of our creatureliness" (p. 432) and also that "the human inclination to distance from other animals is motivated by concerns about death" (p. 433). These conclusions suggest that speciesism may reflect this type of protest, and exaggerated perceptions of differences between humans and other species may be motivated, in part, by existential anxiety.

Terror management theory predicts that such dynamics may be moderated by people's level of self-esteem. According to the theory, self-esteem is important to people because it serves to further substantiate a sense of value and allay the fear of death (Pyszczynski et al., 2004). Consequently, recognition of the real similarities between humans and many other animals may be especially threatening to those with low self-esteem. Beatson and Holloran (2007) tested this idea and found that students with low self-esteem who had been made to think about death and the similarities between humans and great apes subsequently showed more negative attitudes toward animals than did the others. In contrast, students with high self-esteem were unaffected by considering death, but they showed more positive attitudes toward animals when asked to contemplate the similarities between humans and great apes. This shows that people whose self-esteem is vulnerable may be the people most likely to use beliefs in human uniqueness as a psychological defense that provides a sense of significance.

Findings such as these are important because they show that the same types of factors that can generate prejudice against other human groups (e.g., threat to cultural values, mortality salience) can generate negativity toward nonhuman animals (see also Goldenberg, Heflick, Vaes, Motyl, & Greenberg, 2009). They are also important because they emphasize the human need to distance oneself from other animals. The tendency to deny human animal nature and to distance humanity from animals is arguably dangerous to humans and animals alike. Not only is it likely to justify the use and abuse of animals, but it may also lead people to engage in dangerous activities to deny their creatureliness. As Goldenberg et al. (2001) described, women starve themselves to the point of death to be beautiful, people undergo dangerous surgery to alter their physical appearance and deny the reality of physical aging, girls in some cultures have their genitals surgically mutilated in an effort to negate their sexuality, and so on. Goldenberg, Arndt, Hart, and Routledge (2008) confirmed that discomfort with creatureliness and its associated mortality can contribute to neglect of bodily health. They found that among people who had contemplated their eventual death, reading an essay about human–animal similarities (vs. one about human uniqueness) reduced women's intentions to perform breast self-examinations.

Overall, research on the psychodynamic analysis of attitudes toward other species has underscored the existence of a motivation to assuage existential anxiety through a focus on differences between humans and other animals and a concomitant devaluation of nonhuman animals. This directly parallels other research from terror management theorists showing that the same factors create expressions of human-to-human prejudice (see Chapter 3). This perspective points to the important role of cultural worldviews such as religion in sustaining beliefs in human uniqueness and superiority. These ideological influences are considered in more detail next.

Midrange Influence: Ideology

Hierarchical thinking that places humans over other animals in importance has a long history in Western philosophy and religion. Aristotle (384–322 BCE) declared humans to be the most rational of all animals, and thus he placed humans on top of all other animals in a hierarchy of worthiness. This notion was subsequently popularized in Western thought as the Great Chain of Being (*scala natura*)—God is on top, followed by other spiritual beings such as angels. Humans, a mix of spirit and animals, were placed below pure spirit yet above other animals. Below animals were plants and minerals.

The influential philosopher Descartes (1596–1650) believed that the human soul resided in the pineal gland of the brain (now known to be involved in endocrine functions such as the regulation of sleep in humans and hibernation in some other animals). He reasoned that the pineal gland is an attribute unique to humans, and because he viewed it as the seat of the soul, he concluded that nonhuman animals had no soul and hence no conscious awareness. This belief justified his practice of nailing live dogs to wooden boards by their paws to dissect them and dismissing their cries of pain as being no more meaningful than the audible tick of a mechanical clock (Singer, 2002).

Religion is evident in the philosophical ideas that have shaped Western thought about nonhuman animals. In fact, the Judeo-Christian tradition has been blamed as the source of human conceit (e.g., L. White, 1967), particularly in response to the passages of Genesis that describe humans as being given dominion over animals and nature. These passages can be interpreted as teaching human domination and superiority (e.g., L. White, 1967), yet other theological models imply an ethic of responsibility and care and teach that nature is itself sacred (Tarakeshwar, Swank, Pargament, & Mahoney, 2001).

Although religious teachings seem to support either dismissive or respectful attitudes toward nonhuman animals, research conducted in predominantly Christian contexts has shown that religiosity is often associated with less positive attitudes toward nonhuman animals. Traditionally, religious people tend to view humans and other animals in more dichotomous terms than do less traditional or nonreligious people (Templer, Connelly, Bassman, & Hart, 2006), and most measures of personal religiosity have been found to correlate positively with anthropocentrism, the ideology that humans are inherently superior to nonhuman animals and nature (Bizumic & Duckitt, 2007; Chandler & Dreger, 1993; Snodgrass & Gates, 1998). However, people who score higher on a measure of quest religiosity and who view religion as an open-ended and questioning search for truth in which doubt and change are valuable (Batson & Schoenrade, 1991) show lower anthropocentrism than those who are less quest oriented (Snodgrass & Gates, 1998). Thus, it is primarily more conventional and conservative forms of religiosity that seem to be linked to higher levels of speciesism.

This research has shown that the hierarchical thinking of Aristotle's Great Chain of Being that ranks humans as inherently superior to other animals is also evident in conventional religiosity in Western Christian samples. Thus, religious ideology is one of the carriers of speciesism, which parallels the considerable body of research showing that prejudice against human groups is often manifest in broad ideologies, including but not limited to religion, that foster hierarchical thinking (see Chapter 4, this volume). Other carriers of speciesism involve socialization practices through which children are taught to accept human superiority and to avoid focusing on the perspectives of other species.

Midrange Influence: Socialization Factors

Chapter 5 addressed the ways in which beliefs relevant to prejudice that are prevalent in a society can become socialized through parenting practices, information in the media, and so on. Similar processes are evident with respect to attitudes toward animals, in particular, to the paradox whereby people generally report positive attitudes toward animals (Beatson & Halloran, 2007) and yet support practices that involve considerable cruelty (Mason & Finelli, 2006). Plous (2003) identified a number of processes that allow people to dissociate their participation in cruel practices in the production of meat from their self-image, including the strategic use of language. For example, he described how hunters talk about "harvesting" animals in the way that farmers harvest crops; how children in 4-H clubs are taught to talk about chicks and calves, not babies; or beak trimming in place of debeaking. Similarly, in research contexts researchers identify animals by number and teach their students to do so as well.

The remoteness of most animal industries also contributes to a lack of widespread knowledge of how animals used for food are treated. Plous (2003) reported results of a survey in which he asked 143 college students whether a series of eight statements were true or false (e.g., "The unwanted chicks of laying hens are often ground alive to make pet food" and "Most goose down comes from geese that have been plucked alive"). Although in fact all eight statements were true, the most common number identified as true by the students was zero.

Children's storybooks typically depict farm animals as frolicking freely in fields rather than penned in cages. Such indirect teaching appears to shape children's attitudes. Plous (2003) reported another survey in which elementary school children tended to view farm animals as less likely to experience unhappiness than either pets or wild animals.

People also construct justifications for their use of animals, and these justifications become part of the system of thought within which children are socialized. In a study of the types of justifications people tend to offer for the use of animals, Hyers (2006) found the following, in order of popularity: necessity (e.g., the belief that it is necessary to eat animals to be healthy), hedonic pleasure (e.g., to advance one's status by wearing fur), the belief that there is an essential food chain of which people are a part, cultural traditions, religious belief, assumptions about human nature, the idea that use of animals is an intrinsic part of the system, and animal nature (e.g., beliefs that non-human animals lack consciousness).

Because these justifications become embedded in social traditions within which children are raised, speciesism often becomes an unquestioned aspect of the cultural milieu. Part of the reason that these justifications are prevalent may be that they serve human interests. Group interests generate human-to-human prejudice (see Chapter 6, this volume), and they appear to generate speciesism as well. This issue is considered next.

Proximal Influence: Self- and Group Interests

Earlier chapters described how the stereotypes that people form about other human groups, and attitudes toward those groups, arise from the relative status of groups and whether relationships between groups are cooperative or competitive. I reviewed research showing that high-status groups that cooperate with one's own group are viewed as capable and admired; low-status groups that compete with one's group are viewed as incompetent and unlikable, and they are held in contempt; high-status groups that compete with one's group are viewed as capable but they are envied; and low-status groups that cooperate with one's group are viewed as lacking capability but likable, and they are held in affection but viewed paternalistically (Cuddy et al., 2007; Fiske et al., 2002; Glick & Fiske, 1996, 2001). The significance of this research is that it shows that stereotypes about and attitudes toward human groups follow from the social position of those groups and their relationship with the attitude holder.

Attitudes toward nonhuman animals may similarly reflect the relative status of animal groups and the type of interdependence that exists between those animals and humans. Kwan and Cuddy (2008) demonstrated that Western people tend to see animals as falling into four general categories that parallel human groupings found in the research noted earlier and correspond to the functional nature of the human–animal relation. Pets, who help people in many ways, such as fostering emotional and physical health and working as assistants to people with disabilities, police, and therapists (Knight & Herzog, 2009; Wells, 2009), tend to be viewed positively, for example being seen as friendly and capable. Pests, such as worms, salamanders, rats, and ants, that tend to cause inconveniences for people, are viewed with contempt, being seen as unfriendly and lacking capability. Predator animals that can harm people, such as leopards, wolves, snakes, and crocodiles, are viewed with enviable ambivalence, being seen as capable but unfriendly. Prey animals that people eat, such as cows, goats, chickens, and pigs, are viewed with more paternalism, being seen as friendly but lacking capability.

These patterns of attitudes seem to parallel the human use of or relationship with animals and perhaps provide justifications for human treatment of them. For example, the fact that pets and prey are both viewed as friendly but only pets are seen as capable may reflect the fact that people tend to eat prey but not pets. Eating prey may be justified by viewing them as lacking capability. In fact, vegetarians (who do not eat animals) and Chinese participants (who are more likely to eat many different animals) do not tend to categorize animals in terms of these four categories (Kwan & Cuddy, 2008). People who use animals differently view those animals differently.

Attitudes toward different types of animals also seem to reflect people's desire to protect their own interests for status and security. For example, in Kwan and Cuddy's (2008) research, predators (who can hurt people) were viewed negatively, and people reported that they would be willing to use these animals as adornment (e.g., by wearing snakeskin shoes), perhaps an indication of a desire to achieve status or security by demonstrating dominance over a worthy opponent. The desire to protect other human interests also shapes attitudes toward animals. For example, animals tend to be deemed to be unworthy of just treatment if protecting them would interfere with humans' material interests (Opotow, 1993).

In brief, attitudes toward nonhuman animals parallel the ways that humans use them and the threats that people feel from them. Together with research illustrating the roles of emotional threat, ideology, and socialization practices in generating attitudes toward nonhuman animals, this work suggests that many of the factors that shape human prejudice also shape attitudes toward nonhumans.

Is Speciesism Prejudice?

Empirically, there are connections between speciesism and human prejudice. Some evidence has suggested that people who are more prejudiced may also endorse more speciesism. People who view humans as inherently superior to both nature and other animals (those who are anthropocentric) also tend to be more ethnocentric (they devalue other cultures relative to their own; Bizumic & Duckitt, 2007; Chandler & Dreger, 1993). In addition, people who are high in social dominance orientation, who tend to view some human groups as superior to others, also tend to view humans and animals as especially distinct (Costello & Hodson, 2009). Other evidence has shown that people who report more empathy for nonhuman animals also extend more empathy toward humans than do those who show less empathy for animals (Ascione & Weber, 1996; Dixon-Preylo & Arikawa, 2008; Paul, 2000; N. Taylor & Signal, 2005). Similarly, vegetarians score higher on empathy for humans than do omnivores (Dixon-Preylo & Arikawa, 2008). Moreover, this empathy may extend to behavior: People involved in the animal movements tend also to be involved in other social justice movements (Selby, 2000). Abundant evidence has shown that abuse of animals often coexists with abuse of vulnerable people (e.g., children; for reviews, see Ascione, 2005, 2008; Ascione & Arkow, 1999; Ascione & Shapiro, 2009; Beirne, 2004). Moreover, recent evidence has shown that adolescents who witness animal abuse in the home are more likely than others to engage in bullying outside the home (Gullone & Robertson, 2008). As a whole, such patterns demonstrate a web of connections among various forms of domination and abuse on the one hand and care and empathy on the other.

If attitudes toward human and animal others are connected, it is possible that fostering change in one will shape the other. This was demonstrated directly by Costello and Hodson (2009), who showed that giving people information that emphasized how animals are similar to humans led people to endorse more humanized and positive attitudes toward immigrants than did emphasizing human–animal differences. The researchers reasoned that this occurred because immigrants are often likened to animals and so "if outgroup dehumanization begins with heightened disregard for 'inferior' animals, perhaps we can cut the dehumanization process off at its roots by narrowing the human-animal divide" (Costello & Hodson, 2009, p. 5).

There is also evidence that increasing empathy for nonhuman animals among children may have beneficial effects on their responses toward other humans. Ascione and Weber (1996) conducted an evaluation of a 40-hr humane education program conducted in a Grade 4 setting. The program focused on education about companion animals, farm animals, and wild animals using a mix of pedagogical tools. A comparison of students who received the program with those who did not showed that both immediately after the program and 1 year later, students in the experimental group showed increases in empathy toward both nonhuman animals and humans. Similar positive changes in attitudes toward both animals and humans were found in a recent study of the effectiveness of a literature-based humane education program with schoolchildren (Arbour, Signal, & Taylor, 2009).

Theoretically, the various parallels between speciesism and human prejudice are noteworthy because they show that prejudice is part of a broader phenomenon whereby psychological and social dynamics shape the way in which people situate themselves relative to others. Moreover, the existence of parallels between speciesism and human-to-human prejudice coupled with the general lack of attention to the former underscores the human propensity to justify and perpetuate one's prejudices, a theme that has emerged repeatedly throughout this book with respect to human prejudice. Analyzing speciesism alongside human prejudice does not require that they be defined as exactly the same thing. In fact, the preceding chapters have shown that human prejudices take many forms, and it is not always easy to determine which phenomena qualify as prejudice. Nevertheless, speciesism involves an evaluative response to a socially constructed category of beings, and research has suggested that this evaluation may spring from many of the same sources as does human-to-human prejudice, and it may have some similar consequences in terms of generating and justifying harmful treatment. Therefore, researching it may deepen the understanding not only of speciesism but of human-to-human prejudice as well.

9

REDUCING PREJUDICE AND PROMOTING SOCIAL CHANGE

Since the 1970s, many types of interventions aimed at reducing prejudice have been implemented in schools, workplace settings, the media, and the community (Stephan & Stephan, 2005). Many of these programs involve getting people of diverse backgrounds together to collaborate on some task because people tend to develop positive attitudes toward those with whom they have cooperative relationships (Allport, 1954/1979). Other approaches, such as multicultural education or diversity training programs, are based on the assumption that prejudice often reflects ignorance and that providing information about differences will reduce prejudice. Yet other strategies target things that individuals can do themselves to work on their own attitudes. Although the majority of programs in actual use are not evaluated systematically, sufficient research exists to provide confidence that most approaches have the potential to show at least modest success, and some are remarkably effective at reducing prejudice (Paluck & Green, 2009). However, there is also evidence to suggest that reducing prejudice may at times have unintended consequences that serve to perpetuate, rather than challenge, inequality (S. C. Wright & Lubensky, 2009). Therefore, understanding the processes of social change requires attention not only to prejudice reduction but also to direct efforts to reduce inequality such as collective action.

CONTACT HYPOTHESIS

Efforts to reduce prejudice frequently bring people from diverse backgrounds together to get to know one another in the hope that increased familiarity will lead to increased understanding and liking. The assumption is logical. Both common sense and empirical evidence make it clear that people tend to like others with whom they are more acquainted and familiar. Yet, it is also clear that in situations in which prejudice is firmly entrenched, contact between people from different groups can also fuel the flames of hatred. For example, in the early days after the desegregation of schools in the United States, in which ethnic majority and minority students were placed in newly integrated schools, tensions mounted, and minority students became increasingly marginalized in their new classes (Aronson, 2000). Clearly, simple contact is not enough.

In his 1954 classic book, *The Nature of Prejudice*, Gordon Allport (1954/1979) explored this issue and proposed what has come to be known as the *contact hypothesis*. He proposed that

> prejudice . . . may be reduced by equal status contact between majority and minority groups in the pursuit of common goals. The effect is greatly enhanced if this contact is sanctioned by institutional supports (i.e., by law, custom, or local atmosphere), and is of a sort that leads to the perception of common interests and common humanity between members of the two groups. (p. 281)

In other words, not just any contact will do. It must be structured to support equality, cooperation, and friendship. This reasoning is also a logical outgrowth of realistic group conflict theory (LeVine & Campbell, 1972; Sherif & Sherif, 1953/1966), which posits that competitive intergroup relations foster prejudice (see Chapter 6, this volume). The corollary, demonstrated to be valid by Sherif and Sherif (1953/1966), is that cooperative intergroup relations facilitate the healing of prejudice. This logic has been used to develop a wide range of types of programs, such as cooperative learning groups in schools (e.g., Aronson, 1978) and reconciliation initiatives in war-torn parts of the world (Staub, 2005).

One popular program that follows the principles of the contact hypothesis is the *jigsaw* classroom, which was developed by Elliot Aronson (1978) and his colleagues in response to tensions in the schools in the United States during the transition from segregated to desegregated schools. The technique was developed to respond to what appeared to be a destructive tendency toward competitiveness in the classroom. Students appeared to vie for the acknowledgment and approval of teachers, a situation that gave some students added confidence yet left others feeling left out and stigmatized. True to its name, the jigsaw classroom treats each student in the class as a piece of a puzzle so that each student is necessary to the successful completion of a project. In the first stage of the technique, students are given an assignment to be completed in small groups. For example, in a science lesson students might be asked to prepare a presentation on amphibians. The project is broken into subtopics such as varieties of amphibians, the role of amphibians in the ecosystem, extinct and threatened species, and so on. Each student is given one of the subtopics to study. Students are then placed in "expert groups" in which they share what they have learned about their subtopic, ensuring that each student is a true expert. Once each student is up to speed on his or her subtopic, class members are placed in jigsaw groups that are made up of individuals from diverse backgrounds (e.g., ethnicity), each of whom is expert on one of the subtopics. Each student then shares his or her information so that each jigsaw group has the material needed for a complete project on amphibians. Key to the success of the technique is the fact that each student in the jigsaw group is needed. Therefore, each student has an equally valuable contribution, and cooperation is required for success in the project.

In a reflection on the development and implementation of this program, Aronson (1990) reported that in classes that implemented the jigsaw technique, positive results were immediately observed in terms of students' level of activity and interest in the classroom. Students learned to listen to one another, and unpopular students seemed to be given more attention and respect. Moreover, systematic comparisons of students in classrooms using the jigsaw technique with those that did not use the technique showed that students in jigsaw classrooms liked one another more, liked school better, had higher self-esteem, and performed better on tests than did students in traditional classrooms (Aronson, 1990). Although not every intervention using the technique has clear success (e.g., Bratt, 2008), reviews of evaluations of the technique have shown that the jigsaw classroom typically has positive outcomes, including increased numbers of students who develop cross-ethnic friendships (Stephan & Stephan, 2001). According to Aronson (2004), such effects occur because the jigsaw exercise creates a situation in which students are more likely to participate in class, learn to attend to one another and so grow in perspective taking and empathy, and provide one another with more rewarding social experiences.

A different and novel application and test of the contact hypothesis was conducted by D. P. Green and Wong (2008), who arranged for a contact situation to be incorporated into an Outward Bound course offered to teenage students in North Carolina. Students participated in a rigorous 2- to 3-week course that included activities such as rock climbing, hiking, instruction in wilderness survival, and activities geared toward self-reflection and personal growth. The researchers arranged for some of the groups to be ethnically mixed with European American, African American, and Latino Americans attending together and others to be homogeneous, with only European American students. One month after the end of the program, students were interviewed about their experience in the course. In addition to many questions regarding the content of the program, they were asked questions regarding their ethnic attitudes, such as how they would feel about living in an ethnically mixed neighborhood or dancing in public with a member of a different ethnic group. In support of the contact hypothesis, students who had participated in ethnically mixed groups evidenced significantly more favorable attitudes on these questions than did those who had participated in the homogeneous groups.

The contact hypothesis has also been applied to situations in which groups differing dramatically in power and privilege have experienced violence and even genocide. Psychologist Ervin Staub worked with Hutu and Tutsi people in Rwanda after the 1994 genocide, trying to foster healing and reconciliation. During the Rwandan genocide, Hutus killed approximately 700,000 people, mainly Tutsis but also some politically moderate Hutus. The genocide was the culmination of years of resentment and tension that followed from the Belgian colonial rule of Rwanda, during which Belgians fostered a sense of difference between Tutsis and Hutus and gave Tutsis power over Hutus. The aftermath of the genocide includes a nation of people who are devastated by severe emotional trauma and have disrupted relationships, identity, and spirituality; changes in worldview; and feelings of vulnerability and threat (Staub, Pearlman, Gubin, & Hagengimana, 2005). In an effort to foster healing, Staub et al. (2005) developed a community-based program in which both Hutu and Tutsi people learned together about genocide and its effects and engaged in group dialogue. In an educational component, lectures about genocide and its effects were provided in an effort to help people understand the context of genocide and to recognize that they are not alone in their suffering. In the experiential component, trained facilitators from local community organizations guided group discussions among Hutus and Tutsis in an empathic manner. Participants were encouraged to share their painful experiences. Two months after the experience, participants were questioned about their ability to cope and their feelings about the other group. Compared with a control group who did not participate in the program, participants showed reduced levels of trauma and also a more positive orientation toward members of the other ethnic group (both Hutu and Tutsi) and a greater willingness to reconcile.

A review of several decades of research involving hundreds of tests of the contact hypothesis showed that contact between members of different groups is quite effective at reducing prejudice against many different groups in many different contexts (Pettigrew & Tropp, 2006). Not only does contact typically improve attitudes toward people in the contact situation, the improved attitudes often generalize to groups as a whole (e.g., a Catholic person who learned to like the Protestant members of her group in a contact situation is likely to develop more favorable attitudes toward Protestants as a whole). Moreover, positive effects generated during programs based on the contact hypothesis are often enduring over time.

Naturally, some programs work better than others, and it appears that the benefits of contact are enhanced when situations are structured in particular ways (Pettigrew & Tropp, 2006). First, as Allport (1954/1979) reasoned, it is useful for groups in the contact situation to be of equal status. Although intergroup contact is often used to reduce prejudice between groups that differ in social status, these differences can be minimized or eliminated in the contact situation. Paluck and Green (2009) cited research by Cook (1971, 1978) that effectively reduced prejudice by bringing African American and European American men together to work on the railway during the 1960s. Although this was a time when status differences between these groups were pronounced, the technique was probably effective in part because in the employment setting, the men worked as equals. Second, intergroup contact is most successful at reducing prejudice when people must work together toward a shared goal because this fosters cooperation, and people tend to come to like those with whom they cooperate. Third, it is helpful if the norms communicated in the contact situation by those who guide the program support intergroup respect. For example, teachers using cooperative learning techniques do well to set clear norms regarding appropriate language, behavior, and so on. Fourth, prejudice is more effectively reduced if groups in a contact situation work cooperatively, not competitively, with other groups. For example, in some applications of the jigsaw classroom, after jigsaw groups work together cooperatively, separate jigsaw groups compete with one another with respect to the quality of their final product. Exercises that omit the competitive element are more effective at reducing prejudice (Paluck & Green, 2009). Finally, contact situations that have an informal element and allow for the development of friendships are most likely to foster positive attitude change (e.g., Molina & Whittig, 2006).

Why does intergroup contact work to reduce prejudice? A good deal of research has examined the processes by which prejudice is reduced in contact situations. In a meta-analysis of this research (a technique by which many studies are pooled to determine combined effects), Pettigrew and Tropp (2008) found that reduced anxiety about contact with different others and increased empathy through learning the perspective of others were strong mediators of the effect of contact on reduced prejudice. To a lesser degree, increased knowledge of other groups also facilitated improved attitudes. Other research has suggested additional dynamics of importance, such as improved communication with members of other groups (Nagda, 2006); increased self-disclosure in contact situations, which facilitates positive relationships through increased trust;

value placed on the contact and empathy (R. N. Turner, Hewstone, & Voci, 2007); and recognition that people from different backgrounds share some other aspects of social identity in common (Crisp & Hewstone, 2007). Other likely changes include reinforcement of people's egalitarian self-standards or distress at recognition of one's own subtle biases and subsequent motivation to reduce them (see Dovidio et al., 2004).

One notable quality of prejudice reduction techniques such as the jigsaw classroom or the Outward Bound experience organized by D. P. Green and Wong (2008) is that participants in the programs are focused on goals and activities other than the reduction of prejudice. The programs reduce prejudice indirectly, without drawing explicit attention to the process. The fact that prejudice reduction is an indirect outcome of such programs is beneficial for a few reasons. First, considerable evidence has suggested that when people are directly instructed not to engage in prejudiced thinking (e.g., not to stereotype), they tend to experience an unintended rebound effect in which they actually are subsequently more likely to stereotype others (Macrae, Bodenhausen, Milne, & Jetten, 1994), perhaps because trying not to think about something tends to make related thoughts come to mind (Wegner, 1994). Try not to think about frogs on lily pads, and you will likely visualize just that. Second, indirect strategies of prejudice reduction may be more effective than more direct techniques in changing the attitudes of especially prejudiced people who view negative attitudes as justified (Esses & Hodson, 2006). Indirect techniques such as the jigsaw classroom or Outward Bound program generate positive attitudes through naturally occurring interactions, and so people are less inclined to react against a perception that their beliefs are under attack. Third, programs that reduce prejudice while focusing participants on other activities and goals provide an opportunity to achieve multiple goals in one setting. In the Outward Bound program organized by D. P. Green and Wong (2008), the students learned about nature, developed physical skills, and engaged in personal development in addition to developing more progressive intergroup attitudes.

Although these types of programs are successful and desirable for several reasons, they are not always possible to implement. Fortunately, some simpler types of contact are also successful at reducing prejudice. For example, S. C. Wright, Aron, McLaughlin-Volpe, and Ropp (1997) showed that prejudice can be reduced when people simply learn that someone from their own group is friends with a member of the other targeted group, a phenomenon they labeled *extended contact*. Even in conflict situations in which prejudice is typically exacerbated, knowledge of cross-group friendships is associated with improved attitudes. This extended contact has been shown to be associated with lower prejudice in many contexts, including between Catholics and Protestants in Northern Ireland (Paolini, Hewstone, Cairns, & Voci, 2004), between White

Europeans and South Asians in the United Kingdom (R. N. Turner et al., 2007), and toward people with disabilities among schoolchildren (Cameron & Rutland, 2006). Recently, the reasons why such simple vicarious contact might reduce prejudice were demonstrated by R. N. Turner, Hewstone, Voci, and Vonofakou (2008). They showed that extended contact reduces prejudice because it encourages people to understand themselves as individuals who have a relationship with the relevant group; it communicates that it is normative for one's group to have friendly relations with the other group and also that it is normative for the other group to have friendly relations with one's own group; and it also serves to alleviate the anxiety people may feel because of unfamiliarity with the other group. This simple form of contact is not a panacea, however. For example, it seems to improve prejudiced attitudes primarily among majority group members and may not alter attitudes among minority groups (Binder et al., 2009).

In summary, applications of the contact hypothesis have been quite successful at reducing many types of prejudice with different groups in various contexts. The requirements of the traditional contact hypothesis—that members of different groups interact, ideally under conditions of equal status, cooperation, normative support for diversity, and with potential for the development of friendships—are sufficiently flexible to allow for programs to be modified to suit multiple purposes and contexts. Moreover, simple things such as learning about cross-group friendships are also of some value. Indeed, recent work has suggested that even simulated contact, in which people are encouraged to imagine having positive interactions with members of other groups, may be effective at reducing prejudice (Crisp & Turner, 2009). Overall, the contact hypothesis and its spin-offs show considerable promise for changing attitudes.

MULTICULTURAL, ANTIBIAS, AND DIVERSITY EDUCATION

In contrast to prejudice reduction programs based on the contact hypothesis that often reduce prejudice indirectly, multicultural, antibias, and diversity education programs are explicit in their goal of reducing prejudice. For example, multicultural education programs used in schools are geared toward educating people about different cultures with the hope that increased knowledge will translate into more positive attitudes. Similarly, antibias programs implemented in schools, communities, and places of work teach people about the nature of inequality and prejudice and encourage participants to develop their own plan for reducing and responding to it. Diversity training programs used in employment settings aim to demonstrate that differences contribute positively to the workplace.

These types of programs are an outgrowth of the increased value placed on multiculturalism in recent decades. According to D. M. Taylor and Moghaddam (1994), grassroots movements that involved demands for respect for minority groups prompted political and social change that led to increased value of multiculturalism. In several Western nations, this was reflected politically with the adoption of official multicultural policies. For example, as mentioned in Chapter 6, in Canada in the 1970s, then Prime Minister Pierre Trudeau introduced a federal multiculturalism policy that is now an important part of the Canadian social fabric. It is substantiated in the Canadian Multiculturalism Act of 1988, which is geared toward preserving and enhancing multiculturalism by directing all government departments to provide leadership in promoting cultural diversity and intercultural respect in Canada. This manifests in many ways, from laws against discrimination to provision of funding for projects that are intended to strengthen cultural development and integration. For example, Citizenship and Immigration Canada (2010) has hosted competitions for youth who have produced antiracism videos. In the United States, where the ethos traditionally supported a view of assimilation in which a new nation was made up of a blend of different backgrounds, there is no official federal policy of multiculturalism. Nevertheless, in both countries, as in many others, multiculturalism exists as a system of thought to which many ascribe, and it consequently supports the development of a variety of educational programs that foster respect for diversity (see Stephan & Vogt, 2004).

Multicultural education is based on the assumption that intergroup relations will be improved when people are educated about other groups' histories, cultures, and religions. It may also focus on different group markers that intersect with ethnicity such as social class (Banks, 2006). Multicultural education in the schools involves both adaptations to standard curriculum and novel activities geared toward fostering intercultural understanding. Traditional pedagogical strategies may be used to address curricula from various groups' perspectives, for example covering a minority group's interpretation of historical events and addressing issues of inequality (Stephan & Stephan, 2005). New content may also be presented, such as occurs when classes learn about the traditions, food, dress, religion, and so forth of different groups. Resource materials for educators review a mix of strategies for ensuring classroom inclusiveness and for teaching about the nature of prejudice and the value of diversity (O. M. Wright, 2000).

One example of this type of program comes from the work of the World of Difference Institute of the Anti-Defamation League. The Anti-Defamation League is an organization founded in 1913 in the United States to combat anti-Semitism. Currently, the aim of the league is to build "bridges of communication, understanding and respect among diverse groups" (Anti-Defamation League, 2009, para. 2) both within the United States and internationally. The

World of Difference Institute focuses on achieving this goal through work with teachers and students, corporations, community groups, and law enforcement agencies (Bettmann & Friedman, 2004). One program, A Classroom of Difference, is geared toward students in preschool through 12th grade. Teachers participate in a workshop hosted by the World of Difference Institute. Several activities facilitate development of awareness of diversity and prejudice among teachers. For example, in the activity "Four Questions," participants complete sentences such as "If I had to describe myself in terms of my culture and heritage in four words, I would say I am a: ___" (Bettmann & Friedman, 2004, p. 85). After completing the sentences, teachers engage in related group discussions. During the discussions, a facilitator reads some of the words provided by participants and requests that everyone who feels that the word describes him or her stand up. In so doing, people recognize that similar attributes may describe people of different backgrounds and also that people with similar backgrounds may understand themselves differently. Teachers who participate in this type of workshop are given an antibias study guide that provides instructional units that give students a similar experience exploring culture and prejudice using comparable exercises (adapted to age level) and curricular supplements.

Stephan and Stephan (2005) reviewed research on the effectiveness of multicultural education programs used in elementary and high school, university, and teacher and counseling educational contexts. Their review showed that the programs were typically effective when used with adolescents and adults. Key to this effectiveness seems to be that the material is age appropriate, that information that can be used to combat stereotypes is included, and that education about the groups at issue is provided. Stephan and Stephan (2005) also found that when used with young children, multicultural education was not effective at reducing prejudice. This finding is consistent with developmental research showing that children need to develop the cognitive flexibility to understand differences in a nonstereotypic manner before such programs are likely to be effective (Aboud & Levy, 2000). For young children whose thinking is necessarily guided by fewer and less flexible categories, multicultural education may foster stereotyping. In contrast, helping to develop young children's ability to think in a complex and flexible manner—for example, by teaching them how to sort objects in multiple ways—is an effective way to reduce their prejudice because this skill can then be used to think about human groups in a more complex way (Aboud & Levy, 2000).

Fewer research studies have examined the effectiveness of similar programs used in employment settings. Often called *diversity training*, such programs are typically short term in length (e.g., 2- to 3-day seminars) and emphasize how diversity in the workplace can be valuable. They are commonly used; for example, about two thirds of U.S. employment settings have some form of diversity training (Paluck, 2006). Carefully constructed evaluations of these programs—those that used controlled comparison groups—have shown less success than with traditional multicultural education programs, with a mix of positive and negative effects emerging (Stephan & Stephan, 2005). Several reasons for the lesser success of these programs relative to others are possible. Their short duration, the fact that they are often mandatory, or their use in work contexts in which they may not be viewed as relevant to the mission of the organization may possibly be responsible for the mixed outcomes. It is also a concern that many of the programs implemented in the workplace are not based on the theory of intergroup relations and that a lack of communication exists between those who study prejudice reduction and those who design and implement diversity training programs (Paluck, 2006). For example, theory-driven research on prejudice reduction has shown that indirect approaches are often most successful, whereas diversity training programs are very direct. Some people, especially those whose attitudes are more in need of adjustment, may be resistant to such direct approaches.

Although multicultural education and diversity training are common in the schools and workplace, other venues have been used to positive effect, such as the media. For example, the television program *Sesame Street* portrays a diverse neighborhood in which people (and various critters) interact amicably, develop life skills, learn about culture and diversity, and learn to respond in a healthy manner to life's ups and downs. According to its website, the program helps to promote respect and understanding among children around the world (*Sesame Street*, 2009). Does research support these assertions? With respect to teaching respect for differences, there is some evidence supporting the effectiveness of coproductions of *Sesame Street* in other parts of the world. Comparisons of the attitudes of children who have and have not watched *Sesame Street*–based programs have shown that exposure seems to support the development of knowledge of culture and a prosocial orientation toward members of other groups (Cole, Labin, & del Rocio Galarza, 2008).

Various media outlets have been used effectively to shape attitudes. Paluck (2009) evaluated the effectiveness of a radio soap opera produced in Rwanda. The program used characters who modeled positive attitudes and experiences regarding relations between ethnic groups in Rwanda. A large group of Rwandans, including prisoners and genocide survivors who listened to the program, showed greater positive willingness to engage in reconciliation and healing, and also more empathy toward members of the other group, than did people who did not listen to this program. Such findings are especially encouraging given the wide potential such programs have to reach people and their relative ease of implementation.

INDIVIDUAL STRATEGIES

Previous chapters have shown how prejudice is pervasive and how subtle manifestations of it can be experienced even by people who value equality and do not wish to be prejudiced. Consequently, prejudice often manifests in subtle yet still potentially hurtful ways. For example, people may not recognize how their evaluations of others can be tainted by implicit stereotyping or how their nonverbal behavior may seem to communicate prejudice. Because subtle biases are common, it is also useful to consider strategies that individuals can use to minimize the potential for unintended bias. Research has suggested that individuals can learn to understand their responses to others in a way that leads to greater self-control and positive behavior change (Monteith & Mark, 2009).

One thing that individuals can do themselves to reduce the likelihood that others in a social setting will do or say inappropriate things is to set a clear norm for respectful behavior. Social norms, and conformity to them, are powerful shapers of people's behavior, and behavior reflective of prejudice is no exception. Indeed, in a review of research examining the role of people's conformity to perceived social norms in the expression of prejudice, Crandall and Stangor (2005) concluded that conformity "seems to form the very core of the majority of people's prejudices" (p. 305). Happily, there is evidence that a norm of nonprejudice may be a stronger influence on people's behavior than a norm of prejudice. Experiments by Monteith, Deneed, and Tooman (1996) demonstrated this. They had some research participants listen to a person who expressed prejudiced or nonprejudiced opinions about either African Americans or gay men, whereas others were not exposed to a norm in this way. They found that participants who heard nonprejudiced expressions subsequently expressed less prejudice than occurred in the control group who did not hear others' views; this conformity was stronger than was conformity to the prejudiced norm. Moreover, this tendency to conform to a nonprejudiced norm occurred among people who had been deemed either high or low in prejudice. Over time, adjustments to behavior to conform to a norm may create shifts in people's attitudes because people often adjust their attitudes to match their behavior to maintain a sense of personal consistency (Festinger, 1957).

People sometimes find that stereotypes occasionally pop into mind when they interact with a member of another group, even if they think the stereotype is inappropriate. Devine (1989) suggested that this type of stereotyping is like a bad habit, that it occurs because stereotypes are deeply engrained in people's culture and socialization experiences. Like any bad habit, it is possible to break. For example, some research has shown that people who examine their own biases subsequently behave in a more positive manner toward other groups (Son Hing, Li, & Zanna, 2002). In this research, people's tendency to reveal unconscious stereotyping was assessed, and people who did and did not reveal unconscious prejudice were asked to remember an occasion on which they had revealed prejudice. Subsequently, they were given an opportunity to allocate funding to student organizations. The task of recalling prejudice had the effect of leading people who showed evidence of unconscious prejudice to experience guilt and also to support funding for a minority student group. Other research has shown that people who are intrinsically motivated to reduce their own bias are also likely to engage in efforts to change their prejudiced thought or feelings rather than simply hide them from others to appear nonprejudiced (Plant & Devine, 2009). Together, such findings have suggested that rather than trying to deny one's biases, one step in the process of reducing prejudice may be for people to recognize their own potential for prejudice.

Evidence is mixed with respect to whether it is helpful to attempt to take the perspective of members of groups against which one has some bias. Some research has shown that even simple, momentary shifts in people's focus of attention, in which they are encouraged to take another's perspective, can change attitudes in a positive manner. For example, in one study, people watched a video depicting a minority group individual discussing the challenges of being a member of a disadvantaged group, under instructions to either take the speaker's perspective or to remain objective and detached. People who took the speaker's perspective subsequently evidenced more positive attitudes toward this minority group than did people who remained detached (Vescio, Sechrist, & Paolucci, 2003). Similar types of experiments have shown the positive value of having people focus on emotions rather than thoughts (Esses & Dovidio, 2002) or specifically on feelings of empathy for the other (Batson, Chang, Orr, & Rowland, 2002) when considering the plight of disadvantaged groups. However, other evidence has shown that for people who are generally low in prejudice, perspective taking can backfire by disrupting the natural flow of their behavior, subsequently creating less positive impressions in interpersonal encounters (Vorauer et al., 2009).

Practices within organizations may shape how effectively people regulate their own behavior in intergroup encounters. In the workplace, subtle evaluative biases can lead to hiring discrimination in such a way that people are unaware that they are making biased judgments and decisions (Jackson et al., 2001). Evaluating job applicants is a complex process in which many different factors play a role. Subtle factors such as feelings evoked by a name on an application may shape how people interpret more important details of an application. Practices that ensure that people are accountable for their decisions seem to be effective in reducing these types of biases (e.g., Dobbs & Crano, 2001). This suggests that practices in organizations that involve open and inclusive decision making are likely to be helpful in reducing the effects of subtle prejudice. In addition, requiring the use of specific criteria for making evaluations, rather than relying on global judgments, which are more subject to bias, is likely to be of help in maintaining fairness.

Prejudice can also be reduced when people focus on their multiple social identities, such as when an ethnic minority woman recognizes that she shares an identity (gender) with women from other ethnic groups. Anything that leads people to categorize themselves or others differently has the potential to alter attitudes toward other people because people tend to form positive attitudes toward those who are categorized as part of their group. In particular, when members of different groups are led to think of themselves as all belonging to a common higher order group, attitudes toward former outgroup members will improve (Gaertner & Dovidio, 2000). For example, Esses, Dovidio, Semenya, and Jackson (2005) attempted to reduce prejudice against immigrants to Canada among people high in social dominance orientation, who are typically quite prejudiced against immigrants (Sidanius & Pratto, 1999), by encouraging these people to think about the ways in which immigrants and members of the host population share a common national identity (e.g., by pointing to their own immigrant past or highlighting the shared future all residents share with new immigrants). This is a sensible approach because people high in social dominance orientation tend to protect the interests of their group. Therefore, encouraging them to think of their group in a more inclusive manner may improve attitudes toward "new" group members. Indeed, highly dominance-oriented people who were encouraged to focus on a common identity with immigrants subsequently showed more favorable attitudes toward immigrants than did people who were not. Other research has shown that creating a sense of "we-ness" with others effectively reduces prejudice even when people retain a strong sense of their original group identity and generate a dual identity that includes the original group and the higher order one (e.g., Chinese Canadian; Gaertner & Dovidio, 2009). This is important because many people value their ethnic identity and other group memberships and it shows that prejudice reduction does not require that people denounce these identities.

LIMITATIONS OF PREJUDICE REDUCTION

An important caution about prejudice reduction has recently been leveled by S. C. Wright and Lubensky (2009). These psychologists pointed out that the benefits gained by reducing prejudice among members of advantaged groups may be offset by the problems created for disadvantaged groups. Their concern is especially relevant to prejudice reduction efforts that involve interactions between groups such as those based on the contact hypothesis. Contact situations geared toward reducing prejudice typically involve structured interactions between members of advantaged and disadvantaged groups, and these encounters often successfully improve intergroup attitudes among members of both groups. The concern is that by creating a situation in which members of disadvantaged groups are likely to feel an increased social identification with and warmth toward the advantaged group, they may become less inclined to identify with their own group and less likely to act on behalf of their group to challenge inequality through collective action. In fact, S. C. Wright and Lubensky (2009) found that among African American and Latino university students, intergroup contact made people less likely to identify with their own ethnic group. Although this resulted in more favorable attitudes toward European Americans, it also had the effect of creating lowered inclinations to endorse collective action on behalf of their own group. By reducing prejudice, contact programs may inadvertently feed into the perpetuation of inequality by creating contentment where discontent is warranted.

A related caution about prejudice reduction is that efforts to improve attitudes may have different effects on members of high- and low-status groups. Henry and Hardin (2006) examined the relation between intergroup contact and both implicit and explicit prejudice among African American and European American people in the United States and Christians and Muslims in Lebanon. They found that among all groups, people who reported having more intergroup contact showed lower explicit prejudice. However, more intergroup contact was associated with lower implicit prejudice only among the lower status groups (African Americans in the United States and Muslims in Lebanon) and not among the higher status groups. Members of the higher status groups retained their implicit prejudices. The researchers reasoned that because there are more negative associations with low-status groups than with high-status groups in society, implicit prejudice against low-status groups becomes more entrenched, and unlearning it is especially challenging.

This pattern of prejudice reduction could lead to the perpetuation of disadvantage because members of lower status groups change more in their attitudes than do members of advantaged groups. Members of advantaged groups, who may have more power to perpetuate inequality, retain subtle biases. Moreover, because explicit prejudice is reduced among advantaged group members, their expressions of prejudice are likely to turn more hidden or indirect. Consequently, it may become less obviously offensive to members of low-status groups, and this could lead to a lessened tendency of disadvantaged group members to advocate on their own behalf to challenge it (see Ellemers & Barreto, 2009). On the basis of their finding that intergroup contact was associated with reduced explicit (vs. implicit) prejudice only among members of higher status groups, Henry and Hardin (2006) concluded that effectively reducing implicit prejudice against low-status groups will likely require institutional changes involving broad-based improvements in underprivileged groups' social status (e.g., affirmative action) because this would effectively create more positive societal associations with these groups. In other words, reducing implicit prejudice may require creating greater equality.

COLLECTIVE ACTION

Collective action involves activities that are aimed at reducing inequality by improving the status or conditions of underprivileged groups or proactive efforts to prevent injustice (van Zomeren & Iyer, 2009). Examples of behaviors that make up collective action include commonly socially accepted actions like provision of education, consciousness raising, lobbying, negotiation, voting, writing protest letters, or signing petitions or more controversial actions such as protesting, engaging in strikes or riots, and even illegal activities like bombings (S. C. Wright, 2009). Needless to say, people's beliefs and values shape the types of problems they deem important to address and the actions viewed as appropriate to achieve that goal. Collective actions of interest to psychologists who study prejudice and inequality typically involve activities such as advocating for policy changes that create greater equality, working in organizations to reduce or prevent discrimination, participating in community activist groups that promote the interests of disadvantaged groups, and the like.

What makes collective action collective is not the number of people participating in it but rather the intent, which is to benefit a group rather than specific individuals in it. Therefore, individuals can engage in solo collective action provided that they understand their behavior as directed toward creating change at the group level (S. C. Wright, 2009). For example, when Martin Luther King Jr. gave his famous "I Have a Dream" speech, he was engaging in collective action because he was promoting civil rights for the sake of the well-being of African American people as a group. More recently, Barack Obama was arguably engaging in collective action during his election speeches when through his "Yes We Can" motto he galvanized the energy of a diverse group of people who had previously felt disempowered socially. Nevertheless, collective action does often involve group activity. For example, the recent annual G-8 summits, during which leaders of eight of the world's most powerful nations meet, typically inspire demonstrators to organize as a group to address various social justice issues of international significance.

Who participates in collective action? It often appears to be members of underprivileged groups who advocate for their own group through collective action. For example, leaders in the early feminist movement were female. This makes sense because it is people who experience disadvantage who are most inclined to have a vested interest in changing inequality. Yet, members of more privileged groups also sometimes campaign on behalf of others—for example, men involved in the contemporary international White Ribbon Campaign work collectively to end men's violence against women (White Ribbon Campaign, 2010). Collective action by members of more privileged groups can be valuable given that these groups have additional power to create change (Iyer & Ryan, 2009).

What motivates people to get involved in collective action? Research has shown that emotions such as anger play a role (e.g., van Zomeren, Spears, Fisher & Leach, 2004). Among members of disadvantaged groups, a sense of relative deprivation—the belief that one's group is deprived in important ways relative to other groups—can generate anger and resentment, and these emotions tend to motivate collective action (Crosby, 1976; Runciman, 1966). However, anger may only generate productive collective action if the behavior provides an effective way to release anger and other routes to do so are not viable (Stürmer & Simon, 2009). Also, other emotions can mitigate against collective action tendencies. For example, fear of negative outcomes of engagement with collective action (e.g., backlash) can also inhibit people's participation (Miller, Cronin, Garcia, & Branscombe, 2009). Nevertheless, emotional responses to injustice do appear to be important motivators of collective action. This can occur among members of relatively more advantaged groups as well as more deprived groups, when people feel angry on behalf of others. For example, a study of American and British citizens found that people who felt anger and shame in relation to the occupation of Iraq were more likely to protest against it and advocate for compensation to Iraq (Iyer, Schmader, & Lickel, 2007).

Members of high- and low-status groups may at times have different reasons for getting engaged in collective action. In a recent demonstration of this, Iyer and Ryan (2009) surveyed a large international group of working adults. They asked the participants to read an article about the glass cliff—the phenomenon whereby women are more likely to be given risky leadership positions than are men, arguably setting them up to fail—and then report their beliefs about this issue as well as their willingness to get involved at their place of work to monitor and prevent it. They found that women who felt more identified with their gender group (those for whom gender was important to their identity) saw the glass cliff as more of a problem, felt more anger about it, and were more willing to engage in collective action to prevent it than were women who were less identified with their gender. In contrast, among men, identification with their gender group did not predict collective action tendencies. Other factors, such as how pervasive they believed the problem to be and how much sympathy they felt for women, did. This shows that identifying with one's group may predict collective action primarily among members of groups that can benefit from it. In fact, among members of higher status groups, it may be those who are less identified with their group who are more incensed by others' disadvantage and more inclined to work to prevent or challenge it (Gordijn, Yzerbyt, Wigboldus, & Dumont, 2006).

The nature of the social context also shapes people's willingness to engage in collective action. According to social identity theory (Tajfel & Turner, 1979, 1986; see Chapter 6, this volume), members of disadvantaged groups will be more likely to engage in collective action when inequality is deemed to be illegitimate, when change is viewed as possible, and when group boundaries are impermeable; that is, people cannot improve their lot by changing the group they belong to, only by improving the status of their group. Evidence supports these claims (see van Zomeren & Iyer, 2009; S. C. Wright, 2009). It is important to note that people's beliefs about these factors shape their responses to inequality because they imply that efforts to support collective action would benefit from challenging beliefs that inequality is legitimate or inevitable and fostering perceptions of possible alternate, more equitable, realities (S. C. Wright, 2009).

Does collective action work? Whether it effectively creates change depends on a host of factors, such as the type of problem addressed and the form of collective action used (Louis, 2009). Nevertheless, in a review of sociological research that addressed the extent to which collective action was effective in reaching specific goals such as policy change, Louis (2009) found that results were frequently successful and also noted that some outcomes may be indirect in that collective action may shift public opinion, which, in turn, may ultimately create change. Collective action also has psychological effects. For example, it can alter public impressions of oppressed groups, generating more empowered images of them (S. C. Wright, 2009). It may also improve psychological well-being among members of disadvantaged groups by providing a vehicle through which people cope actively with their oppression (Outten, Schmitt, Garcia, & Branscombe, 2009).

In summary, many different approaches to reducing prejudice exist, and many of those that are based in theory have been shown by research to be effective. Some of the most effective programs work indirectly by encouraging a climate in which people from different backgrounds work together cooperatively. Prejudice reduction on its own is unlikely to be sufficient to eliminate inequality, however, because it may undermine the motivation to engage in collective action among members of underprivileged groups and it may leave intact implicit forms of prejudice among more privileged groups. Therefore, an important challenge for those interested in reducing both prejudice and inequality will be to create interventions that effectively approach both goals. To this end, collective action that is geared toward preventing or reducing inequality has been shown to be of interest to members of both disadvantaged and advantaged groups, and it shows promise at achieving some of its important goals.

CONCLUDING COMMENTS

The preceding chapters have described how prejudice is just one problem nested in a web of related social issues including not only inequality but also environmental issues, peace and conflict, intraspecies conceit, and so on. Therefore, efforts to reduce prejudice and create equality are arguably compatible with other initiatives, such as those that promote environmental responsibility, those that advocate for peace, those that advocate for the humane treatment of nonhumans, and so on. Recently, calls have been made for interventions that address such goals in unison (e.g., Thomas & Beirne, 2002). Encouragingly, many of the programs reviewed in this final chapter can be adapted to address multiple goals simultaneously. This is important given the many challenges we face in the 21st century, such as declining natural resources and an ecosystem in crisis, growing gaps between rich and poor in many places, wars, proliferation of inhumane factory farms and their unhealthy effects, and the consequent need for communities to work together to address such problems (Stokols, Misra, Runnerstrom, & Hipp, 2009). Programs aimed at generating peace, a humane approach to the natural world, or resolving specific community-based challenges like housing or transportation, if structured to promote equal-status cooperative contact among people from diverse backgrounds, are likely to be promising ways to improve intergroup relations while working toward other forms of healing change in the world.

REFERENCES

Aboud, F. E. (2003). The formation of in-group favoritism and out-group prejudice in young children: Are they distinct attitudes? *Developmental Psychology, 39,* 48–60. doi:10.1037/0012-1649.39.1.48

Aboud, F. E. (2005). The development of prejudice in childhood and adolescence. In J. F. Dovidio, P. Glick, & L. A. Rudman (Eds.), *On the nature of prejudice: Fifty years after Allport* (pp. 310–326). Malden, MA: Blackwell.

Aboud, F. E. (2008). A social-cognitive developmental theory of prejudice. In S. M. Quintana & C. McKown (Eds.), *Handbook of race, racism, and the developing child* (pp. 55–71). Hoboken, NJ: Wiley.

Aboud, F. E., & Amato, M. (2001). Developmental and socialization influences on intergroup bias. In R. Brown & S. Gaertner (Eds.), *Blackwell handbook of social psychology: Intergroup processes* (pp. 65–85). Malden, MA: Blackwell.

Aboud, F. E., & Levy, S. R. (2000). Interventions to reduce prejudice and discrimination in children and adolescents. In S. Oskamp (Ed.), *Reducing prejudice and discrimination* (pp. 269–293). Mahwah, NJ: Erlbaum.

Adams, C. J. (2000). *The sexual politics of meat: A feminist-vegetarian critical theory.* New York, NY: Continuum.

Adorno, T. W., Frenkel-Brunswik, E., Levinson, D. J., & Sanford, R. N. (1950). *The authoritarian personality.* New York, NY: Harper & Row.

Adriaens, P. R., & De Block, A. (2006). The evolution of a social construction: The case of male homosexuality. *Perspectives in Biology and Medicine, 49,* 570–585. doi:10.1353/pbm.2006.0051

Allport, G. W. (1979). *The nature of prejudice.* Cambridge, MA: Perseus Books. (Original work published 1954)

Altemeyer, B. (1982). *Right-wing authoritarianism.* Winnipeg, Manitoba, Canada: University of Manitoba Press.

Altemeyer, B. (1988). *Enemies of freedom: Understanding right-wing authoritarianism.* San Francisco, CA: Jossey-Bass.

Altemeyer, B. (2006). *The authoritarians.* Retrieved from http://home.cc.umanitoba.ca/~altemey/

Altemeyer, B., & Hunsberger, B. (2005). Fundamentalism and authoritarianism. In R. F. Paloutzian & C. L. Park (Eds.), *Handbook of the psychology of religion and spirituality* (pp. 378–393). New York, NY: Guilford Press.

Amodio, D. M. (2008). The social neuroscience of intergroup relations. *European Review of Social Psychology, 19,* 1–54. doi:10.1080/10463280801927937

Amodio, D. M. (2009). Intergroup anxiety effects on the control of racial stereotypes: A psychoneuroendocrine analysis. *Journal of Experimental Social Psychology, 45,* 60–67. doi:10.1016/j.jesp.2008.08.009

Amodio, D. M., Devine, P. G., & Harmon-Jones, E. (2007). Mechanisms for the regulation of intergroup responses. In E. Harmon-Jones & P. Winkielman (Eds.), *Social neuroscience: Integrating biological and psychological explanations of social behavior* (pp. 353–375). New York, NY: Guilford Press.

Anderson, P. E. (2008). *The powerful bond between people and pets: Our boundless connections to companion animals*. Westport, CT: Praeger.

Anti-Defamation League. (2009). *About the Anti-Defamation League*. Retrieved from http://www.adl.org/about.asp?s=topmenu

Arbour, R., Signal, T., & Taylor, N. (2009). Teaching kindness: The promise of humane education. *Society & Animals, 17,* 136–148. doi:10.1163/156853009X418073

Aronson, E. (1978). *The jigsaw classroom*. Beverly Hills, CA: Sage.

Aronson, E. (1990). Applying social psychology to desegregation and energy conservation. *Personality and Social Psychology Bulletin, 16,* 118–132. doi:10.1177/0146167290161009

Aronson, E. (2000). *Nobody left to hate: Teaching compassion after Columbine*. New York, NY: Worth.

Aronson, E. (2004). Reducing hostility and building compassion: Lessons from the jigsaw classroom. In A. Miller (Ed.), *The social psychology of good and evil* (pp. 469–488). New York, NY: Guilford Press.

Ascione, F. (2005). *Children and animals: Exploring the roots of kindness and cruelty*. West Lafayette, IL: Purdue University Press.

Ascione, F. (2008). *The international handbook of animal abuse and cruelty*. West Lafayette, IL: Purdue University Press.

Ascione, F. R., & Arkow, P. (1999). *Child abuse, domestic violence, and animal abuse*. West Lafayette, IL: Purdue University Press.

Ascione, F. R., & Shapiro, K. (2009). People and animals, kindness and cruelty: Research directions and policy implications. *Journal of Social Issues, 65,* 569–587. doi:10.1111/j.1540-4560.2009.01614.x

Ascione, F. R., & Weber, C. V. (1996). Children's attitudes about the humane treatment of animals and empathy: One-year follow-up of a school-based intervention. *Anthrozoos, 9,* 188–195. doi:10.2752/089279396787001455

Ashmore, R. D., & Del Boca, F. K. (1981). Conceptual approaches to stereotypes and stereotyping. In D. L. Hamilton (Ed.), *Cognitive processes in stereotyping and intergroup behavior* (pp. 1–35). Hillsdale, NJ: Erlbaum.

Associated Press. (2007, April 11). Hundreds killed in attacks on eastern Chad. *The Washington Post,* p. A10.

Aviram, R. B. (2006). Object relations and prejudice: From in-group favoritism to out-group hatred. *International Journal of Applied Psychoanalytic Studies, 4*(1), 4–14. doi:10.1002/aps.121

Bagley, C., & Tremblay, P. (1998). On the prevalence of homosexuality and bisexuality in a random survey of 750 men aged 18 to 27. *Journal of Homosexuality, 36*(2), 1–18. doi:10.1300/J082v36n02_01

Baker, K., & Raney, A. A. (2007). Equally super? Gender stereotyping of superheros in children's animated programs. *Mass Communication & Society, 10*, 25–41.

Banaji, M., & Greenwald, A. G. (1994). Implicit stereotyping and prejudice. In M.P. Zanna & J. M. Olson (Eds.), *The psychology of prejudice: The Ontario Symposium* (Vol. 7, pp. 149-169). Hillsdale, NJ: Erlbaum.

Bandura, A. (1973). *Aggression: A social learning analysis*. Oxford, England: Prentice-Hall.

Bandura, A. (1977). *Social learning theory*. Oxford, England: Prentice-Hall.

Banks, J. A. (2006). Improving race relations in schools: From theory and research to practice. *Journal of Social Issues, 62*, 607–614. doi:10.1111/j.1540-4560. 2006.00476.x

Bar-Tal, D. (1996). Development of social categories and stereotypes in early childhood: The case of "the Arab" concept formation, stereotype and attitudes by Jewish children in Israel. *International Journal of Intercultural Relations, 20*, 341–370. doi:10.1016/0147-1767(96)00023-5

Bar-Tal, D., & Teichman, Y. (2005). *Stereotypes and prejudice in conflict: Representations of Arabs in Israeli Jewish society*. New York, NY: Cambridge University Press. doi:10.1017/CBO9780511499814

Bartholow, B. D., Dickter, C. L., & Sestir, M. (2006). Stereotype activation and control of prejudiced responses: Cognitive control of inhibition and its impairment by alcohol. *Journal of Personality and Social Psychology, 90*, 272–287. doi:10.1037/ 0022-3514.90.2.272

Batson, C. D., Chang, J., Orr, R., & Rowland, J. (2002). Empathy, attitudes and action: Can feeling for a member of a stigmatized group motivate one to help the group? *Personality and Social Psychology Bulletin, 28*, 1656–1666. doi:10.1177/ 014616702237647

Batson, C. D., & Schoenrade, P. A. (1991). Measuring religion as quest: 1) Validity concerns. *Journal for the Scientific Study of Religion, 30*, 416–429. doi:10.2307/ 1387277

Bauman, H. D. L. (2004). Audism: Exploring the metaphysics of oppression. *Journal of Deaf Studies and Deaf Education, 9*, 239–246. doi: 10.1093/deafed/enh025

Beaton, A. M., & Tougas, F. (2001). Reactions to affirmative action: Group membership and social justice. *Social Justice Research, 14*, 61–78. doi:10.1023/ A:1012575724550

Beatson, R. M., & Halloran, M. J. (2007). Humans rule! The effects of creatureliness reminders, mortality salience and self-esteem on attitudes toward animals. *British Journal of Social Psychology, 46*, 619–632. doi:10.1348/014466606X147753

Becker, E. (1973). *The denial of death*. New York, NY: Free Press.

Beirne, P. (2004). From animal abuse to interhuman violence? A critical review of the progression thesis. *Society and Animals, 12*, 39-65.

Bekoff, M. (2002). *Minding animals: Awareness, emotions, and heart*. New York, NY: Oxford University Press.

Bell, D. W., & Esses, V. M. (2002). Ambivalence and response amplification: A motivational perspective. *Personality and Social Psychology Bulletin, 28*, 1143–1152. doi:10.1177/01461672022811012

Bell, D. W., Esses, V. M., & Maio, G. R. (1996). The utility of an open-ended measure to assess intergroup ambivalence. *Canadian Journal of Behavioural Science, 28*, 12–18. doi:10.1037/0008-400X.28.1.12

Berkowitz, L., & Harmon-Jones, E. (2004). Toward an understanding of the determinants of anger. *Emotion, 4*, 107–130. doi:10.1037/1528-3542.4.2.107

Bernd, S., & Pettigrew, T. F. (1990). Social identity and perceived group homogeneity: Evidence for the ingroup homogeneity effect. *European Journal of Social Psychology, 20*, 269–286.

Berry, J.W. (1984). Multicultural policy in Canada: A social psychological analysis. *Canadian Journal of Behavioural Science, 16*, 353–370.

Bettmann, E. H., & Friedman, L. J. (2004). The Anti-Defamation League's A World of Difference Institute. In W. G. Stephan & W. P. Vogt (Eds.), *Education programs for improving intergroup relations* (pp. 75–94). New York, NY: Teachers College Press.

Bhandar, B. (2000). *A guilty verdict against the odds: Privileging white femininity in the trial of Kelly Ellard for the murder of Reena Virk.* Retrieved from http://www.rajweb.com/cassa/eMag/Articles/Articles3.htm

Bigler, R. S., Jones, L. C., & Lobliner, D. B. (1997). Social categorization and the formation of intergroup attitudes in children. *Child Development, 68*, 530–543. doi:10.2307/1131676

Bigler, R. S., & Liben, L. S. (2006). A developmental intergroup theory of social stereotypes and prejudice. In R. V. Kail (Ed.), *Advances in child development and behavior* (Vol. 34, pp. 39–89). San Diego, CA: Elsevier.

Bigler, R. S., & Liben, L. S. (2007). Developmental intergroup theory: Explaining and reducing children's social stereotyping and prejudice. *Current Directions in Psychological Science, 16*, 162–166. doi:10.1111/j.1467-8721.2007.00496.x

Binder, J., Zagefka, H., Brown, R., Funke, F., Kessler, T., Mummendey, A., . . . Leyens, J.-P. (2009). Does contact reduce prejudice or does prejudice reduce contact? A longitudinal test of the contact hypothesis among majority and minority groups in three European countries. *Journal of Personality and Social Psychology, 96*, 843–856. doi:10.1037/a0013470

Bitacola, L., Jackson, L. M., Esses, V. M., & Janes, L. (2010, June). *Social dominance orientation and environmental decision making.* Poster presented at the biennial meeting of the Society for the Psychological Study of Social Issues, New Orleans, LA.

Bizumic, B., & Duckitt, J. (2007). Varieties of group self-centeredness and dislike of the specific other. *Basic and Applied Social Psychology, 29*, 195–202.

Blatz, C. W., & Ross, M. (2009). Principled ideology or racism: Why do modern racists oppose race-based social justice programs? *Journal of Experimental Social Psychology, 45*, 258–261. doi:10.1016/j.jesp.2008.08.008

Blumer, H. (1958). Race prejudice as a sense of group position. *Pacific Sociological Review, 1*, 3–7.

Bobo, L. (1983). White's opposition to busing: Symbolic racism or realistic group conflict? *Journal of Personality and Social Psychology, 45*, 1196–1210. doi:10.1037/0022-3514.45.6.1196

Bobo, L. D., & Tuan, M. (2006). *Prejudice in politics: Group position, public opinion, and the Wisconsin Treaty rights dispute*. Cambridge, MA: Harvard University Press.

Bobocel, D. R., Son Hing, L. S., Davey, L. M., Stanley, D. J., & Zanna, M. P. (1998). Justice-based opposition to social policies: Is it genuine? *Journal of Personality and Social Psychology, 75*, 653–669. doi:10.1037/0022-3514.75.3.653

Bonham, V. L., Warshauer-Baker, E., & Collins, F. S. (2005). Race and ethnicity in the genome era: The complexity of constructs. *American Psychologist, 60*, 9–15. doi:10.1037/0003-066X.60.1.9

Bonoguore, T. (2007, May 31). Ipperwash report released. *The Globe and Mail*. Retrieved from http://www.theglobeandmail.com/news/national/ipperwash-report-released/article761326/

Branscombe, N. R. (1998). Thinking about one's gender groups' privileges or disadvantages: Consequences for well-being in women and men. *British Journal of Social Psychology, 37*(Pt. 2), 167–184.

Branscombe, N. R., Schmitt, M. T., & Schiffhauer, K. (2007). Racial attitudes in response to thoughts of White privilege. *European Journal of Social Psychology, 37*, 203–215. doi:10.1002/ejsp.348

Bratt, C. (2008). The jigsaw classroom under test: No effect on intergroup relations evident. *Journal of Community & Applied Social Psychology, 18*, 403–419. doi:10.1002/casp.946

Breckenridge, J. N., & Zimbardo, P. G. (2007). The strategy of terrorism and the psychology of mass-mediated fear. In B. Borgar, L. M. Brown, L. E. Beutler, J. N. Breckenridge, & P. G. Zimbardo (Eds.), *Psychology of terrorism* (pp. 116–133). New York, NY: Oxford University Press.

Brewer, M. B. (1988). A dual process model of impression formation. In T. K. Srull & R. S. Wyer (Eds.), *Advances in social cognition* (Vol. 1, pp. 1–36). Hillsdale, NJ: Erlbaum.

Brewer, M. B. (1999). The psychology of prejudice: Ingroup love or outgroup hate? *Journal of Social Issues, 55*, 429–444. doi:10.1111/0022-4537.00126

Brown, R. (2000). Social identity theory: Past achievements, current problems, and future challenges. *European Journal of Social Psychology, 30*, 745–778. doi:10.1002/1099-0992(200011/12)30:6{745::AID-EJSP24}3.0.CO;2-O

Brown, R., Maras, P., Masser, B., Vivian, J., & Hewstone, M. (2001). Life on the ocean wave: Testing some intergroup hypotheses in a naturalistic setting. *Group Processes & Intergroup Relations, 4*, 81–97. doi:10.1177/1368430201004002001

Burris, C. T., & Jackson, L. M. (2000). Social identity and the true believer: Responses to threatened self-stereotypes among the intrinsically religious. *British Journal of Social Psychology, 39,* 257–278. doi:10.1348/014466600164462

Buss, D. M., & Kenrick, D. T. (1998). Evolutionary social psychology. In D. T. Gilbert, S. T. Fiske, & G. Lindzey (Eds.), *The handbook of social psychology* (4th ed., pp. 982–1026). New York, NY: McGraw-Hill.

Cameron, L., & Rutland, A. (2006). Extended contact through story telling in school: Reducing children's prejudice toward the disabled. *Journal of Social Issues, 62,* 469–488. doi:10.1111/j.1540-4560.2006.00469.x

Canadian Hearing Society. (2007). *The Canadian Hearing Society Position paper on discrimination and audism.* Toronto, Ontario, Canada: Author.

Caporael, L. R. (2007). Evolutionary theory for social and cultural psychology. In A. W. Kruglanski & E. T. Higgins (Eds.), *Social psychology: Handbook of basic principles* (2nd ed., pp. 3–18). New York, NY: Guilford Press.

Castano, E. (2004). In case of death, cling to the ingroup. *European Journal of Social Psychology, 34,* 375–384. doi:10.1002/ejsp.211

Castano, E., & Giner-Sorolla, R. (2006). Not quite human: Infrahumanization in response to collective responsibility for intergroup killing. *Journal of Personality and Social Psychology, 90,* 804–818. doi:10.1037/0022-3514.90.5.804

Castano, E., & Kofta, M. (2009). Dehumanization: Humanity and its denial. *Group Processes and Intergroup Relations, 12,* 695–697.

Citizenship and Immigration Canada. (2010). *Racism: Stop it!* Retrieved from http://www.cic.gc.ca/english/multiculturalism/march21/index.asp

Chandler, E. W., & Dreger, R. M. (1993). Anthropocentrism: Construct validity and measurement. *Journal of Social Behavior and Personality, 8,* 169–188.

Chovaz, C. J. (1998). Cultural aspects of deafness. In S. S. Kazarian & D. R. Evans (Eds.), *Cultural clinical psychology: Theory, research, and practice* (pp. 377–400). New York, NY: Oxford University Press.

Chovaz, C. J. (2009, October). *Deaf Kids Mental Health Clinic: A first in Canada.* Paper presented at the Fourth World Congress of the Deaf, Brisbane, Queensland, Australia.

Chovaz-McKinnon, C. J. (2007). Mental health services for the Deaf (MHSD). *Psynopsis,* Winter, 7.

Chrisafis, A. (2007, July 7), Cosmetics giant guilty of racism. *The Globe and Mail,* p. A2.

Clark, K. B., & Clark, M. K. (1939). The development of consciousness of self and the emergence of racial identification in Negro preschool children. *Journal of Social Psychology, 10,* 591–599.

Cohen, G. L., Garcia, J., Apfel, N., & Master, A. (2006, September 1). Reducing the racial achievement gap: A social psychological intervention. *Science, 313,* 1307–1310. doi:10.1126/science.1128317

Cole, C. F., Labin, D. B., & del Rocio Galarza, M. (2008). Begin with the children: What research on Sesame Street's international coproductions reveals about using media to promote a new peaceful world. *International Journal of Behavioral Development, 32*, 359–365. doi:10.1177/0165025408090977

Condit, C. M., Parrott, R. L., Bates, B. R., Bevan, J., & Achter, P. J. (2004). Exploration of the impact of messages about genes and race on lay attitudes. *Clinical Genetics, 66*, 402–408. doi:10.1111/j.1399-0004.2004.00327.x

Conway, M., Pizzamiglio, M. T., & Mount, L. (1996). Status, communality and agency: Implications for stereotypes of gender and other groups. *Journal of Personality and Social Psychology, 71*, 25–38. doi:10.1037/0022-3514.71.1.25

Coren, M. (2007, August 18). Doggone fools. *The London Free Press*, p. A10.

Corenblum, B., & Stephan, W. G. (2001). White fears and Native apprehensions: An integrated threat theory approach to intergroup relations. *Canadian Journal of Behavioural Science, 33*, 251–268. doi:10.1037/h0087147

Correctional Services Canada. (1998). *Demographic overview of Aboriginal peoples in Canada and Aboriginal offenders in federal corrections*. Retrieved from http://www.csc-scc.gc.ca/text/prgrm/abinit/who-eng.shtml

Correll, J., Park, B., Judd, C. M., & Wittenbrink, B. (2007). The influence of stereotypes on decisions to shoot. *European Journal of Social Psychology, 37*, 1102–1117. doi:10.1002/ejsp.450

Correll, J., Park, B., Wittenbrink, B., & Judd, C. M. (2002). The police officer's dilemma: Using ethnicity to disambiguate potentially threatening individuals. *Journal of Personality and Social Psychology, 83*, 1314–1329. doi:10.1037/0022-3514.83.6.1314

Costello, K., & Hodson, G. (2010). Exploring the roots of dehumanization: The role of animal-human similarity in promoting immigrant humanization. *Group Processes & Intergroup Relations, 13*, 3–22. doi:10.1177/1368430209347725

Cozzarelli, C., Wilkinson, A. V., & Tagler, M. J. (2001). Attitudes toward the poor and attributions for poverty. *Journal of Social Issues, 57*, 207–227. doi:10.1111/0022-4537.00209

Crandall, C. S. (1991). Do heavyweight students have more difficulty paying for college? *Personality and Social Psychology Bulletin, 17*, 606–611. doi:10.1177/0146167291176002

Crandall, C. S. (1994). Prejudice against fat people: Ideology and self-interest. *Journal of Personality and Social Psychology, 66*, 882–894. doi:10.1037/0022-3514.66.5.882

Crandall, C. S. (1995). Do parents discriminate against their heavyweight daughters? *Personality and Social Psychology Bulletin, 21*, 724–735. doi:10.1177/0146167295217007

Crandall, C. S., & Stangor, C. (2005). Conformity and prejudice. In J. F. Dovidio, P. Glick, & L. A. Rudman (Eds.), *On the nature of prejudice: Fifty years after Allport* (pp. 295–309). Malden, MA: Blackwell.

Crisp, R. J., & Hewstone, M. (2007). Multiple social categorization. *Advances in Experimental Social Psychology, 39*, 163–254. doi:10.1016/S0065-2601(06)39004-1

Crisp, R. J., & Turner, R. N. (2009). Can imagined interactions produce positive perceptions? Reducing prejudice through simulated social contact. *American Psychologist, 64,* 231–240. doi:10.1037/a0014718

Crosby, F. J. (1976). A model of egotistical relative deprivation. *Psychological Review, 83,* 85–113. doi:10.1037/0033-295X.83.2.85

Crosby, F. J., Iyer, A., Clayton, S., & Downing, R. A. (2003). Affirmative action: Psychological data and the policy debates. *American Psychologist, 58,* 93–115. doi:10.1037/0003-066X.58.2.93

Cuddy, A. J. C., Fiske, S. T., & Glick, P. (2007). The BIAS map: Behaviors from intergroup affect and stereotypes. *Journal of Personality and Social Psychology, 92,* 631–648. doi:10.1037/0022-3514.92.4.631

Cunningham, W. A., Johnson, M. K., Raye, C. L., Gatenby, J. C., Gore, J. C., & Banaji, M. R. (2004). Separable neural components in the processing of Black and White faces. *Psychological Science, 15,* 806–813. doi:10.1111/j.0956-7976.2004.00760.x

Czopp, A. M. (2008). When is a compliment not a compliment? Evaluating the expressions of positive stereotypes. *Journal of Experimental Social Psychology, 44,* 413–420. doi:10.1016/j.jesp.2006.12.007

Dambrun, M., Kamiejski, R., Haddadi, N., & Duarte, S. (2009). Why does social dominance orientation decrease with university exposure to the social sciences? The impact of institutional socialization and the mediating role of "geneticism." *European Journal of Social Psychology, 39,* 88–100. doi:10.1002/ejsp.498

Danso, H. A., & Esses, V. M. (2001). Black experimenters and the intellectual test performance of White participants: The tables are turned. *Journal of Experimental Social Psychology, 37,* 158–165. doi:10.1006/jesp.2000.1444

Dawkins, R. (2003). Gaps in the mind. In S. Plous (Ed.), *Understanding prejudice and discrimination* (pp. 537–542). Boston, MA: McGraw-Hill.

Dawkins, R. (2004, September). Race and creation. *Prospect,* pp. 15–16.

De Houwer, J., Thomas, S., & Baeyens, F. (2001). Associative learning of likes and dislikes: A review of 25 years of research on human evaluative conditioning. *Psychological Bulletin, 127,* 853–869. doi:10.1037/0033-2909.127.6.853

Delgado, N., Rodriguez-Peréz, A., Vaes, J., Leyens, J.-P., & Betancor, V. (2009). Priming effects of violence on infrahumanization. *Group Processes & Intergroup Relations, 12,* 699–714. doi:10.1177/1368430209344607

Deo, S. R. (2008). Where have all the Lovings gone? The continuing relevance of the movement for a multi-racial category and racial classification after *Parents Involved in Community Schools v. Seattle School District No. 1. Journal of Gender, Race and Justice, 11,* 409–444.

Devine, P. G. (1989). Stereotypes and prejudice: Their automatic and controlled components. *Journal of Personality and Social Psychology, 56,* 5–18. doi:10.1037/0022-3514.56.1.5

Devine, P. G., & Elliot, A. J. (1995). Are racial stereotypes *really* fading? The Princeton trilogy revisited. *Personality and Social Psychology Bulletin, 21*, 1139–1150. doi:10.1177/01461672952111002

Diebel, L. (2008, June 12). *Harper "sorry" for Native residential schools.* Retrieved from http://www.thestar.com/comment/columnists/article/441820

Dixon, B., & Arikawa, H. (2008). Comparisons of vegetarians and non-vegetarians on pet attitudes and empathy. *Anthrozoos, 21*, 387–395. doi:10.2752/1753 03708X371654

Dobbs, M., & Crano, W. D. (2001). Outgroup accountability in the minimal group paradigm: Implications for aversive discrimination and social identity theory. *Personality and Social Psychology Bulletin, 27*, 355–364. doi:10.1177/ 0146167201273009

Dollard, J., Doob, L. W., Miller, N. E., Mowrer, O. W., & Sears, R. R. (1939). *Frustration and aggression.* New Haven, CT: Yale University Press.

Dovidio, J. F., & Gaertner, S. L. (2004). Aversive racism. In M. P. Zanna (Ed.), *Advances in experimental social psychology, 36* (pp. 1–52). San Diego, CA: Elsevier/ Academic Press. doi:10.1016/S0065-2601(04)36001-6

Dovidio, J. F., & Gaertner, S. L. (2008). New directions in aversive racism research: Persistence and pervasiveness. In C. Willis-Esqueda (Ed.), *Nebraska Symposium on Motivation: Vol. 53. Motivational aspects of prejudice and racism.* (pp. 43–67). New York, NY: Springer.

Dovidio, J. F., Gaertner, S. L., Stewart, T. L., Esses, V. M., Vergert, M., & Hodson, G. (2004). From intervention to outcome: Processes in the reduction of bias. In W. G. Stephan & W. P. Vogt (Eds.), *Education programs for improving intergroup relations: Theory, research, and practice* (pp. 243–265). New York, NY: Teachers College Press.

Dovidio, J. F., Hebl, M., Richeson, J. A., & Shelton, J. N. (2006). Nonverbal communication, race, and intergroup interaction. In V. Manusov & M. L. Patterson (Eds.), *The Sage handbook of nonverbal communication* (pp. 481–500). Thousand Oaks, CA: Sage.

Dovidio, J. F., Kawakami, K., & Gaertner, S. L. (2002). Implicit and explicit prejudice and interracial interactions. *Journal of Personality and Social Psychology, 82*, 62–68. doi:10.1037/0022-3514.82.1.62

Doyle, A. B., & Aboud, F. E. (1995). A longitudinal study of White children's racial prejudice as social cognitive development. *Merrill-Palmer Quarterly, 41*, 210–229.

Dubinski, K. (2007, May 30). Dying. *The London Free Press*, pp. A2–A3.

Duckitt, J., Wagner, C., du Plessis, I., & Birum, I. (2002). The psychological bases of ideology and prejudice: Testing a dual process model. *Journal of Personality and Social Psychology, 83*, 75–93. doi:10.1037/0022-3514.83.1.75

Duncan, B. L. (1976). Differential social perception and attribution of intergroup violence: Testing the lower limits of stereotyping of Blacks. *Journal of Personality and Social Psychology, 34*, 590–598. doi:10.1037/0022-3514.34.4.590

Eagly, A. H. (1987). *Sex differences in social behavior: A social-role interpretation*. Hillsdale, NJ: Erlbaum.

Eagly, A. H., & Chin, J. L. (2010). Diversity and leadership in a changing world. *American Psychologist, 65*, 216–224. doi:10.1037/a0018957

Eagly, A. H., & Karau, S. J. (2002). Role congruity theory of prejudice toward female leaders. *Psychological Review, 109*, 573–598. doi:10.1037/0033-295X.109.3.573

Eagly, A. H., & Mladinic, A. (1989). Gender stereotypes and attitudes toward women and men. *Personality and Social Psychology Bulletin, 15*, 543–558. doi:10.1177/0146167289154008

Eagly, A. H., Mladinic, A., & Otto, S. (1991). Are women evaluated more favourably than men? An analysis of attitudes, beliefs, and emotions. *Psychology of Women Quarterly, 15*, 203–216. doi:10.1111/j.1471-6402.1991.tb00792.x

Eagly, A. H., & Steffen, V. (1984). Gender stereotypes stem from the distribution of women and men into social roles. *Journal of Personality and Social Psychology, 46*, 735–754. doi:10.1037/0022-3514.46.4.735

Economic Council of Canada. (1991). *Economic and social impacts of immigration* (Research report). Ottawa, Ontario, Canada: Minister of Supply and Services Canada.

Edmonds, C., & Killen, M. (2009). Do adolescents' perceptions of parental racial attitudes relate to their intergroup contact and cross-race relationships? *Group Processes & Intergroup Relations, 12*, 5–21. doi:10.1177/1368430208098773

Ellemers, N., & Barreto, M. (2009). Collective action in modern times: How modern expressions of prejudice prevent collective action. *Journal of Social Issues, 65*, 749–768. doi:10.1111/j.1540-4560.2009.01621.x

Ellingson, T. (2001). *The myth of the noble savage*. Berkeley: University of California Press.

Esses, V. M., & Dovidio, J. F. (2002). The role of emotions in determining willingness to engage in intergroup contact. *Personality and Social Psychology Bulletin, 28*, 1202–1214. doi:10.1177/01461672022812006

Esses, V. M., Dovidio, J. F., Jackson, L. M., & Armstrong, T. L. (2001). The immigration dilemma: The role of perceived group competition, ethnic prejudice, and national identity. *Journal of Social Issues, 57*, 389–412. doi:10.1111/0022-4537.00220

Esses, V. M., Dovidio, J. F., Semenya, A. H., & Jackson, L. M. (2005). Attitudes toward immigrants and immigration: The role of national and international identities. In D. Abrams, A. Hogg, & J. M. Marques (Eds.), *The social psychology of inclusion and exclusion* (pp. 317–337). Philadelphia, PA: Psychology Press.

Esses, V. M., Haddock, G., & Zanna, M. P. (1993). Values, stereotypes, and emotions as determinants of intergroup attitudes. In D. M. Mackie & D. L. Hamilton (Eds.), *Affect, cognition, and stereotyping: Interactive processes in group perception* (pp. 137–166). San Diego, CA: Academic Press.

Esses, V. M., & Hodson, G. (2006). The role of lay perceptions of ethnic prejudice in the maintenance and perpetuation of ethnic bias. *Journal of Social Issues, 62,* 453–468. doi:10.1111/j.1540-4560.2006.00468.x

Esses, V. M., & Jackson, L. M. (2008). Applying the unified instrumental model of group conflict to understanding ethnic conflict and violence: The case of Sudan. In V. M. Esses & R. A. Vernon (Eds.), *Why neighbours kill: Explaining the break-down of ethnic relations* (pp. 223–243). Malden, MA: Blackwell. doi:10.1002/9781444303056.ch10

Esses, V. M., Jackson, L. M., & Armstrong, T. L. (1998). Intergroup competition and attitudes toward immigrants and immigration: An instrumental model of group conflict. *Journal of Social Issues, 54,* 699–724.

Esses, V. M., Jackson, L. M., Dovidio, J. F., & Hodson, G. H. (2005). Instrumental relations among groups: Group competition, conflict, and prejudice. In J. F. Dovidio, P. Glick, & L. Rudman (Eds.), *On the nature of prejudice: Fifty years after Allport* (pp. 227–442). Malden, MA: Blackwell. doi:10.1002/9780470773963.ch14

Esses, V. M., Jackson, L. M., Nolan, J. M., & Armstrong, T. L. (1999). Economic threat and attitudes toward immigrants. In S. S. Halli & L. Driedger (Eds.), *Immigrant Canada: Demographic, economic, and social challenges* (pp. 212–229). Toronto, Ontario, Canada: University of Toronto Press.

Esses, V. M., & Lawson, A. (2008, October). Media effects on the dehumaniza-tion of immigrants: The role of the association of immigrants with disease. In A. Waytz (Chair), *Noble savages and savage nobles: Psychological insights into the processes of humanization and dehumanization.* Symposium conducted at the annual meeting of the Society of Experimental Social Psychology, Sacramento, CA.

Fagan, J. F., & Singer, L. T. (1979). The role of simple feature differences in infants' recognition of faces. *Infant Behavior and Development, 2,* 39–45. doi:10.1016/S0163-6383(79)80006-5

Fairbain, W. R. D. (1952). *An object-relations theory of personality.* New York, NY: Basic Books.

Fazio, R. H. (1990). Multiple processes by which attitudes guide behavior: The MODE model as an integrative framework. *Advances in Experimental Social Psychology, 23,* 75–109.

Festinger, L. A. (1957). *A theory of cognitive dissonance.* Stanford, CA: Stanford University Press.

Fidler, M., Coleman, P., & Roberts, A. (2000). Empathic response to animal suf-fering: Societal versus family influence. *Anthrozoos, 13,* 48–51. doi:10.2752/089279300786999978

Fish, J. M. (1995). Why psychologists should learn some anthropology. *American Psy-chologist, 50,* 44–45. doi:10.1037/0003-066X.50.1.44

Fishbein, H. D. (2002). *Peer prejudice and discrimination: The origins of prejudice* (2nd ed.). Mahwah, NJ: Erlbaum.

Fiske, S. T. (2005). Social cognition and the normality of prejudgment. In J. F. Dovidio, P. Glick, & L. A. Rudman (Eds.), *On the nature of prejudice: Fifty years after Allport* (pp. 36–53). Malden, MA: Blackwell.

Fiske, S. T., Cuddy, A. J. C., & Glick, P. (2007). Universal dimensions of social cognition: Warmth and competence. *Trends in Cognitive Sciences, 11*, 77–83. doi:10.1016/j.tics.2006.11.005

Fiske, S. T., Cuddy, A. J. C., Glick, P., & Xu, J. (2002). A model of (often mixed) stereotype content: Competence and warmth respectively follow from perceived status and competition. *Journal of Personality and Social Psychology, 82*, 878–902. doi:10.1037/0022-3514.82.6.878

Fiske, S. T., & Neuberg, S. L. (1990). A continuum of impression formation, from category-based to individuating processes: Influences of information and motivation on attention and interpretation. In M. P. Zanna (Ed.), *Advances in experimental social psychology* (Vol. 23, pp. 1–74). New York, NY: Academic Press.

Fiske, S. T., & Taylor, S. E. (1991). *Social cognition* (2nd ed.). New York, NY: McGraw-Hill.

Fool ducks too. (1945, May 17). *The London Echo*, p. 10.

Foucault, M. (1990). The history of sexuality: An introduction (R. Hurley Trans.). New York, NY: Vintage Books. (Original work published 1978)

Fouts, G., & Burggraf, K. (1999). Television situation comedies: Female body images and body reinforcements. *Sex Roles, 40*, 473–481. doi:10.1023/A:1018875711082

Fouts, G., & Burggraf, K. (2000). Television situation comedies: Female weight, male negative comments, and audience reactions. *Sex Roles, 42*, 925–932. doi:10.1023/A:1007054618340

Fouts, G., & Vaughan, K. (2002). Television situation comedies: Male weight, negative references, and audience reactions. *Sex Roles, 46*, 439–442. doi:10.1023/A:1020469715532

Freud, S. (1955). *Moses and monotheism*. New York, NY: Vintage Books. (Original work published 1939)

Freud, S. (1961). *Civilization and its discontents*. New York, NY: Norton. (Original work published 1929)

Freud, S. (1967). *Group psychology and the analysis of the ego*. New York, NY: Liveright. (Original work published 1921)

Friedman, C. (2007). An object relations approach to studying prejudice with specific reference to anti-Semitism: The long-term use of a lethal apocalyptic projection. *International Journal of Applied Psychoanalytic Studies, 4*, 31–40. doi:10.1002/aps.120

Fritsche, I., & Jonas, E. (2005). Gender conflict and worldview defence. *British Journal of Social Psychology, 44*(Pt. 4), 571–581. doi:10.1348/014466605X27423

Gailliot, G. T., Peruche, M., Plant, E. A., & Baumeister, R. F. (2009). Stereotypes and prejudice in the blood: Sucrose drinks reduce prejudice and stereotyping. *Journal of Experimental Social Psychology, 45*, 288–290. doi:10.1016/j.jesp.2008.09.003

Gaertner, S. L., & Dovidio, J. F. (1986). The aversive form of racism. In J. F. Dovidio & S. L. Gaertner (Eds.), *Prejudice, discrimination and racism* (pp. 61–89). San Diego, CA: Academic Press.

Gaertner, S. L., & Dovidio, J. F. (2000). *Reducing intergroup bias: The common ingroup identity model*. Philadelphia, PA: Psychology Press.

Gaertner, S. L., & Dovidio, J. F. (2009). A common ingroup identity: A categorization-based approach for reducing intergroup bias. In T. D. Nelson (Ed.), *Handbook of prejudice, stereotyping, and discrimination* (pp. 489–505). New York, NY: Psychology Press.

Gallaudet University. (2009). Retrieved from http://www.gallaudet.edu

Garcia, M. (2005, April 21). Muslims detained at border sue homeland border security. *The Washington Post*, p. A8.

Gardner, R. A., & Gardner, B. T. (1969, August 15). Teaching language to a chimpanzee. *Science, 165*, 664–672. doi:10.1126/science.165.3894.664

Gelman, S. A., & Heyman, G. D. (1999). Carrot-eaters and creature believers: The effects of lexicalization on children's inferences about social categories. *Psychological Science, 10*, 489–493. doi:10.1111/1467-9280.00194

George, L. (2007, May 14). R U there, Allah? *Macleans*. Retrieved from http://www.macleans.ca/culture/entertainment/article.jsp?content=20070514_105167_105167

Gilbert, D. T., & Hixon, J. G. (1991). The trouble of thinking: Activation and application of stereotypic beliefs. *Journal of Personality and Social Psychology, 60*, 509–517. doi:10.1037/0022-3514.60.4.509

Gill, M. J. (2004). When information does not deter stereotyping: Prescriptive stereotyping can foster bias under conditions that deter descriptive stereotyping. *Journal of Experimental Social Psychology, 40*, 619–632. doi:10.1016/j.jesp.2003.12.001

Glick, P., & Fiske, S. T. (1996). The Ambivalent Sexism Inventory: Differentiating hostile and benevolent sexism. *Journal of Personality and Social Psychology, 70*, 491–512. doi:10.1037/0022-3514.70.3.491

Glick, P., & Fiske, S. T. (1999). The Ambivalence Toward Men Inventory: Differentiating hostile and benevolent beliefs about men. *Psychology of Women Quarterly, 23*, 519–536. doi:10.1111/j.1471-6402.1999.tb00379.x

Glick, P., & Fiske, S. T. (2001). Ambivalent stereotypes as legitimizing ideologies: Differentiating paternalistic and envious prejudice. In J. T. Jost & B. Major (Eds.), *The psychology of legitimacy: Emerging perspectives on ideology, justice, and intergroup relations* (pp. 278–306). Cambridge, England: Cambridge University Press.

Glick, P., Fiske, S. T., Mladinic, A., Saiz, J. L., Abrams, D., Masswer, B., . . . López, W. L. (2000). Beyond prejudice as simple antipathy: Hostile and benevolent sexism across cultures. *Journal of Personality and Social Psychology, 79*, 763–775. doi:10.1037/0022-3514.79.5.763

Glick, P., Lameiras, M., & Rodriguez Castro, Y. (2002). Education and Catholic religiosity as predictors of hostile and benevolent sexism toward women and men. *Sex Roles*, *47*, 433–441. doi:10.1023/A:1021696209949

Goetz, D., & James, P. (2001). What can evolutionary theory say about ethnic phenomena? In P. James & D. Goetz (Eds.), *Evolutionary theory and ethnic conflict* (pp. 3–18). Westport, CT: Praeger.

Goff, P. A., Eberhardt, J. L., Williams, M. J., & Jackson, M. C. (2008). Not yet human: Implicit knowledge, historical dehumanization, and contemporary consequences. *Journal of Personality and Social Psychology*, *94*, 292–306. doi:10.1037/0022-3514.94.2.292

Goldenberg, J. L., Arndt, J., Hart, J., & Routledge, C. (2008). Uncovering an existential barrier to breast self-exam behaviour. *Journal of Experimental Social Psychology*, *44*, 260–274. doi:10.1016/j.jesp.2007.05.002

Goldenberg, J. L., Heflick, N., Vaes, J., Motyl, M., & Greenberg, J. (2009). Of mice and men, and objectified women: A terror management account of infrahumanization. *Group Processes & Intergroup Relations*, *12*, 763–776. doi:10.1177/1368430209340569

Goldenberg, J. L., Pyszczynski, T., Greenberg, J., Solomon, S., Kluck, B., & Cornwell, R. (2001). I am not an animal: Mortality salience, disgust, and the denial of human creatureliness. *Journal of Experimental Psychology: General*, *130*, 427–435. doi:10.1037/0096-3445.130.3.427

Gordijn, E. H., Yzerbyt, V., Wigboldus, D., & Dumont, M. (2006). Emotional reactions to harmful intergroup behaviour. *European Journal of Social Psychology*, *36*, 15–30. doi:10.1002/ejsp.296

Government of Ontario. (2009). *Education Act*. Retrieved from http://www.e-laws.gov.on.ca/html/statutes/english/elaws_statutes_90e02_e.htm#BK105

Grandin, T. (2005). *Animals in translation: Using the mysteries of autism to decode animal behavior*. New York, NY: Scribner.

Grandin, T. (2009). *Animals make us human: Creating the best life for animals*. Boston, MA: Houghton Mifflin/Harcourt.

Green, D. A., & Kesselman, J. R. (2006). *Dimensions of inequality in Canada*. Vancouver, British Columbia, Canada: University of British Columbia Press.

Green, D. P., Glaser, J., & Rich, A. (1998). From lynching to gay bashing: The elusive connection between economic conditions and hate. *Journal of Personality and Social Psychology*, *75*, 82–92. doi:10.1037/0022-3514.75.1.82

Green, D. P., & Wong, J. S. (2008). Tolerance and the contact hypothesis: A field experiment. In E. Borgida, C. Federico, & J. L. Sullivan (Eds.), *Political psychology of democratic citizenship* (pp. 228–246). London, England: Oxford University Press.

Green, E. (2009). Who can enter? A multilevel analysis on public support for immigration criteria across 20 European countries. *Group Processes & Intergroup Relations*, *12*, 41–60. doi:10.1177/1368430208098776

Greenberg, B. S., Eastin, M., Hofschire, L., Lachlan, K., & Brownell, K. D. (2003). Portrayals of overweight and obese individuals on commercial television. *American Journal of Public Health, 93*, 1342–1348. doi:10.2105/AJPH.93.8.1342

Greenberg, J., Pyszcznski, T., Solomon, S., Rosenblatt, A., Veeder, M., Kirkland, S., & Lyon, D. (1990). Evidence for terror management II: The effects of mortality salience reactions to those who threaten or bolster the cultural worldview. *Journal of Personality and Social Psychology, 58*, 308–318. doi:10.1037/0022-3514.58.2.308

Greenberg, J., Schimel, J., Martens, A., Solomon, S., & Pyszcznyski, T. (2001). Sympathy for the devil: Evidence that reminding Whites of their mortality promotes more favourable reactions to White racists. *Motivation and Emotion, 25*, 113–133. doi:10.1023/A:1010613909207

Greenwald, A. G., & Banaji, M. R. (1995). Implicit social cognition: Attitudes, self-esteem and stereotypes. *Psychological Review, 102*, 4–27. doi:10.1037/0033-295X.102.1.4

Greenwald, A. G., Poehlman, T. A., Uhlmann, E. L., & Banaji, M. R. (2009). Understanding and using the Implicit Associations Test III: Meta-analysis of predictive validity. *Journal of Personality and Social Psychology, 97*, 17–41. doi:10.1037/a0015575

Guimond, S., Dambrun, M., Michinov, N., & Duarte, S. (2003). Does social dominance generate prejudice? Integrating individual and contextual determinants of intergroup cognitions. *Journal of Personality and Social Psychology, 84*, 697–721. doi:10.1037/0022-3514.84.4.697

Gullone, E., & Robertson, N. (2008). The relationship between bullying and animal abuse behaviors in adolescents: The importance of witnessing animal abuse. *Journal of Applied Developmental Psychology, 29*, 371–379. doi:10.1016/j.appdev.2008.06.004

Gunst, L. (1995). *Born fi' dead.* New York, NY: Henry Holt.

Guthrie, R. V. (2004). *Even the rat was White: A historical view of psychology* (2nd ed.). Boston, MA: Pearson.

Haines, E. L., & Jost, J. T. (2000). Placating the powerless: Effects of legitimate and illegitimate explanation on affect, memory, and stereotyping. *Social Justice Research, 13*, 219–236. doi:10.1023/A:1026481205719

Hall, D. L., Matz, D. C., & Wood, W. (2010). Why don't we practice what we preach? A meta-analytic review of religious racism. *Personality and Social Psychology Review, 14*, 126–139. doi:10.1177/1088868309352179

Hamilton, W. D. (1964). The genetic evolution of social behavior I and II. *Journal of Theoretical Biology, 7*, 1–16. doi:10.1016/0022-5193(64)90038-4

Harris, S. (2004). *The end of faith: Religion, terror, and the future of reason.* New York, NY: Norton.

Hart, A. J., Whalen, P. J., Shine, L. M., McInerney, S. C., Fischer, H., & Rauch, S. L. (2000). Differential response in the human amygdala to racial outgroup versus ingroup face stimuli. *Neuroreport, 11,* 2351–2355. doi:10.1097/00001756-200008030-00004

Haslam, N. (2006). Dehumanization: An integrative review. *Personality and Social Psychology Review, 10,* 252–264. doi:10.1207/s15327957pspr1003_4

Haslam, N., Kashima, Y., Loughan, S., Shi, J., & Suiter, C. (2008). Subhuman, inhuman and superhuman: Contrasting humans with nonhumans in three cultures. *Social Cognition, 26,* 248–258. doi:10.1521/soco.2008.26.2.248

Haslam, N., Rothschild, L., & Ernst, D. (2000). Essentialist beliefs about social categories. *British Journal of Social Psychology, 39,* 113–127. doi:10.1348/014466600164363

Hebl, M. R., King, E. G., Glick, P., Singletary, S. L., & Kazama, S. (2007). Hostile and benevolent reactions toward pregnant women: Complementary interpersonal punishments and rewards that maintain traditional roles. *Journal of Applied Psychology, 92,* 1499–1511. doi:10.1037/0021-9010.92.6.1499

Henry Louis Gates, Jr. (2009). Retrieved from http://en.wikipedia.org/wiki/Henry_Louis_Gates,_Jr.

Henry, P. J., & Hardin, C. D. (2006). The contact hypothesis revisited: Status bias in the reduction of implicit prejudice in the United States and Lebanon. *Psychological Science, 17,* 862–868. doi:10.1111/j.1467-9280.2006.01795.x

Herek, G. M. (2000). The psychology of sexual prejudice. *Current Directions in Psychological Science, 9,* 19–22. doi:10.1111/1467-8721.00051

Herouxville Town Charter. (2007). *Publication of standards.* Retrieved from http://herouxville-quebec.blogspot.com

Hickman, C. B. (1997). The devil and the one drop rule: Racial categories, African Americans, and the U.S. Census. *Michigan Law Review, 95,* 1161–1265. doi:10.2307/1290008

Himes, S. M., & Thompson, J. K. (2007). Fat stigmatization in television shows and movies: A content analysis. *Obesity, 15,* 712–718. doi:10.1038/oby.2007.635

Hinojosa, V. J., & Park, J. Z. (2004). Religion and the paradox of racial inequality attitudes. *Journal for the Scientific Study of Religion, 43,* 229–238. doi:10.1111/j.1468-5906.2004.00229.x

Hirschfeld, L. A. (2001). On a folk theory of society: Children, evolution, and mental representations. *Personality and Social Psychology Review, 5,* 107–117. doi:10.1207/S15327957PSPR0502_2

Ho, A. K., & Sidanius, J. (2010). Preserving positive identities: Public and private regard for one's ingroup and susceptibility to stereotype threat. *Group Processes & Intergroup Relations, 13,* 55–67. doi:10.1177/1368430209340910

Hoffman, M. L. (1981). Is altruism a part of human nature? *Journal of Personality and Social Psychology, 40,* 121–137. doi:10.1037/0022-3514.40.1.121

Hofmann, W., Gawronski, B., Gschwendner, T., Le, H., & Schmitt, M. (2005). A meta-analysis on the correlation between the Implicit Association Test and explicit self-report measures. *Personality and Social Psychology Bulletin, 31,* 1369–1385. doi:10.1177/0146167205275613

Holtz, P., & Wagner, W. (2009). Essentialism and attribution of monstrosity in racist discourse: Right-wing Internet postings about Africans and Jews. *Journal of Community and Applied Social Psychology, 19*, 411–425.

Homer-Dixon, T. F., Boutwell, J. H., & Rathjens, G. W. (1993). Environmental change and violent conflict. *Scientific American, 268*, 38–45. doi:10.1038/scientificamerican0293-38

Hood, E. (2005). Shift in sex ratio: Male numbers sink in Great Lakes region. *Environmental Health Perspectives, 113*, A686–A687. doi:10.1289/ehp.113-a686b

Hood, R. W., Jr., Morris, R. J., & Watson, P. J. (1986). Maintenance of religious fundamentalism. *Psychological Reports, 59*, 547–559.

Hovland, C. I., & Sears, R. (1940). Minor studies in aggression: VI: Correlation of lynchings with economic indices. *Journal of Psychology, 9*, 301–310.

Human Rights Committee. (2006). *Concluding observations of the Human Rights Committee.* Retrieved from http://www.unhchr.ch/tbs/doc.nsf/(Symbol)/CCPR.C.CAN.CO.5.En?OpenDocument

Hunsberger, B., & Jackson, L. M. (2005). Religion, meaning, and prejudice. *Journal of Social Issues, 61*, 807–826. doi:10.1111/j.1540-4560.2005.00433.x

Hyers, L. L. (2006). Myths used to legitimize the exploitation of animals: An application of social dominance theory. *Anthrozoos, 19*, 194–210. doi:10.2752/089279306785415538

Immigration Watch Canada. (2009). Retrieved from http://immigrationwatchcanada.org

Intergovernmental Panel on Climate Change. (2007). Frequently asked questions. In S. Solomon, D. Qin, M. Manning, Z. Chen, M. Marquis, K. B. Avery, . . . H. L. Miller (Eds.), *Climate Change 2007: The physical science basis. Contribution of working group I to the fourth assessment report of the Intergovernmental Panel on Climate Change* (pp. 93–127). Cambridge, England: Cambridge University Press. Retrieved from http://www.ipcc.ch/publications_and_data/ar4/wg1/en/faqs.html

Ipsos Reid. (2001). *Paws and claws: A syndicated study on pet ownership.* Toronto, Ontario, Canada: Author.

Islam, M. R., & Jahjah, M. (2001). Predictors of young Australians' attitudes toward Aboriginals, Asians and Arabs. *Social Behavior and Personality, 29*, 569–579. doi:10.2224/sbp.2001.29.6.569

Ito, T. A., Willadsen-Jensen, E., & Correll, C. (2007). Social neuroscience and social perception: New perspectives on categorization, prejudice, and stereotyping. In E. Harmon-Jones & P. Winkielman (Eds.), *Social neuroscience: Integrating biological and psychological explanations of social behavior* (pp. 401–421). New York, NY: Guilford Press.

Iyer, A., & Ryan, M. K. (2009). Why do men and women challenge gender discrimination in the workplace? The role of group status and in-group identification in predicting pathways to collective action. *Journal of Social Issues, 65*, 791–814. doi:10.1111/j.1540-4560.2009.01625.x

Iyer, A., Schmader, T., & Lickel, B. (2007). Why individuals protest the perceived transgressions of their country: The role of anger, shame, and guilt. *Personality and Social Psychology Bulletin, 33*, 572–587. doi:10.1177/0146167206297402

Jackman, M. R. (1994). *The velvet glove: Paternalism and conflict in gender, class, and race relations.* Berkeley: University of California Press.

Jackman, M. R. (2001). License to kill: Violence and legitimacy in expropriative social relations. In J. T. Jost & B. Major (Eds.), *The psychology of legitimacy: Emerging perspectives on ideology, justice, and intergroup relations* (pp. 437–467). New York, NY: Cambridge University Press.

Jackson, L. M., Bitacola, L., Esses, V. M., & Janes, L. (2010, June). *Social dominance orientation and environmental decision making.* Poster presented at the biennial meeting of the Society for the Psychological Study of Social Issues, New Orleans, LA.

Jackson, L. M., & Esses, V. M. (1997). Of scripture and ascription: The relation between religious fundamentalism and intergroup helping. *Personality and Social Psychology Bulletin, 23*, 893–906. doi:10.1177/0146167297238009

Jackson, L. M., & Esses, V. M. (2000). Effects of perceived economic competition on people's willingness to help empower immigrants. *Group Processes & Intergroup Relations, 3*, 419–435. doi:10.1177/1368430200003004006

Jackson, L. M., Esses, V. M., & Burris, C. T. (2001). Contemporary sexism and discrimination: The importance of respect for men and women. *Personality and Social Psychology Bulletin, 27*, 48–61. doi:10.1177/0146167201271005

Jafri, B. (2008). Organizing at school. In A. Gosine & C. Teelucksingh (Eds.), *Environmental justice and racism in Canada* (pp. 130–135). Toronto, Ontario, Canada: Emond Montgomery.

Janes, L., Jackson, L. M., & Esses, V. M. (2010, January). *Social dominance orientation and perceptions of resource entitlement.* Paper presented at the annual meeting of the Society for Personality and Social Psychology, Las Vegas, NV.

Janes, L., Jackson, L. M., Esses, V. M., & Sibanda, C. (2009, June). *Resource entitlement: Is environmental damage to foreign nations more acceptable if Canada stands to benefit?* Poster presented at the 70th Annual Convention of the Canadian Psychological Association, Montreal, Quebec, Canada.

Jayaratne, T. E., Ybarra, O., Sheldon, J. P., Brown, T. N., Feldbaum, M., Pfeffer, C. A., . . . Petty, E. M. (2006). White Americans' genetic lay theories of race differences and sexual orientation: Their relationship with prejudice toward Blacks and gay men and lesbians. *Group Processes & Intergroup Relations, 9*, 77–94. doi:10.1177/1368430206059863

Jena Six. (2009). Retrieved from http://www.wikipedia.org/wiki/Jena_six

Johnson, G. R. (2001). The roots of ethnic conflict: An evolutionary perspective. In P. James & D. Goetz (Eds.), *Evolutionary theory and ethnic conflict* (pp. 19–38). Westport, CT: Praeger.

Jones, J. M. (1997). *Prejudice and racism* (2nd ed.). New York, NY: McGraw-Hill.

Jorde, L. B., & Wooding, S. P. (2004). Genetic variation, classification, and "race." *Nature Genetics, 36*(11, Suppl.), S28–S33. doi:10.1038/ng1435

Jost, J. T. (2006). The end of the end of ideology. *American Psychologist, 61,* 651–670. doi:10.1037/0003-066X.61.7.651

Jost, J. T., & Banaji, M. R. (1994). The role of stereotyping in system justification and the production of false consciousness. *British Journal of Social Psychology, 33,* 1–27.

Jost, J. T., Banaji, M. R., & Nosek, B. A. (2004). A decade of system-justification theory: Accumulated evidence of conscious and unconscious bolstering of the status quo. *Political Psychology, 25,* 881–919. doi:10.1111/j.1467-9221.2004.00402.x

Jost, J. T., Burgess, D., & Mosso, C. O. (2001). Conflicts of legitimation among self, group, and system: The integrative potential of system justification theory. In J. T. Jost & B. Major (Eds.), *The psychology of legitimacy: Emerging perspectives on ideology, justice, and intergroup relations* (pp. 363–388). Cambridge, England: Cambridge University Press.

Jost, J. T., Kivetz, Y., Rubini, M., Guermandi, G., & Mosso, C. (2005). System justifying functions of regional and ethnic stereotypes: Cross-national evidence. *Social Justice Research, 18,* 305–333. doi:10.1007/s11211-005-6827-z

Jost, J. T., & Major, B. (2001). Emerging perspectives on the psychology of legitimacy. In J. T. Jost & B. Major (Eds.), *The psychology of legitimacy: Emerging perspectives on ideology, justice, and intergroup relations* (pp. 3–32). Cambridge, England: Cambridge University Press.

Jost, J. T., & Thompson, E. P. (2000). Group-based dominance and opposition to equality as independent predictors of self-esteem, ethnocentrism and social political attitudes among African Americans and European Americans. *Journal of Experimental Social Psychology, 36,* 209–232. doi:10.1006/jesp.1999.1403

Jussim, L., Cain, T. R., Crawford, J. T., Harber, K., & Cohen, F. (2009). The unbearable accuracy of stereotypes. In T. D. Nelson (Ed.), *Handbook of prejudice, stereotyping and discrimination* (pp. 199–227). New York, NY: Psychology Press.

Jussim, L., & Harber, K. D. (2005). Teacher expectations and self-fulfilling prophecies: Knowns and unknowns, resolved and unresolved controversies. *Personality and Social Psychology Review, 9,* 131–155. doi:10.1207/s15327957pspr0902_3

Kamans, E., Gordijn, E. H., Oldenhuis, H., & Otten, S. (2009). What I think you see is what you get: Influence of prejudice on assimilation to negative meta-stereotypes among Dutch Moroccan teenagers. *European Journal of Social Psychology, 39,* 842–851. doi:10.1002/ejsp.593

Katz, P. A. (2003). Racists or tolerant multiculturalists? How do they begin? *American Psychologist, 58,* 897–909. doi:10.1037/0003-066X.58.11.897b

Katz, P. A., & Seavey, C. (1973). Labels and children's perception of faces. *Child Development, 44,* 770–775. doi:10.2307/1127722

Kawakami, K., Phills, C. E., Dovidio, J. F., & Steele, J. R. (2007). (Close) distance makes the heart grow fonder: Improving implicit racial attitudes and interracial interactions through approach behaviors. *Journal of Personality and Social Psychology, 92,* 957–971. doi:10.1037/0022-3514.92.6.957

Keita, S. O. Y., Kittles, R. A., Royal, C. D. M., Bonney, G. E., Furbert-Harris, P., Dunston, G. M., & Rotimi, C. M. (2004). Conceptualizing human variation. *Nature Genetics, 36*(11, Suppl.), S17–S20. doi:10.1038/ng1455

Kelman, H. C. (2001). Reflections on social and psychological processes of legitimization and delegitimization. In J. T. Jost & B. Major (Eds.), *The psychology of legitimacy: Emerging perspectives on ideology, justice, and intergroup relations* (pp. 54–73). Cambridge, England: Cambridge University Press.

Kiesner, J., Maass, A., Cadinu, M., & Vallese, I. (2003). Risk factors for ethnic prejudice during early adolescence. *Social Development, 12,* 288–308. doi:10.1111/1467-9507.00234

Kinsey, A. C., Pomeroy, W. B., & Martin, C. E. (1948). *Sexual behavior in the human male.* Philadelphia, PA: W. B. Saunders.

Klein, M. (1949). *The psychoanalysis of children.* London, England: Hogarth Press/Institute of Psychoanalysis.

Knight, S., & Herzog, H. (2009). All creatures great and small: New perspectives on psychology and human-animal interactions. *Journal of Social Issues, 65,* 451–461. doi:10.1111/j.1540-4560.2009.01608.x

Knight, S., Vrij, A., Bard, K., & Brandon, D. (2009). Science versus human welfare? Understanding attitudes toward animal use. *Journal of Social Issues, 65,* 463–483. doi:10.1111/j.1540-4560.2009.01609.x

Kohler, N. (2007, October 8). Doomsday: Alberta stands accused. *Macleans.* Retrieved http://www.macleans.ca/article.jsp?content=20071008_110103_110103&source=srch

Kovel, J. (2003). Racism and ecology. *Socialism and Democracy, 17,* 99–107. doi:10.1080/08854300308428343

Kurzban, R., & Leary, M. R. (2001). Evolutionary origins of stigmatization: The functions of social exclusion. *Psychological Bulletin, 127,* 187–208. doi:10.1037/0033-2909.127.2.187

Kwan, V. S. Y., & Cuddy, A. J. C. (2008, October). *(Non-human) animal stereotypes: Reflections of anthropomorphism and cultural differences in system-justification.* Paper presented at the Annual Meeting of the Society for Experimental Social Psychology, Sacramento, CA.

LaFrance, M., & Banaji, M. (1992). Toward a reconsideration of the gender-emotion relationship. In M. Clark (Ed.), *Emotion and social behavior* (pp. 178–201). Newbury Park, CA: Sage.

La Prairie, C. (2002). Aboriginal over-representation in the criminal justice system: A tale of nine cities. *Canadian Journal of Criminology, 44,* 181–208.

Layton, C. (2009, June). Draft AODA employment standard released. *Arch Alert,* pp. 1–3.

LeDoux, J. E. (2000). Emotion circuits in the brain. *Annual Review of Neuroscience, 23,* 155–184. doi:10.1146/annurev.neuro.23.1.155

Letheren, L. (2009, June). Eddy Morten v. Air Canada's blanket policy for Deaf-Blind passengers discriminatory. *Arch Alert,* pp. 3–5.

LeVine, R. A., & Campbell, D. T. (1972). *Ethnocentrism: Theories of conflict, ethnic attitudes, and group behavior*. New York, NY: Wiley.

Levy, B. R., & Leifheit-Limson, E. (2009). The stereotype-matching effect: Greater influence on functioning when age stereotypes correspond to outcomes. *Psychology and Aging, 24*, 230–233. doi:10.1037/a0014563

Lewington, J. (2008, March 12). Asian protestors want Ford to apologize for remarks. *The Globe and Mail*, p. A12.

Leyens, J. P., Cortes, B. P., Demoulin, S., Dovidio, J. F., Fiske, S. T., Gaunt, R., . . . Vaes, J. (2003). Emotional prejudice, essentialism and nationalism: The 2002 Tajfel Lecture. *European Journal of Social Psychology, 33*, 703–717. doi:10.1002/ejsp.170

Louis, W. R. (2009). Collective action—and then what? *Journal of Social Issues, 65*, 727–748. doi:10.1111/j.1540-4560.2009.01623.x

Maass, A., & Cadinu, M. (2003). Stereotype threat: When minority members underperform. *European Review of Social Psychology, 14*, 243–275. doi:10.1080/10463280340000072

Maass, A., Ceccarelli, R., & Rudin, S. (1996). Linguistic intergroup bias: Evidence for ingroup protective motivation. *Journal of Personality and Social Psychology, 71*, 512–526. doi:10.1037/0022-3514.71.3.512

Macrae, C. N., & Bodenhausen, G. V. (2000). Social cognition: Thinking categorically about others. *Annual Review of Psychology, 51*, 93–120. doi:10.1146/annurev.psych.51.1.93

Macrae, C. N., Bodenhausen, G. V., Milne, A. B., & Jetten, J. (1994). Out of mind but back in sight: Stereotypes on the rebound. *Journal of Personality and Social Psychology, 67*, 808–817. doi:10.1037/0022-3514.67.5.808

Mahalingam, R. (2003). Essentialism, culture, and power: Representations of social class. *Journal of Social Issues, 59*, 733–749.

Mahalingam, R. (2007). Essentialism, power, and the representation of social categories: A folk sociology perspective. *Human Development, 50*, 300–319. doi:10.1159/000109832

Mair, R. (2007). Harriet Nahanee did not die in vain. *The Tyee*. Retrieved from http://thetyee.ca/Views/2007/03/05/Eagleridge/

Malkowski, G. (2005). *Submission to the standing committee on social policy with respect to Bill 118: accessibility for Ontarioans with disabilities act, 2004*. Toronto, Ontario, Canada: Canadian Hearing Society.

Malkowski, G. (2006, November). *Human rights violations: Deaf people*. Presentation given at the Deaf Legal Clinic Recruitment and Training Session of the Law Society of Upper Canada, Toronto, Ontario, Canada.

Malkowski, G. (2008). Struggles, challenges and accomplishments of Deaf, Deafened and Hard of Hearing people. In Psychiatric Patient Advocate Office, *Honouring the past, shaping the future: 25 years of progress in mental health advocacy and protection* (25th Anniversary Report 1983–2008, pp. 62–64). Toronto, Ontario, Canada: Queen's Printer for Ontario.

Malkowski, G. (2009). Audism. *Canadian Hearing Report, 3*(4), 28–30.

Marcu, A., Lyons, E., & Hegarty, P. (2007). Dilemmatic human-animal boundaries in Britain and Romania: Post-materialist and materialist dehumanization. *British Journal of Social Psychology, 46*, 875–893. doi:10.1348/014466607X174356

Marlow, J. (2006). *Darfur diaries: Stories of survival.* New York, NY: Nation Books.

Marques, J. M., Yzerbyt, V. Y., & Leyens, J. P. (1988). The black sheep effect: Extremity of judgment toward ingroup members as a function of group identification. *European Journal of Social Psychology, 18*, 1–16. doi:10.1002/ejsp.2420180102

Mason, J., & Finelli, M. (2006). Brave new farm? In P. Singer (Ed.), *In defense of animals: The second wave* (pp. 104–122). Malden, MA: Blackwell.

Masserman, J. H., Wechkin, S., & Terris, W. (1964). "Altruistic" behavior in rhesus monkeys. *American Journal of Psychiatry, 121*, 584–585.

Maxim, P. S., White, J. P., Beavon, D., & Whitehead, P. C. (2001). Dispersion and polarization of income among Aboriginal and non-Aboriginal Canadians. *Canadian Review of Sociology and Anthropology/Revue Canadienne de Sociologie et d'Anthropologie, 38*, 465–476.

McConahay, J. G. (1986). Modern racism, ambivalence, and the Modern Racism Scale. In J. F. Dovidio & S. L. Gaertner (Eds.), *Prejudice, discrimination, and racism* (pp. 91–125). San Diego, CA: Academic Press.

McIntosh, P. (2003). White privilege: Unpacking the invisible knapsack. In S. Plous (Ed.), *Understanding prejudice and discrimination* (pp. 191–196). Boston, MA: McGraw-Hill.

McLaren, L. M. (2003). Anti-immigrant prejudice in Europe: Contact, threat perception, and preferences for the expulsion of migrants. *Social Forces, 81*, 909–936. doi:10.1353/sof.2003.0038

Mehl, M. R., Vazire, S., Ramirez-Esparza, N., Slatcher, R. B., & Pennebaker, J. W. (2007, July 6). Are women really more talkative than men? *Science, 317*, 82. doi:10.1126/science.1139940

Merskin, D. (2004). The construction of Arabs as enemies: Post-September 11 discourse of George W. Bush. *Mass Communication & Society, 7*, 157–175. doi:10.1207/s15327825mcs0702_2

Merton, R. K. (1948). The self-fulfilling prophecy. *Antioch Review, 8*, 193–210.

Midgley, D. (2005). *The essential Mary Midgley.* New York, NY: Routledge.

Milgram, S. (1974). *Obedience to authority: An experimental view.* New York, NY: Harper & Row.

Miller, D. A., Cronin, T., Garcia, A. L., & Branscombe, N. R. (2009). The relative impact of anger and efficacy on collective action is affected by feelings of fear. *Group Processes & Intergroup Relations, 12*, 445–462. doi:10.1177/1368430209105046

Moghaddam, F. M. (2005). The staircase to terrorism: A psychological exploration. *American Psychologist, 60*, 161–169. doi:10.1037/0003-066X.60.2.161

Moghaddam, F. M. (2008). *Multiculturalism and intergroup relations.* Washington, DC: American Psychological Association. doi:10.1037/11682-000

Mohai, P., & Saha, R. (2007). Racial inequality in the distribution of hazardous waste: A nation-level reassessment. *Social Problems, 54*, 343–370. doi:10.1525/sp. 2007.54.3.343

Mohipp, C., & Morry, M. M. (2004). The relationship of symbolic beliefs and prior contact to heterosexuals' attitudes to gay men and lesbians. *Canadian Journal of Behavioural Science, 36*, 36–44. doi:10.1037/h0087214

Molina, L. E., & Whittig, M. A. (2006). Relative importance of contact conditions in explaining prejudice reduction in a classroom context: Separate and equal? *Journal of Social Issues, 62*, 489–509. doi:10.1111/j.1540-4560.2006.00470.x

Monteith, M. J., Deneed, N. F., & Tooman, G. D. (1996). The effect of social norm activation on the expression of opinions concerning gay men and blacks. *Basic and Applied Social Psychology, 18*, 267–288. doi:10.1207/s15324834basp1803_2

Monteith, M. J., & Mark, A. Y. (2009). The self-regulation of prejudice. In T. D. Nelson (Ed.), *Handbook of prejudice, stereotyping, and discrimination* (pp. 507–524). New York, NY: Psychology Press.

Morrison, M. A., Morrison, T. G., Harriman, R. L., & Jewell, L. M. (2008). Old-fashioned and modern prejudice toward Aboriginals in Canada. In M. E. Morrison & T. G. Morrison (Eds.), *The psychology of modern prejudice* (pp. 277–305). New York, NY: Nova Science.

Morton, T. A., Postmes, T., Haslam, S. A., & Hornsey, M. J. (2009). Theorizing gender in the face of social change: Is there anything essential about essentialism? *Journal of Personality and Social Psychology, 96*, 653–664. doi:10.1037/a0012966

Mouchetant-Rostaing, Y., Giard, M. H., Delpuech, C., Echallier, J. F., & Pernier, J. (2000). Early signs of visual categorization for biological and non-biological stimuli in humans. *Neuroreport, 11*, 2521–2525. doi:10.1097/00001756-200008030-00035

Musselman, C., & Akamatsu, C. T. (1999). Interpersonal communication skills of deaf adolescents and their relationship to communication history. *Journal of Deaf Studies and Deaf Education, 4*, 305–320. doi:10.1093/deafed/4.4.305

Nagda, B. A. (2006). Breaking barriers, crossing borders, building bridges: Communication processes in intergroup dialogues. *Journal of Social Issues, 62*, 553–576. doi:10.1111/j.1540-4560.2006.00473.x

Narter, D. B. (2006). The development of prejudice in children. In B. E. Whitely Jr. & M. E. Kite, *The psychology of prejudice and discrimination* (pp. 260–299). Belmont, CA: Thomson Wadsworth.

Neuberg, S. L., & Cottrell, C. A. (2006). Evolutionary bases of prejudices. In M. Schaller, J. A. Simpson, & D. T. Kenrick (Eds.), *Evolution and social psychology* (pp. 163–187). Madison, CT: Psychosocial Press.

Neuberg, S. L., Smith, D. M., & Asher, T. (2000). Why people stigmatize: Toward a biocultural framework. In T. Heatherton, R. Kleck, J. G. Hull, & M. Hebl (Eds.), *The social psychology of stigma* (pp. 31–61). New York, NY: Guilford Press.

Newcomb, T. M. (1961). *The acquaintance process*. New York, NY: Holt, Rinehart & Winston.

Nicol, A. M., Charbonneau, D., & Boies, K. (2007). Right-wing authoritarianism and social dominance orientation in a Canadian military sample. *Military Psychology, 19*, 239–257.

Nisbett, R. E. (2005). Heredity, environment and race differences in IQ: A commentary on Rushton and Jensen (2005). *Psychology, Public Policy, and Law, 11*, 302–310. doi:10.1037/1076-8971.11.2.302

Obama, B. (2008, January 20). Inaugural address. *The Globe and Mail*. Retrieved from http://www.theglobeandmail.com

Öhman, A. (2005, July 29). Conditioned fear of a face: A prelude to ethnic enmity? *Science, 309*, 711–713. doi:10.1126/science.1116710

Olson, J. M., & Janes, L. M. (2002). Vigilance for differences: Heightened impact of differences on surprise. *Personality and Social Psychology Bulletin, 28*, 1084–1093. doi:10.1177/01461672022811007

Olson, M. A., & Fazio, R. H. (2001). Implicit attitude formation through classical conditioning. *Psychological Science, 12*, 413–417. doi:10.1111/1467-9280.00376

Olson, M. A., & Fazio, R. H. (2002). Implicit acquisition and manifestation of classically conditioned attitudes. *Social Cognition, 20*, 89–103. doi:10.1521/soco.20.2.89.20992

Olson, M. A., & Fazio, R. H. (2006). Reducing automatically activated racial prejudice through implicit evaluative conditioning. *Personality and Social Psychology Bulletin, 32*, 421–433. doi:10.1177/0146167205284004

Olsson, A., Ebert, J. P., Banaji, M. R., & Phelps, E. A. (2005, July 29). The role of social groups in the persistence of learned fear. *Science, 309*, 785–787. doi:10.1126/science.1113551

Ong, A. D., Fuller-Rowell, T., & Burrow, A. (2009). Racial discrimination and the stress process. *Journal of Personality and Social Psychology, 96*, 1259–1271. doi:10.1037/a0015335

Opotow, S. (1990). Moral exclusion and injustice: An introduction. *Journal of Social Issues, 46*(1), 1–20. doi:10.1111/j.1540-4560.1990.tb00268.x

Opotow, S. (1993). Animals and the scope of justice. *Journal of Social Issues, 49*(1), 71–85. doi:10.1111/j.1540-4560.1993.tb00909.x

Opotow, S. (1994). Predicting protection: Scope of justice and the natural world. *Journal of Social Issues, 50*(3), 49–63. doi:10.1111/j.1540-4560.1994.tb02419.x

Opotow, S. (2005). Hate, conflict, and moral exclusion. In R. J. Sternberg (Ed.), *The psychology of hate* (pp. 121–153). Washington, DC: American Psychological Association.

Osterhout, L., Bersick, M., & McLaughlin, J. (1997). Brain potentials reflect violations of gender stereotypes. *Memory & Cognition, 25*, 273–285.

Ostrom, T. M., & Sedikides, C. (1992). Outgroup homogeneity effects in minimal and natural groups. *Psychological Bulletin, 112*, 536–552. doi:10.1037/0033-2909.112.3.536

Outten, H. R., Schmitt, M. T., Garcia, D. M., & Branscombe, N. R. (2009). Coping options: Missing links between minority group identification and psychological well-being. *Applied Psychology: An International Review, 58*, 146–170. doi:10.1111/j.1464-0597.2008.00386.x

Paluck, E. L. (2006). Diversity training and intergroup contact: A call to action research. *Journal of Social Issues, 62*(3), 577–595. doi:10.1111/j.1540-4560.2006.00474.x

Paluck, E. L. (2009). Reducing intergroup prejudice and conflict using the media: A field experiment in Rwanda. *Journal of Personality and Social Psychology, 96*, 574–587. doi:10.1037/a0011989

Paluck, E. L., & Green, D. P. (2009). Prejudice reduction: What works? A review and assessment of research and practice. *Annual Review of Psychology, 60*, 339–367. doi:10.1146/annurev.psych.60.110707.163607

Panksepp, J. (1998). *Affective neuroscience: The foundations of human and animal emotions.* New York, NY: Oxford University Press.

Paolini, S., Hewstone, M., Cairns, E., & Voci, A. (2004). Effects of direct and indirect cross-group friendships on judgments of Catholics and Protestants in Northern Ireland: The mediating role of an anxiety reduction mechanism. *Personality and Social Psychology Bulletin, 30*, 770–786. doi:10.1177/0146167203262848

Pargament, K. I., Trevino, K., Mahoney, A., & Silberman, I. (2007). They killed our Lord: The perception of Jews as desecrators of Christianity as a predictor of anti-Semitism. *Journal for the Scientific Study of Religion, 46*, 143–158. doi:10.1111/j.1468-5906.2007.00347.x

Passer, M. W., Smith, R. E., Atkinson, M. L., Mitchell, J. B., & Muir, D. W. (2008). *Psychology: Frontiers and applications* (3rd Canadian ed.). Toronto, Ontario, Canada: McGraw-Hill.

Patterson, F. G. (1978). The gesture of a gorilla: Language acquisition in another pongid. *Brain and Language, 5*, 72–97. doi:10.1016/0093-934X(78)90008-1

Paul, E. S. (2000). Empathy with animals and with humans: Are they linked? *Anthrozoos, 13*, 194–202. doi:10.2752/089279300786999699

Payne, B. K. (2001). Prejudice and perception: The role of automatic and controlled processes in misperceiving a weapon. *Journal of Personality and Social Psychology, 81*, 181–192. doi:10.1037/0022-3514.81.2.181

Payne, B. K., & Bishara, A. J. (2009). An integrative review of process dissociation and related models in social cognition. *European Review of Social Psychology, 20*, 272–314. doi:10.1080/10463280903162177

Pehrson, S., Brown, R., & Zagefka, H. (2009). When does national identification lead to rejection of immigrants? Cross-sectional and longitudinal evidence for the role of essentialist in-group definitions. *British Journal of Social Psychology, 48*, 61–76. doi:10.1348/014466608X288827

Pepperberg, I. M. (2006). Grey parrot numerical competence: A review. *Animal Cognition, 9*, 377–391. doi:10.1007/s10071-006-0034-7

Pepperberg, I. M. (2008). Difficulties with "humaniqueness." *Behavioral and Brain Sciences, 31*, 143–144. doi:10.1017/S0140525X08003695

Pepperberg, I. M., & Brezinsky, M. V. (1991). Relational learning by an African grey parrot (*Psittacus Erithacus*): Discriminations based on relative size. *Journal of Comparative Psychology, 105*, 286–294. doi:10.1037/0735-7036.105.3.286

Perdue, C. W., Dovidio, J. F., Gurtman, M. B., & Tyler, R. B. (1990). Us and them: Social categorization and the process of intergroup bias. *Journal of Personality and Social Psychology, 59*, 475–486. doi:10.1037/0022-3514.59.3.475

Pettigrew, T. F., Allport, G. W., & Barnett, E. O. (1958). Binocular resolution and perception of race in South Africa. *British Journal of Social Psychology, 49*, 265–278.

Pettigrew, T. F., & Tropp, L. R. (2006). A meta-analytic test of intergroup contact theory. *Journal of Personality and Social Psychology, 90*, 751–783. doi:10.1037/0022-3514.90.5.751

Pettigrew, T. F., & Tropp, L. R. (2008). How does intergroup contact reduce prejudice? Meta-analytic test of three mediators. *European Journal of Social Psychology, 38*, 922–934. doi:10.1002/ejsp.504

Petrinovich, L., O'Neill, P., & Jorgensen, M. (1993). An empirical study of moral intuitions: Toward an evolutionary ethics. *Journal of Personality and Social Psychology, 64*, 467–478. doi:10.1037/0022-3514.64.3.467

Phelps, E. A., O'Connor, K. J., Cunningham, W. A., Funayama, E. S., Gatenby, J. C., Gore, J. C., & Banaji, M. R. (2000). Performance on indirect measures of race evaluation predicts amygdala activation. *Journal of Cognitive Neuroscience, 12*, 729–738. doi:10.1162/089892900562552

Pinker, S. (2002). *The blank slate: The modern denial of human nature*. New York, NY: Penguin.

Plant, E. A., & Devine, P. G. (2009). The active control of prejudice: Unpacking the intentions guiding control efforts. *Journal of Personality and Social Psychology, 96*, 640–652. doi:10.1037/a0012960

Plous, S. (2003). Is there such a thing as prejudice toward animals? In S. Plous (Ed.), *Understanding prejudice and discrimination* (pp. 509–536). New York, NY: McGraw-Hill.

Plummer, D. C. (2001). The quest for modern manhood: Masculine stereotypes, peer culture and the social significance of homophobia. *Journal of Adolescence, 24*, 15–23. doi:10.1006/jado.2000.0370

Pollan, M. (2006). *The omnivore's dilemma: A natural history of four meals*. New York, NY: Penguin Press.

Pope John Paul II. (1995, June 29). *Letter of Pope John Paul II to women*. Retrieved from http://www.vatican.va/holy_father/john_paul_ii/letters/documents/hf_jp-ii_let_29061995_women_en.html

Poteat, V. P. (2007). Peer socialization of homophobic attitudes and behavior during adolescence. *Child Development, 78*, 1830–1842. doi:10.1111/j.1467-8624.2007.01101.x

Poteat, V. P., Espelage, D. L., & Green, H. D., Jr. (2007). The socialization of dominance: Peer groups' contextual effects on homophobic and dominance attitudes. *Journal of Personality and Social Psychology, 92,* 1040–1050. doi:10.1037/0022-3514.92.6.1040

Powlishta, K. K. (1995). Gender bias in children's perceptions of personality traits. *Sex Roles, 32,* 17–28. doi:10.1007/BF01544755

Pratto, F. (1999). The puzzle of continuing group inequality: Piecing together psychological, social, and cultural forces in social dominance theory. In M. P. Zanna (Ed.), *Advances in experimental social psychology* (Vol. 31, pp. 191–263). San Diego, CA: Academic Press.

Pratto, F., & John, O. P. (1991). Automatic vigilance: The attention-grabbing power of negative social information. *Journal of Personality and Social Psychology, 61,* 380–391. doi:10.1037/0022-3514.61.3.380

Pratto, F., Sidanius, J., & Levin, S. (2006). Social dominance theory and the dynamics of intergroup relations: Taking stock and looking forward. *European Review of Social Psychology, 17,* 271–320. doi:10.1080/10463280601055772

Pratto, F., Sidanius, J., Stallworth, L. M., & Malle, B. F. (1994). Social dominance orientation: A personality variable predicting social and political attitudes. *Journal of Personality and Social Psychology, 67,* 741–763. doi:10.1037/0022-3514.67.4.741

Pratto, F., & Walker, A. (2001). Dominance in disguise: Power, beneficence and exploitation in personal relationships. In A. Y. Lee-Chai & J. A. Bargh (Eds.), *The use and abuse of power: Multiple perspectives on the causes of corruption* (pp. 93–114). Philadelphia, PA: Psychology Press.

Prentice, D. A., & Miller, D. T. (2007). Psychological essentialism of human categories. *Current Directions in Psychological Science, 16,* 202–206. doi:10.1111/j.1467-8721.2007.00504.x

Pyszczynski, T., Greenberg, J., Solomon, S., Arndt, J., & Schmiel, J. (2004). Why do people need self-esteem? A theoretical and empirical review. *Psychological Bulletin, 130,* 435–468. doi:10.1037/0033-2909.130.3.435

Quillian, L. (1995). Prejudice as a response to perceived group threat: Population composition and anti-immigrant and racial prejudice in Europe. *American Sociological Review, 60,* 586–611. doi:10.2307/2096296

Rahman, Q., & Wilson, G. D. (2003). Born gay? The psychobiology of human sexual orientation. *Personality and Individual Differences, 34,* 1337–1382. doi:10.1016/S0191-8869(02)00140-X

Ramsey, J. L., Langlois, J. H., & Marti, N. C. (2005). Infant categorization of faces: Ladies first. *Developmental Review, 25,* 212–246. doi:10.1016/j.dr.2005.01.001

Reiss, D., & Marino, L. (2001). Mirror self-recognition in the bottlenose dolphin: A case of cognitive convergence. *Proceedings of the National Academy of Sciences, 98,* 5937–5942. doi:10.1073/pnas.101086398

Reyna, C., Henry, P. J., Korfmacher, W., & Tucker, A. (2006). Examining the principles in principled conservatism: The role of responsibility stereotypes as cues for deservingness in racial policy decisions. *Journal of Personality and Social Psychology, 90,* 109–128. doi:10.1037/0022-3514.90.1.109

Reynolds, K. J., Turner, J. C., & Haslam, S. A. (2000). When are we better than them and they worse than us? A closer look at social discrimination in positive and negative domains. *Journal of Personality and Social Psychology, 78*, 64–80. doi:10.1037/0022-3514.78.1.64

Riek, B. M., Mania, E. W., & Gaertner, S. L. (2006). Intergroup threat and outgroup attitudes: A meta-analytic review. *Personality and Social Psychology Review, 10*, 336–353. doi:10.1207/s15327957pspr1004_4

Ritchey, P. N., & Fishbein, H. D. (2001). The lack of an association between adolescent friends' prejudices and stereotypes. *Merrill-Palmer Quarterly, 47*, 188–206. doi:10.1353/mpq.2001.0012

Roccas, S. (2005). Religion and value systems. *Journal of Social Issues, 61*, 747–759. doi:10.1111/j.1540-4560.2005.00430.x

Rodgers, S., Kenix, L. J., & Thorson, E. (2007). Stereotypical portrayals of emotionality in news photographs. *Mass Communication & Society, 10*, 119–138.

Rokeach, M., & Rothman, G. (1965). The principle of belief congruence and the congruity principle as models of cognitive interaction. *Psychological Review, 72*, 128–142. doi:10.1037/h0021702

Roney, C. (2009, July). *The psychology of free-market ideology: Links between economic and social conservatism.* Paper presented at the International Society for Political Society, Dublin, Ireland.

Roney, C., & Alexander, B. (2002, June). *The psychology of free-market ideology.* Paper presented at the annual meeting of the Canadian Psychological Association, Vancouver, British Columbia, Canada.

Rosenthal, R., & Jacobson, L. (1968). *Pygmalion in the classroom: Teacher expectations and student intellectual development.* New York, NY: Holt.

Royal, C. D. M., & Dunston, G. (2004). Changing the paradigm from "race" to human genome variation. *Nature Genetics, 36*(11, Suppl.), S5–S7. doi:10.1038/ng1454

Rubin, K. H., Bukowski, W. M., & Parker, J. G. (2006). Peer interactions, relationships, and groups. In W. Damon, R. M. Lerner, & N. Eisenberg (Eds.), *Handbook of child psychology: Vol. 3. Social, emotional and personality development* (6th ed., pp. 1003–1067). Hoboken, NJ: Wiley.

Rudman, L. A. (2004). Social justice in our minds, homes, and society: The nature, causes, and consequences of implicit bias. *Social Justice Research, 17*, 129–142. doi:10.1023/B:SORE.0000027406.32604.f6

Rudman, L. A., & Fairchild, K. (2004). Reactions to counterstereotypic behavior: The role of backlash in cultural stereotype maintenance. *Journal of Personality and Social Psychology, 87*, 157–176. doi:10.1037/0022-3514.87.2.157

Rudman, L. A., Phelan, J. E., & Heppen, J. B. (2007). Developmental sources of implicit attitudes. *Personality and Social Psychology Bulletin, 33*, 1700–1713. doi:10.1177/0146167207307487

Runciman, W. G. (1966). *Relative deprivation and social justice: A study of attitudes to social inequality in twentieth-century England.* Berkeley: University of California Press.

Rushton, P. J., & Jensen, A. R. (2005). Thirty years of research on race differences in cognitive ability. *Psychology, Public Policy, and Law, 11*, 235–294. doi:10.1037/1076-8971.11.2.235

Rydell, R. J., McConnell, A. R., & Beilock, S. L. (2009). Multiple social identities and stereotype threat: Imbalance, accessibility and working memory. *Journal of Personality and Social Psychology, 96*, 949–966. doi:10.1037/a0014846

Ryder, R. D. (2006). Speciesism in the laboratory. In P. Singer (Ed.), *In defense of animals: The second wave* (pp. 87–103). Malden, MA: Blackwell.

Sampson, E. E. (1999). *Dealing with differences. An introduction to the social psychology of prejudice*. Fort Worth, TX: Harcourt-Brace.

Sanchez, D. T., & Garcia, J. (2009). When race matters: Racially stigmatized others and perceiving race as a biological construction affect biracial people's daily well-being. *Personality and Social Psychology Bulletin, 35*, 1154–1164. doi:10.1177/0146167209337628

Santiago-Rivera, A. L., Talka, K., & Tully, A. W. (2006). Environmental racism: A call to the profession for community intervention and social action. In R. L. Toporek, L. H. Gerstein, N. A. Fouad, G. Roysircar, & T. Isreal (Eds.), *Handbook for social justice in counseling psychology: Leadership, vision, and action* (pp. 185–199). Thousand Oaks, CA: Sage.

Savage-Rumbaugh, S., Shanker, S. G., & Taylor, T. J. (1998). *Apes, language, and the human mind*. New York, NY: Oxford University Press.

Schaller, M. (2003). Ancestral environments and motivated social perception: Goal like blasts from the evolutionary past. In S. J. Spencer, S. Fein, M. P. Zanna & J. M. Olson (Eds.), *Motivated social perception: The Ontario Symposium* (Vol. 9, pp. 215–231). Mahwah, NJ: Erlbaum.

Schaller, M., Park, J. H., & Mueller, A. (2003). Fear of the dark: Interactive effects of beliefs about danger and ambient darkness on ethnic stereotypes. *Personality and Social Psychology Bulletin, 29*, 637–649. doi:10.1177/0146167203029005008

Schmitt, M. T., Branscombe, N., & Kappen, D. M. (2003). Attitudes toward group-based inequality: Social dominance or social identity? *British Journal of Social Psychology, 42*, 161–186. doi:10.1348/014466603322127166

Schwartz, S. H., & Huismans, S. (1995). Value priorities and religiosity in four western religions. *Social Psychology Quarterly, 58*, 88–107. doi:10.2307/2787148

Sean Bell. (2008). *The New York Times*. Retrieved from http://topics.nytimes.com/topics/reference/timestopics/people/b/sean_bell/index.html

Sears, D. O., & Henry, P. J. (2003). The origins of symbolic racism. *Journal of Personality and Social Psychology, 85*, 259–275. doi:10.1037/0022-3514.85.2.259

Sears, D. O., & Henry, P. J. (2005). Over thirty years later: A contemporary look at symbolic racism. In M. P. Zanna (Ed.), *Advances in experimental social psychology* (Vol. 37, pp. 95–150). New York, NY: Academic Press.

Selby, D. (2000). Humane education: Widening the circle of compassion and justice. In T. Goldstein (Ed.), *Weaving connections: Educating for peace, social and environmental justice* (PAGES) (pp. 268–296). Toronto, Ontario, Canada: Sumach Press.

Semyonov, M., & Lewin-Epstein, N. (2009). The declining racial earnings' gap in United States: Multi-level analysis of males' earnings, 1960-2000. *Social Science Research, 38,* 296–311. doi:10.1016/j.ssresearch.2008.11.001

Sesame Street. (2009). Retrieved from http://www.sesamestreet.org

Shaheen, J. G. (2009). *Reel bad Arabs: How Hollywood vilifies a people.* Northhampton, MA: Olive Branch Press.

Sherif, M., Harvey, O. J., White, B. J., Hood, W. R., & Sherif, C. W. (1961). *Intergroup conflict and cooperation. The Robbers Cave experiment.* Norman, OK: University of Oklahoma Book Exchange.

Sherif, M., & Sherif, C. W. (1966). *Groups in harmony and tension: An integration of studies on intergroup relations.* New York, NY: Harper. (Original work published 1953)

Sidanius, J., & Pratto, F. (1999). *Social dominance: An intergroup theory of social hierarchy and oppression.* New York, NY: Cambridge University Press.

Sidanius, J., Pratto, F., & Bobo, L. (1994). Social dominance orientation and the political psychology of gender: A case of invariance? *Journal of Personality and Social Psychology, 67,* 998–1011. doi:10.1037/0022-3514.67.6.998

Sidanius, J., Levin, S., Federico, C. M., & Pratto, F. (2001). Legitimizing ideologies: The social dominance approach. In J. T. Jost & B. Major (Eds.), *The psychology of legitimacy: Emerging perspectives on ideology, justice, and intergroup relations* (pp. 307–331). Cambridge, England: Cambridge University Press.

Singer, P. (2002). *Animal liberation.* New York, NY: HarperCollins.

Singer, P. (2007). Animal liberation or animal rights? In L. Kalof & A. Fitzgerald (Eds.), *The animals reader: Essential classic and contemporary writings* (pp. 14–22). Oxford, England: Berg. (Reprinted from *The Monist: An International Quarterly Journal of General Philosophical Inquiry, 70,* 3–14.)

Smedley, A., & Smedley, B. D. (2005). Race as biology is fiction, racism as a social problem is real: Anthropological and historical perspectives on the social construction of race. *American Psychologist, 60,* 16–28.

Smedley, B. D., Stith, A. Y., & Nelson, A. R. (2003). *Unequal treatment: Confronting racial and ethnic disparities in health care.* Washington, DC: National Academies Press.

Smith, E. R. (1993). Social identity and social emotions: Toward new conceptualizations of prejudice. In D. M. Mackie & D. L. Hamilton (Eds.), *Affect, cognition, and stereotyping: Interactive processes in group perception* (pp. 297–315). San Diego, CA: Academic Press.

Sniderman, P. M., Piazza, T., Tetlock, P. E., & Kendrick, A. (1991). The new racism. *American Journal of Political Science, 35,* 423–447. doi:10.2307/2111369

Snodgrass, C. E., & Gates, L. (1998). Doctrinal orthodoxy, religious orientation, and anthropocentrism. *Current Psychology: Developmental, Learning, Personality, Social, 17,* 222–236.

Solomon, S., Greenberg, J., & Pyszczynski, T. (1991). Terror management theory of self-esteem. In C. R. Snyder & D. R. Forsyth (Eds.), *Handbook of social and clinical psychology: The health perspective* (pp. 21–40). Elmsford, NY: Pergamon Press.

Solomon, S., Greenberg, J., & Pyszczynski, T. (2000). Pride and prejudice: Fear of death and social behavior. *Current Directions in Psychological Science, 9,* 200–204. doi:10.1111/1467-8721.00094

Sommers, S. R., Apfelbaum, E. P., Dukes, K. N., Toosi, N., & Wand, E. J. (2006). Race and media coverage of Hurricane Katrina: Analysis, implications, and future research questions. *Analyses of Social Issues and Public Policy, 6,* 39–55. doi:10.1111/j.1530-2415.2006.00103.x

Son Hing, L. S., Chung-Yan, G. A., Hamilton, L. K., & Zanna, M. P. (2008). A two-dimensional model that employs explicit and implicit attitudes to characterize prejudice. *Journal of Personality and Social Psychology, 94,* 971–987. doi:10.1037/0022-3514.94.6.971

Son Hing, L. S., Li, W., & Zanna, M. P. (2002). Inducing hypocrisy to reduce prejudicial responses among aversive racists. *Journal of Experimental Social Psychology, 38,* 71–78. doi:10.1006/jesp.2001.1484

Stanley, D., Phelps, E., & Banaji, M. (2008). The neural basis of implicit attitudes. *Current Directions in Psychological Science, 17,* 164–170. doi:10.1111/j.1467-8721.2008.00568.x

Staub, E. (1989). *The roots of evil: The origins of genocide and other group violence.* New York, NY: Cambridge University Press.

Staub, E. (2005). Healing, reconciliation, forgiving and the prevention of violence after genocide or mass killing: An intervention and its experimental evaluation in Rwanda. *Journal of Social and Clinical Psychology, 24,* 297–334. doi:10.1521/jscp.24.3.297.65617

Staub, E., Pearlman, L. A., Gubin, A., & Hagengimana, A. (2005). Healing, reconciliation, forgiving and the prevention of violence after genocide or mass killing: An intervention and its experimental evaluation in Rwanda. *Journal of Social and Clinical Psychology, 24,* 297–334. doi:10.1521/jscp.24.3.297.65617

Steele, C. M., & Aronson, J. (1995). Stereotype threat and the intellectual test performance of African Americans. *Journal of Personality and Social Psychology, 69,* 797–811. doi:10.1037/0022-3514.69.5.797

Stelzl, M., Janes, L., & Seligman, C. (2008). Champ or chump: Strategic utilization of dual social identities of others. *European Journal of Social Psychology, 38,* 128–138. doi:10.1002/ejsp.446

Stephan, W. G., Renfro, C. L., Esses, V. M., Stephan, C. W., & Martin, T. (2005). The effect of feeling threatened on attitudes toward immigrants. *International Journal of Intercultural Relations, 29,* 1–19. doi:10.1016/j.ijintrel.2005.04.011

Stephan, W. G., & Stephan, C. W. (2000). An integrated theory of prejudice. In S. Oskamp (Ed.), *Reducing prejudice and discrimination* (pp. 23–45). Mahwah, NJ: Erlbaum.

Stephan, W. G., & Stephan, C. W. (2001). *Improving intergroup relations*. Thousand Oaks, CA: Sage.

Stephan, W. G., & Stephan, C. W. (2005). Intergroup relations program evaluation. In J. F. Dovidio, P. Glick, & L. A. Rudman (Eds.), *On the nature of prejudice: Fifty years after Allport* (pp. 431–446). Malden, MA: Blackwell.

Stephan, W. G., & Vogt, W. P. (2004). *Education programs for improving intergroup relations: Theory, research, and practice*. New York, NY: Teachers College Press.

Stephan, W. G., Ybarra, O., & Bachman, G. (1999). Prejudice toward immigrants. *Journal of Applied Social Psychology, 29*, 2221–2237. doi:10.1111/j.1559-1816. 1999.tb00107.x

Steptoe, A. (2000). Control and stress. In G. Fink (Ed.), *Encyclopedia of stress* (pp. 526–531). San Diego, CA: Academic Press.

Sternberg, R. J., Grigorenko, E. L., & Kidd, K. K. (2005). Intelligence, race, and genetics. *American Psychologist, 60*, 46–59. doi:10.1037/0003-066X.60.1.46

Stokols, D., Misra, S., Runnerstrom, M. G., & Hipp, J. A. (2009). Psychology in an age of ecological crisis: From personal angst to collective action. *American Psychologist, 64*, 181–193. doi:10.1037/a0014717

Stürmer, S., & Simon, B. (2009). Pathways to collective protest: Calculation, identification, or emotion? A critical analysis of the role of group-based anger in social movement participation. *Journal of Social Issues, 65*, 681–705. doi:10.1111/j.1540-4560.2009.01620.x

Tajfel, H. (1978). Social categorization, social identity, and social comparison. In H. Tajfel (Ed.), *Differentiation between social groups: Studies in the social psychology of intergroup relations* (pp. 61–76). London, England: Academic Press.

Tajfel, H., & Turner, J. (1979). An integrative theory of intergroup conflict. In W.G. Austin & S. Worchel (Eds.), *The social psychology of intergroup relations* (pp. 33–48). Belmont, CA: Wadsworth.

Tajfel, H., & Turner, J. (1986). The social identity theory of intergroup behavior. In W. G. Austin & S. Worchel (Eds.), *Psychology of intergroup relations* (2nd ed., pp. 7–27). Chicago, IL: Nelson-Hall.

Tarakeshwar, N., Swank, A. G., Pargament, K. I., & Mahoney, A. (2001). The sanctification of nature and theological conservatism: A study of opposing religious correlates of environmentalism. *Review of Religious Research, 42*, 387–404. doi:10.2307/3512131

Taylor, D. M. (1997). The quest for collective identity: The plight of disadvantaged ethnic minorities. *Canadian Psychology, 38*, 174–190. doi:10.1037/0708-5591.38.3.174

Taylor, D. M., & Moghaddam, F. M. (1994). *Theories of intergroup relations: International social psychological perspectives* (2nd ed.). Westport, CT: Praeger.

Taylor, N., & Signal, T. D. (2005). Empathy and attitudes to animals. *Anthrozoos, 18*, 18–27. doi:10.2752/089279305785594342

Templer, D. I., Connelly, H. J., Bassman, L., & Hart, J. (2006). Construction and validation of an animal-human continuity scale. *Social Behavior and Personality, 34*, 769–776. doi:10.2224/sbp.2006.34.7.769

Thomas, S. C., & Beirne, P. (2002). Humane education and humanistic philosophy: Toward a new curriculum. *Journal of Humanistic Counseling, Education and Development, 41*, 190–199.

Tolman, E. C. (1948). Cognitive maps in rats and men. *Psychological Review, 55*, 189–208. doi:10.1037/h0061626

Tooby, J., & Cosmides, L. (1992). The psychological foundations of culture. In J. H. Barkow, L. Cosmides, & J. Tooby (Eds.), *The adapted mind: Evolutionary psychology and the generation of culture* (pp. 19–136). New York, NY: Oxford University Press.

Tougas, F., Brown, R., Beaton, A. M., & Joly, S. (1995). Neosexism: Plus ca change, plus c'est pareil. *Personality and Social Psychology Bulletin, 21*, 842–849. doi:10.1177/0146167295218007

Trivers, R. L. (1972). Parental investment and sexual selection. In B. Campbell (Ed.), *Sexual selection and the descent of man* (pp. 136–188). Chicago, IL: Aldine-Atherton.

Turner, J. C., & Reynolds, K. J. (2001). The social identity perspective in intergroup relations: Theories, themes, and controversies. In R. Brown & S. Gaertner (Eds.), *Blackwell handbook of social psychology: Intergroup processes* (pp. 133–152). Malden, MA: Blackwell.

Turner, R. N., Hewstone, M., & Voci, A. (2007). Reducing explicit and implicit prejudice via direct and extended contact: The mediating role of self-disclosure and intergroup anxiety. *Journal of Personality and Social Psychology, 93*, 369–388. doi:10.1037/0022-3514.93.3.369

Turner, R. N., Hewstone, M., Voci, A., & Vonofakou, C. (2008). A test of the extended intergroup contact hypothesis: The mediating role of intergroup anxiety, perceived ingroup and outgroup norms, and inclusion of the outgroup in the self. *Journal of Personality and Social Psychology, 95*, 843–860. doi:10.1037/a0011434

United Nations Environment Programme. (2007). *Sudan post-conflict environmental assessment.* Retrieved from http://unep.org/sudan/

van Zomeren, M., & Iyer, A. (2009). Introduction to the social and psychological dynamics of collective action. *Journal of Social Issues, 65*, 645–660. doi:10.1111/j.1540-4560.2009.01618.x

van Zomeren, M., Spears, R., Fisher, A. H., & Leach, C. W. (2004). Put your money where your mouth is! Explaining collective action tendencies through group-based anger and group efficacy. *Journal of Personality and Social Psychology, 87*, 649–664. doi:10.1037/0022-3514.87.5.649

Verkuyten, M. (2003). Discourses about ethnic group (de-)essentialism: Oppressive and progressive aspects. *British Journal of Social Psychology, 42*, 371–391. doi:10.1348/014466603322438215

Vescio, T. K., Sechrist, G. B., & Paolucci, M. P. (2003). Perspective taking and prejudice reduction: The meditational role of empathy arousal and situational attributions. *European Journal of Social Psychology, 33,* 455–472. doi:10.1002/ejsp.163

Vorauer, J. D., Main, K. J., & O'Connell, G. B. (1998). How do individuals expect to be viewed by members of lower status groups? Content and implications of meta-stereotypes. *Journal of Personality and Social Psychology, 75,* 917–937. doi:10.1037/0022-3514.75.4.917

Vorauer, J. D., Martens, V., & Sasaki, S. J. (2009). When trying to understand detracts from trying to behave: Effects of perspective in intergroup interaction. *Journal of Personality and Social Psychology, 96,* 811–827. doi:10.1037/a0013411

Vorauer, J. D., & Turpie, C. A. (2004). Disruptive effects of vigilance on dominant group members' treatment of outgroup members: Choking versus shining under pressure. *Journal of Personality and Social Psychology, 87,* 384–399. doi:10.1037/0022-3514.87.3.384

Waldau, P. (2006). Religion and animals. In P. Singer (Ed.), *In defense of animals: The second wave* (pp. 69–83). Malden, MA: Blackwell.

Walton, G. M., & Cohen, G. L. (2003). Stereotype lift. *Journal of Experimental Social Psychology, 39,* 456–467. doi:10.1016/S0022-1031(03)00019-2

Watts, M. W. (1996). Political xenophobia in the transition from socialism: Threat, ideology and racism among East German youth. *Political Psychology, 17,* 97–126. doi:10.2307/3791945

Weber, M. (1958). *The Protestant ethic and the spirit of capitalism.* New York, NY: Scribner's. (Original work published 1904)

Wegner, D. M. (1994). Ironic processes of mental control. *Psychological Review, 101,* 34–52. doi:10.1037/0033-295X.101.1.34

Weizman, F., Wiener, N. I., Wiesenthal, D. L., & Ziegler, M. (1991). Eggs, eggplants and eggheads: A rejoinder to Rushton. *Canadian Psychology, 32,* 43–50. doi:10.1037/h0078958

Wells, D. L. (2009). The effects of animals on human health and well-being. *Journal of Social Issues, 65,* 523–543. doi:10.1111/j.1540-4560.2009.01612.x

Welsh, A., & Ogloff, J. R. P. (2000). Full parole and the Aboriginal experience: Accounting for the racial discrepancies in release rates. *Canadian Journal of Criminology, 42,* 469–491.

Wessler, S. L., & DeAndrade, L. L. (2006). Slurs, stereotypes and student interventions: Examining the dynamics, impact and prevention of harassment in middle and high school. *Journal of Social Issues, 62,* 511–532. doi:10.1111/j.1540-4560.2006.00471.x

Wheeler, M. E., & Fiske, S. T. (2005). Controlling racial prejudice: Social-cognitive goals affect amygdala and stereotype activation. *Psychological Science, 16,* 56–63. doi:10.1111/j.0956-7976.2005.00780.x

White, J. B., & Langer, E. J. (1999). Horizontal hostility: Relations between similar minority groups. *Journal of Social Issues, 55,* 537–559. doi:10.1111/0022-4537.00132

White, J. B., Schmitt, M. T., & Langer, E. J. (2006). Horizontal hostility: Multiple minority groups and differentiation from the mainstream. *Group Processes & Intergroup Relations, 9*, 339–358. doi:10.1177/1368430206064638

White, L. (1967, March 10). The historical roots of our ecological crisis. *Science, 155*, 1203–1207. doi:10.1126/science.155.3767.1203

White Ribbon Campaign. (2010). Retrieved from http://www.whiteribbon.ca

Whitley, B. E., Jr. (1990). The relationship of heterosexuals' attributions for the causes of homosexuality to attitudes toward lesbians and gay men. *Personality and Social Psychology Bulletin, 16*, 369–377. doi:10.1177/0146167290162016

Whitley, B. E., Jr., & Kite, M. E. (2006). *The psychology of prejudice and discrimination*. Belmont, CA: Thomson Wadsworth.

Wild, H. A., Barrett, S. E., Spence, M. J., O'Toole, A. J., Cheng, Y. D., & Brooke, J. (2000). Recognition and sex categorization of adults' and children's faces: Examining performance in the absence of sex-stereotyped cues. *Journal of Experimental Child Psychology, 77*, 269–291. doi:10.1006/jecp.1999.2554

Williams, M. J., & Eberhardt, J. (2008). Biological conceptions of race and the motivation to cross racial boundaries. *Journal of Personality and Social Psychology, 94*, 1033–1047. doi:10.1037/0022-3514.94.6.1033

Wilson, S. (2007, November). *Intensive animal agriculture, environmental injustice, and public health*. Symposium conducted at the 135th Annual Meeting and Exposition of the American Public Health Association, Washington, DC. Retrieved from http://apha.confex.com/apha/135am/techprogram/session_21407.htm

Wood, P. B., & Bartoski, J. P. (2004). Attribution style and public policy attitudes toward gay rights. *Social Science Quarterly, 85*, 58–74. doi:10.1111/j.0038-4941.2004.08501005.x

Woodward, J. S., & Allen, T. (1993). Models of deafness compared: A sociolinguistic study of deaf and hard of hearing teachers. *Sign Language Studies, 79*, 113–126.

Word, C. O., Zanna, M. P., & Cooper, J. C. (1974). The nonverbal mediation of self-fulfilling prophecies in interracial interaction. *Journal of Experimental Social Psychology, 10*, 109–120. doi:10.1016/0022-1031(74)90059-6

Wright, O. M. (2000). Multicultural and anti-racist education: The issue is equity. In T. Goldstein & D. Selby (Eds.), *Weaving connections: Educating for peace, social and environmental justice* (pp. 57–98). Toronto, Ontario, Canada: Sumach Press.

Wright, S. C. (2009). The next generation of collective action research. *Journal of Social Issues, 65*, 859–879. doi:10.1111/j.1540-4560.2009.01628.x

Wright, S. C., Aron, A., McLaughlin-Volpe, T., & Ropp, S. A. (1997). The extended contact effect: Knowledge of cross-group friendships and prejudice. *Journal of Personality and Social Psychology, 73*, 73–90. doi:10.1037/0022-3514.73.1.73

Wright, S. C., & Lubensky, M. E. (2009). The struggle for social equality: Collective action versus prejudice reduction. In S. Demoulin, J. P. Leyens, & J. F. Dovidio (Eds.), *Intergroup misunderstandings: Impact of divergent social realities* (pp. 291–310). New York, NY: Psychology Press.

Wynter, S. (1992). No humans involved: An open letter to my colleagues. *Voices of the African Diaspora*, 8, 13–18.

Zelditch, M., Jr. (2001). Theories of legitimacy. In J. T. Jost & B. Major (Eds.), *The psychology of legitimacy: Emerging perspectives on ideology, justice, and intergroup relations* (pp. 33–53). Cambridge, England: Cambridge University Press.

INDEX

Aamjiwaang reserve, 137, 138
Aboud, F. E., 85, 93, 94
Abuse, 157
    of animals, 147, 148, 152, 157
    of Native Canadians, 7, 8, 115
Accessibility, 28, 105
Achievement orientation, stereotypes
    of, 18
Achter, P. J., 43–44
Adolescents. *See* Children and
    adolescents
Adorno, T. W., 58
Advantage, 23
Advantaged groups. *See also specific*
    headings
    awareness of stereotypes, 132–133
    collective action by, 174
    conservative ideologies among, 74
    discrimination against, 21
    essentialist views of, 43–44
    implicit prejudice in, 172–173
    ingroup bias by, 73
    privileges of, 23–24, 111
    and social construction of race, 36
    stereotype lift, 134
Affective conditioning, 126
Affective processes, 124–128
Affirmative action programs, 15
African Americans
    awareness of stereotypes, 132
    discrimination-related deaths, 79–80
    ingroup devaluation among, 73
    ingroup preference in, 86
    and Obama election, 7, 8
    prejudice against, 83
    as scapegoats, 60
    during slavery in U.S., 18
    social status of, 172–173
    stereotypes about, 119–121
Age, 31
Age-based trends, 93–96
Aggression, 51, 59–61, 119–120
Allport, G. W., 12, 37, 160, 163
Altemeyer, B., 58
Ambivalence, 57
Ambivalent prejudice, 12, 75–80

American Sign Language (ASL), 26, 27,
    149
Amygdala, 51, 127–128
Ancestral history, 34
Androgens, 40
Anger, 174
Animal agriculture, 147–148
Animals, 138–139, 147–151. *See also*
    Speciesism
Anterior cingulate cortex, 123
Anthropocentrism, 113, 141–142, 154
Antibias education, 165–168
Anti-Defamation League, 166
Anti-Semitism, 65–66, 166
Apartheid, 36–37, 69
Apes, 149
Arab people
    children's descriptions of, 83–84
    media depictions since 9/11, 10, 89
    in Sudan, 29–30, 143
Aristotle, 153, 154
Arndt, J., 153
Aron, A., 164
Aronson, E., 160, 161
Aronson, J., 131–133
Ascione, F. R., 158
Asian people, 75, 77
ASL. *See* American Sign Language
Athabasca oil sands, 137
Attachments, 58–59
Attitudes
    based on group membership, 20–21
    conditioned, 126–127
    disrespectful, 20, 148
    environmental, 141–142
    and essentialism, 44–45
    negative, 14
    parental transmission of, 87–88
    peer influences on, 91–92
    positive, 18–20, 44, 171
    system justification theory, 73–74
    toward nonhuman animals. *See*
        Speciesism
Audism, 24–28
Authoritarian personality, 58
Automatic stereotyping, 122

Aversive racism, 124–125
Aviram, R. B., 59
Avoidance, selective, 52
Awareness, 145–146

Banaji, M. R., 126
Bandura, A., 87
Barnett, E. O., 37
Bar-Tal, D., 83, 84
Basic categories, 31
Bates, B. R., 43–44
Bauman, H. D. L., 28
Beatson, R. M., 152
Beliefs. *See also* Ideology(-ies)
 about difference, 42
 cultural, 36
 and group hierarchy, 68
 in human uniqueness, 151–153
 and positive social identity, 110
 prejudice-supporting, 65–66
 religious, 66
 in socialization processes, 154–155
 symbolic, 13–14
 and values, 13–14
Bell, Sean, 117, 119–120
Benevolent stereotypes, 78–79
Bevan, J., 43–44
Bhandar, B., 81
Bias
 ingroup. *See* Ingroup bias
 linguistic, 26–27
Bigler, R. S., 97, 99, 100
Biological factors, 123
Biological perspectives
 and positive attitudes, 44
 on race categories, 38–39
 on sexual orientation, 40
Biological taxonomy, 149
Bisexuality, 41
Bitacola, L., 141
Black Africans, 29–30, 143
Black heritage, 37. *See also* African
 Americans
Black sheep effect, 111
Blatz, C. W., 15
Bobo, L. D., 115
Boies, K., 72
Brahmins, 99
Brain activity
 emotional prejudice, 127–128

emotion in mammals, 150
mental modules, 49
prejudice within ingroups, 52
social neuroscience, 12–13
in stereotyping, 122–123
Branscombe, N. R., 23
Brown, R., 43, 106
Burgess, D., 72
Bush, George W., 32, 89

Campbell, D. T., 105
Canada. *See also* White Canadians
 First Nations in, 7–9
 multiculturalism policy, 110, 166
 rights of persons with disabilities, 28
Castano, E., 146
Categories and categorization
 of humans vs. animals, 149
 by infants, 84–85
 positive attitude formation, 171
 process of, 30
 psychological salience of, 96–98
 of race, 30–32, 38–39
 in South Africa, 36–37
 and stereotypes, 98–101
 values associated with, 85–86
 by young children, 97, 98
Catholic Church, 79
Census data, 37
Charbonneau, D., 72
Childhood experiences, 125
Children and adolescents, 81–101
 attitudes toward nonhuman animals,
  155, 157–158
 developmental intergroup approach,
  96–101
 developmental trends, 83–86
 multicultural education for, 167
 peer influence on, 91–92
 Reena Virk case, 81–82
 social–cognitive developmental
  perspective, 92–96
 socialization perspective, 87–91
Chimpanzees, 149
Chippewa nation, 114
Christian tradition
 anti-Semitism in, 66
 cultural discrimination, 22
 fundamentalist, 108
 ideology of, 153–154

racialization of Jews, 38
stereotypes in, 119
Citizenship and Immigration
Canada, 166
Civilization and Its Discontents
(S. Freud), 53
Clark, K. B., 73
Clark, M. K., 73
Classical conditioning, 125–126
Classic psychoanalytic theory, 48,
53–57
Classification, 31–33, 95–97
Classroom context
competition in, 160–161
expectations in, 129–130
prejudice reduction programs for,
166–167
A Classroom of Difference
(program), 167
Cognitive abilities, 93–94, 149–150
Cohen, G. L., 133, 134
Collective action, 173–176
Collective identity, 109–110
Colonization, 144, 162
Community-based programs, 162
Community standards, 22
Competition
absence of, 109
in classroom, 160–161, 164
in contact situations, 163
silencing voice of, 115
Competition for resources
effects of, 105–107
in environment of evolutionary
adaptedness, 50–51
ideology of, 113
immigrants as source of, 106
and intergroup relations, 138
perceived, 114
unified instrumental model of group
conflict, 114–115
as utilitarian, 113
Competitiveness, 56
Condit, C. M., 43–44
Conditioned fears, 127
Conditioning, 125–127
Conflict, realistic, 105
Conformity, 56, 169
Conscious experience, 54
Conservation ability, 95

Conservative perspectives, 15, 74
Constructionist approach. *See* Social
constructionist approach
Contact hypothesis, 160–165, 171–172
Contemptuous prejudice, 77
Control, of others, 67–68, 72
Controlled stereotyping, 122
Cooper, J. C., 130
Cooperation, 50, 163
Correll, J., 120, 121
Costello, K., 157
Cottrell, C. A., 52
Crandall, C. S., 169
Creatureliness, 152–153
Crimes, hate, 60
Cross-group friendships, 164–165
Cruelty, to animals, 147–148
Cuddy, A. J. C., 156
Cultural beliefs, 36
Cultural discrimination, 22–23, 27
Cultural influences, 88–91
Cultural stereotypes, 120–121
Cultural worldviews, 61–62
Czopp, A. M., 19

Dalits, 99
Dambrun, M., 71
Danso, H. A., 134
Darfur, Sudan, 29–30, 143
Dawkins, R., 35, 139, 149
Deaf community, 25–28
DeAndrade, L. L., 82
Death, 61–62, 152
Dehumanization, 144–146
Deneed, N. F., 169
Deprivation, relative, 174
Descartes, Rene, 153
Descriptive stereotypes, 10
Desegregation, 160–161
Deservingness, 70, 72
Devaluation
of ingroup, 73
of nonhuman animals, 139, 146, 151
by positive affirmation, 44
Developmental intergroup approach,
96–101
Developmental trends, 83–86, 93–96
Devine, P. G., 169
*Diagnostic and Statistical Manual of
Mental Disorders*, 42

Diallo, Amadou, 117, 119–120
Difference(s), 29–45
    Arabs and Black Africans in Sudan,
        29–30
    beliefs about, 42
    children's awareness of, 83–84
    exaggeration of, 112
    genetic, 33–36, 40
    human–animal, 157
    implications, 42–45
    infants' detection of, 84–85
    and language, 97–98
    as meaningful, 96–98
    racial, 31–39
    sexual orientation, 39–42
Disadvantaged groups. See also specific
        headings
    collective action, 173–174
    conservative ideologies among, 74
    contact situations, 171–172
    discrimination against, 21
    expectations about, 129–130
    ingroup bias by, 73
    media attention to, 88–89
    perspective of, 170
    and privilege, 23–24
    and social dominance orientation,
        70–72
    stereotype threat, 131–133
    system justification, 75
Discrimination
    cultural, 22–23, 27
    deaths related to, 79–80
    and essentialism, 43–44
    against First Nation peoples,
        103–104
    in hiring, 130–131, 170–171
    institutional, 21–22, 26
    and prejudice, 21–22
    toward D/deaf people, 25–28
    against women in workplace, 106
Disrespectful attitudes, 20, 148
Distal influences, 48, 151–153
Diversity education, 165–168
Diversity training programs, 159, 167–168
DNA, 34, 35
Dollard, J., 59, 60
Dominance, 67, 70–72
Dominant groups. See also Advantaged
        groups

hierarchy-enhancing myths, 70
    perpetuation of hierarchies by, 67
    perspective of, 36
Dovidio, J. F., 124, 125, 171
Doyle, A. B., 93
Dual identities, 111–112
Duarte, S., 71
Dutch Reformed Church, 69

Eberhardt, J. L., 145
Ebert, J. P., 126
Economic conservatism, 16
Economic factors
    in envious prejudice, 78
    in environmental inequality, 140
    frustration–aggression
        hypothesis, 60
    in prejudice against immigrants,
        106, 107
EEA (environment of evolutionary
        adaptedness), 49
Egalitarianism, 124–125
Egocentrism, 94
Ego justification, 73
Emotional prejudice, 124–128
Emotional threat, 151–153
Emotions
    in collective action, 174
    focus on, 170
    and infrahumanization, 145
    negative, 56–57
    in nonhuman animals, 150
    and prejudice, 12–13, 20, 124–128
    as primary responses, 95
    splitting of, 59
Empathy, 157, 158
Employment settings, 167–168,
        170–171
Entitlement, 142
Environmental damage, 142–144
Environmental inequality, 138–142
Environmental racism, 139
Environment of evolutionary
        adaptedness (EEA), 49
Equality, 70
Erin Brokovich (film), 90
Espelage, D. L., 92
Essentialism, 42–44, 99
Esses, V. M., 106, 134, 138, 171

Ethnic group members. *See also specific headings*
    dehumanization of, 144–145
    identification with group, 172
    interpersonal interaction with, 88
    minority men, 119–120
    misuse of notions about, 30
Ethnic–racial identities, 112
Ethnocentrism, 141–142, 157
European Americans. *See* White Americans
Evaluative conditioning, 126
Evolutionary perspectives, 47–63
Evolutionary theory
    categorization ability, 97
    origins of inequality, 67
    and prejudice, 48–53
    social dominance orientation, 72
    and terror management, 61
Existential anxiety, 61–62, 151–153
Expectations, 129–130
Explicit prejudice, 125, 172–173
Explicit stereotyping, 121, 122
Extended contact, 164–165

Facial recognition, 49–50
Fairchild, K., 111
Fairness, 74
Family groups, 49–50
Father figure, 55–58
Fear, 51, 127, 128
Federico, C. M., 67
Finelli, M., 147
First Nations
    and anthropocentric views, 113
    in Canada, 7–9
    colonization of, 144
    discrimination against, 103–104
    environmental issues, 137–138
    land disputes, 114–115
    social programs for, 15–16
    views of White Canadians, 135
Fish, J. M., 33
Fiske, S. T., 76–79
fMRI (functional magnetic resonance imaging), 127
Fontaine, Phil, 8
Foucault, M., 41
Freud, Sigmund, 53–57, 151
Frustration, 59–61

Frustration and Aggression (J. Dollard), 59
Functional magnetic resonance imaging (fMRI), 127
Fundamentalism, 69, 108

Gaertner, S. L., 124, 125
Gang violence, 107
Gates, Henry Louis, Jr., 8
Gelman, S. A., 98
Gender, 31, 85, 97. *See also* Men; Women
Gender stereotypes, 19, 99
Genetic differences, 33–36, 40
Genetic factors, 48–49
Genocide, 106, 143, 162
Genome variability, 33–36
George, Dudley, 115
Giner-Sorolla, R., 146
Glaser, J., 60
"Glass cliff," 174
Glick, P., 76–79
Global warming, 142, 143
Globe and Mail (newspaper), 75
Goals, 164
Goff, P. A., 145
Goldenberg, J. L., 152, 153
Gorillas, 149
Great Chain of Being, 153, 154
Green, D. A., 23
Green, D. P., 60, 161, 163
Green, H. D., Jr., 92
Greenberg, J., 61
Group conflict perspective, 104–108
Group hierarchies, 66–73
Group interests, 155–157
Group justification, 73
Group membership
    attitudes based on, 20–21
    and ingroup bias, 108–109, 112
    privilege based on, 23–24
    and social dominance orientation, 71
Group mind, 55
Group Psychology and the Analysis of the Ego (S. Freud), 53
Group structure, 104–105
Guimond, S., 71

Habituation paradigm, 84–85
Haines, E. L., 74
Hall, D. L., 112

Harber, K. D., 130
Hardin, C. D., 172
Harper, Stephen, 7, 8
Harris, S., 38
Hart, J., 153
Haslam, N., 145
Hate crimes, 60
Hatred, 160
Hazardous waste sites, 139–140
Hebl, M. R., 78
Henry, P. J., 172
Herouxville Town Charter incident, 22
Heterosexuality, 39, 41–42. *See also*
        Sexual orientation
Hewstone, M., 106, 165
Heyman, G. D., 98
Hierarchies, 66–73
Hierarchy-attenuating myths, 69–70
Hierarchy-enhancing myths, 68–70
Himmler, Heinrich, 38
Hiring discrimination, 130–131, 170–171
Hirshfeld, L. A., 97
Hodson, G., 157
Holloran, M. J., 152
The Holocaust, 38, 65
Holtz, P., 43
Homogeneity, 34, 110–111
Homophobia, 91–92
Homo sapiens, 149
Homosexuality, 41–42. *See also*
        Sexual orientation
Hong Kong residents, 75–76
Hostility, 105
Hovland, C. I., 60
Human–animal relations, 156
Humane Society, 147
Humans
        ancestral history of, 34
        animals vs., 149
        genome variability in, 33–36
        relations with animals, 156
        uniqueness of, 149–153
Humphries, Tom, 25
Hurricane Katrina, 89–90
Hutu people, 162
Hyers, L. L., 155
Hypodescent rules, 37

Identity(-ies)
        affirmation of, 133

collective, 109–110
        dual, 111–112
        ethnic–racial, 112
        multiple social, 171
        personal, 109
        social, 108–112, 171, 172, 175
Ideology(-ies), 65–80. *See also* Beliefs
        ambivalent prejudice, 75–80
        in competition for resources, 113
        of environmental inequality,
            140–141
        Great Chain of Being, 153, 154
        social dominance theory, 66–72
        system justification theory, 72–75
Immigrants and immigration
        economic benefits of, 107
        and dehumanization, 145, 157
        Rwandan, 14
        and scarcity of natural resources, 142
        social dominance orientation, 171
        as source of competition, 106, 107
Immigrant Watch Canada, 142–143
Implicit prejudice, 125–129, 172–173
Implicit stereotypes, 119–124, 169–170
Indirect outcomes, 164, 175
Indirect prejudice, 14–16
Individual strategies, 168–171
Inequality
        D/deaf people, 27
        environmental, 138–142
        and essentialism, 43–44
        justifications for, 16–18, 68
        origins of, 67
        perpetuation of, 172
        and positive stereotypes, 19
        and prejudice, 16–18
        and social construction of race, 36
        and well-being, 23
Infants, 84–85
Infrahumanization, 145–146
Ingroup bias
        in children, 86
        commitment to group, 104–105
        evolutionary theory, 50, 51
        and group membership, 108–109,
            112
        and identification with group, 59
        and prejudice in children, 99–101
Ingroup homogeneity, 111
Instinctive drives, 54

Institutional discrimination, 21–22, 26
Interactive processes, 128–136
Interdependence, 76–77
Intergovernmental Panel on Climate
    Change (IPCC), 142
Intergroup relations, 103–116
    and ambivalent prejudice, 76–77
    attitudes and essentialism, 44–45
    contact hypothesis, 163
    and dehumanization, 145
    in employment settings, 168,
        170–171
    environmental damage, 143–144
    group conflict perspective, 104–108
    metastereotypes in, 135–136
    multicultural education, 166
    social identity perspective, 108–112
    and social status, 172
    unified instrumental model, 112–116
Intergroup vigilance theory, 51
Interpersonal discrimination, 21
Interpersonal encounters, 130–131
IPCC (Intergovernmental Panel on
    Climate Change), 142
"Isms," 25
Iyer, A., 174

Jackman, M. R., 79
Jackson, L. M., 106, 138, 171
Jackson, M. C., 145
Jacobson, L., 129
Jamaica, 107
Janes, L., 111, 140
"Jena Six" incident, 8–9
Jensen, A. R., 32
Jewish people, 38, 65–66
Jigsaw classroom, 160–161, 164
Job interviews, 130–131
John Paul II, Pope, 79
Johnson, Ben, 111
Johnson, G. R., 50
Jones, J. M., 39
Jones, L. C., 100
Jost, J. T., 18, 72–74
Judd, C. M., 121
Judeo-Christian tradition, 153–154. See
    also Christian tradition
Jussim, L., 130
Justifications
    for cultural beliefs, 36

for inequality, 16–18, 68
of nonhuman animal devaluation, 151
system justification theory, 72–75
for use of nonhuman animals, 155, 156

Katz, P. A., 82–83, 86–88, 98
Kawakami, K., 125
Kazama, S., 78
King, E. G., 78
King, Martin Luther, Jr., 173
King, Rodney, 145
Kinsey, A. C., 41
Kinship, 49–50
Kurzban, R., 51–52
Kwan, V. S. Y., 156

Land disputes, 114–115
Language
    and D/deaf children, 26–27
    differences salience, 97–98
    ingroup formation, 50
    media stereotyping, 89–90
    in nonhuman animals, 149–150
Laws, 37
Law students, 71–72
Leaders, 55–56
Leary, M. R., 51–52
Levin, S., 67
LeVine, R. A., 105
Lewington, J., 75
Leyens, J. P., 145
Liben, L. S., 97, 99, 100
Liberation theology, 69
Libido, 54
Linguistic bias, 26–27
Linnaeus, 32, 36
Lippman, Walter, 10
Lobliner, D. B., 100
Louis, W. R., 175
Lubensky, M. E., 171, 172

Mahalingam, R., 43, 99
Mahoney, A., 66
Main, K. J., 134–135
Mammalian brains, 150
Maras, P., 106
Marlow, J., 29–30
Mason, J., 147
Masser, B., 106
Matz, D. C., 112

McIntosh, P., 23
McLaughlin-Volpe, T., 164
Meaningfulness, 100
Media influences, 88–91, 168
Medical system, 21, 26
Men, 55, 67
Mental modules, 49–50
Merton, R. K., 130
Metastereotypes, 134–136
Michinov, N., 71
Midrange influences, 66, 153–155
Milgram, S., 150
Military context, 72
Minimal group experiments, 109
Mining, 140–141
Minority groups. *See specific headings*
Modern prejudice, 15
Moghaddam, F. M., 53, 166
Mohai, P., 140
Mohawk nation, 114
Monteith, M. J., 169
Morality, 150
Morrison, M. A., 144
Mortality salience, 61, 62, 151–152
Morton, Eddy, 24–25
Morton, T. A., 44
Moses and Monotheism (S. Freud), 53
Mosso, C. O., 72
Mueller, A., 51
Mulitiple social identities, 171
Multicultural education, 159, 165–168
Multiple classifications, 96
Myth, 50

Nahanee, Harriet, 115
National Human Genome Center, 39
Natural resources, 107, 142
Natural selection, 49
Natural world, 137–158
    dehumanization, 144–146
    environmental attitudes, 141–142
    environmental inequality, 139–141
    ongoing environmental damage,
        142–144
    speciesism, 146–158
The Nature of Prejudice (G. Allport), 160
Neuberg, S. L., 52
Neurological systems. *See* Brain activity
News media, 89
Nicol, A. M., 72

Nonhuman animals, 138–139. *See also*
    Speciesism
Norms, 163, 169
"Not-in-my-backyard" phenomenon, 141
The Nutty Professor (film), 90

Obama, Barack, 7–8, 173
Obedience, 56
Object relations theory, 58–59
O'Connell, G. B., 134–135
Öhman, A., 128
Olsson, A., 126
"One drop" rules, 37
Opotow, S., 145
Oral language, 27
Osterhout, L., 122
Outgroup homogeneity effect, 110–111
Outgroups, 51, 105
Outward Bound program, 161–162, 164
Overweight people, 90

Paluck, E. L., 163, 168
Panksepp, J., 150
Parental influences, 87–88, 93, 94
Pargament, K. I., 66
Park, B., 121
Park, J. H., 51
Parrott, R. L., 43–44
Paternalistic prejudice, 78–79
Payne, B. K., 121
Peer influences, 91–92
Pehrson, S., 43
Pepperberg, I. M., 150
Perceptions, 11–12, 119–120
Performance gaps, 132–133
Personal identity, 109
Pests, 156
Pets, 147, 156
Pettigrew, T. F., 37, 163
Phelps, E. A., 126
Philosophy, 153
Physical features, 32–36, 95
Piaget, Jean, 93
Plain, Ron, 138
Plous, S., 148, 154, 155
Police violence, 117–118, 120
Pope John Paul II, 79
Positive affirmation, 44
Positive stereotypes, 18–20, 76, 133
Poteat, V. P., 92

Powell, Colin, 32
Powlishta, K. K., 99
Pratto, F., 67
Predators, 156
Prejudice, 7–28. *See also specific headings*
    audism, 24–28
    components of, 10–14
    definition of, 9–10, 20–21
    and discrimination, 21–22
    essentialist views of, 42–44
    indirect, 14–16
    and inequality, 16–18
    and privilege, 23–24
    seemingly positive attitudes, 18–20
Prenatal development, 40
Prescriptive stereotypes, 11
Prey, 156
Primitive categories, 31
Privilege
    and prejudice, 23–24
    protection of, 111
    and social construction of race, 36
    and social dominance orientation,
        70–72
Protestant work ethic, 68
Proximal influences, 104, 155–157
Psychoanalytic theory, 53–57
Psychodynamic perspectives, 48, 53–61
    and authoritarian personality, 58
    classic psychoanalytic theory, 53–57
    and frustration/aggression, 59–61
    object relations theory, 58–59
Pyszczynksi, T., 61

Quillian, L., 106

Race, 31–39
    as basic category, 31
    as classification, 31–33
    human genome variability, 33–36
    infant awareness of, 85
    as social construction, 36–39
Racism
    aversive, 124–125
    environmental, 139
Rahman, Q., 39
Realistic conflict, 105
Realistic group conflict theory, 107, 160
Reducing prejudice. *See* Social change
Relative deprivation, 174

Religion(s). *See also* Christian tradition
    beliefs systems of, 66
    benevolent sexism in, 79
    and ethnic–racial identities, 112
    fundamentalist, 69, 108
    hierarchy enhancement by, 69
    ideologies in, 66
    and minorities' freedoms, 22
    Protestant work ethic, 68
    racialized teachings of, 38
    and speciesism, 153–154
    as threat, 56
Resources
    competition for. *See* Competition for
        resources
    natural, 107, 142
Rich, A., 60
Rodgers, S., 89
Ropp, S. A., 164
Rosenthal, R., 129
Ross, M., 15
Routledge, C., 153
Rudman, L A., 111
Rushton, P. J., 32
Rwanda, 14, 162, 168
Ryan, M. K., 174
Ryder, R. D., 146

Saha, R., 140
Salience
    mortality, 61, 62, 151–152
    psychological, 96–98
Same-sex desires, 39
Sampson, E. E., 38
Scapegoats, 60
Schaller, M., 51
Scorched-earth tactics, 143
Sears, R., 60
Seavey, C., 98
Selective avoidance, 52
Self-esteem, 62, 110, 111, 152
Self-examination, 128
Self-fulfilling prophecies, 129–131
Self-interest, 155–157
Seligman, C., 111
Semenya, A. H., 171
Sexism, 79, 106
Sexual behaviors, 40–41
Sexual orientation
    adolescent stigmatization, 91–92

Sexual orientation, *continued*
  as difference, 39–42
  prejudice toward, 9
  symbolic beliefs about, 14
Shaheen, J. G., 89
Sherif, C. W., 104, 108, 160
Sherif, M., 104, 108, 160
Sidanius, J., 67
Silberman, I., 66
Sin, 41
Singer, P., 146
Singletary, S. L., 78
Skin tones, 32–33, 35, 97, 119
Slavery, 18
Social categories. *See* Categories and
      categorization
Social change, 159–176
  collective action for, 173–176
  contact hypothesis, 160–165
  educational programs for, 165–168
  individual strategies for, 168–171
  limitations of prejudice reduction,
      171–173
Social–cognitive developmental
      perspective, 92–96
Social conditions, 107
Social conservatism, 16
Social constructionist approach
  animals, 149–151
  and essentialism, 43–44
  race, 36–39
  sexual orientation, 40–42
Social context, 71, 100, 175
Social dominance orientation, 66–72
  competition for resources, 113
  and environmental inequality,
      140–141
  and prejudice against immigrants, 171
  and speciesism, 157
  and stereotype lift, 134
Social groups, 94–95
Social identity, 108–112, 171, 172, 175
Social institutions, 36–37
Socialization perspective
  attitudes toward nonhuman animals,
      154–155
  authoritarianism, 58
  prejudice in children and adoles-
      cents, 87–91
  transmission of prejudice, 47–48

Social learning theory, 87
Social neuroscience, 12–13
Social norms, 163, 169
Social programs/policies, 14–16
Social roles, 99–100
Social sciences students, 71–72
Social status, 17–18
  of animal groups, 156
  children's recognition of, 86
  and collective action, 174–175
  and conservative ideologies, 74
  in contact situations, 163
  and envious prejudice, 77–78
  and implicit/explicit prejudice,
      172–173
  and interdependence, 76–77
  and intergroup contact, 172–173
  paternalistic prejudice, 78–79
  perceptions of, 13
  socioeconomic, 67, 77
Socioeconomic status, 67, 77
Solomon, S., 61
Son Hing, L. S., 16
South Africa, 36–37, 69
Speciesism, 146–158
  distal influences, 151–153
  midrange influences, 153–155
  and prejudice, 144, 146–149, 157–158
  proximal influences, 155–157
  social construction of *animal*,
      149–151
Stangor, C., 169
Staub, E., 162
Steele, C. M., 131–133
Stelzl, M., 111
Stephan, C. W., 167
Stephan, W. G., 167
Stereotype content model, 76
Stereotype lift, 134
Stereotypes and stereotyping. *See also*
      specific headings
  of African Americans, 119–121, 132
  automatic, 122
  awareness of, 132–133
  benevolent, 78–79
  and categorization, 98–101
  as cognitive process, 118–124
  cultural, 120–121
  descriptive, 10
  explicit, 121, 122

gender, 19, 99
implicit, 119–124, 169–170
inferred, 100
in media representations, 89–90
meta-, 135–136
multicultural education, 167
of nonhuman animals, 150–151, 156
in police violence, 117–118
positive, 18–20, 76, 133
prescriptive, 11
and self-fulfilling prophecies, 130
as self-protective, 52
similarities in, 17
unconsciously held, 169–170
Stereotype threat, 131–133
Stigmatization, 51–52, 91–92, 130
Stroop test, 123
Sudan, 29–30, 106, 143
Symbolic beliefs, 13–14
Symbolic prejudice, 15
Symbolic threats, 108
Systema Naturae (Linnaeus), 32
System justification theory, 72–75

Tajfel, H., 109
Taylor, D. M., 166
Television programming, 89, 91
Terror management theory, 61–63, 151–152
Testosterone, 40
Theology, 69. *See also* Religion(s)
Threat(s)
emotional, 151–153
by ingroup members, 52
religion as, 56
stereotype, 131–133
symbolic, 108
value-based, 108
to values, 14–15
Tooman, G. D., 169
Toxic waste sites, 139–140
Tradition, 15, 16, 69
Trevino, K., 66
Tropp, L. R., 163
Trudeau, Pierre, 166
Tuan, M., 115
Turner, R. N., 165
Turpie, C. A., 135
Tutsi people, 162

Unambivalent prejudice, 77
Unconscious processes, 53–57
Unified instrumental model, 112–116
United States, 60. *See also* African Americans; White Americans
exposure to environmental pollution in, 139–140
prejudice among children and adolescents, 82
rights of persons with disabilities, 28
school segregation/desegregation in, 73, 160–161
social construction of race in, 37

Value(s)
affirmation of, 133
association with social categories, 85–86
of nonhuman animals, 147
and prejudice, 13–14
threats to, 14–15
Value-based threats, 108
Verkuyten, M., 44
Violence, 117–120
Virk, Reena, 81–82
Visual markers, 32–36, 97
Vivian, J., 106
Voci, A., 165
Vonofakou, C., 165
Vorauer, J. D., 134–135

Wagner, W., 43
Walton, G. M., 134
Weapons effect, 120
Weber, C. V., 158
Wessler, S. L., 82
White Americans
advantages of, 23
ingroup favoritism among, 73
positive stereotyping by, 19
prejudice in children, 83, 86
scapegoating of African Americans by, 60
social status and prejudice reduction, 172–173
unconsciously held stereotypes in, 119–121
White Canadians
metastereotypes held by, 135
support of social programs by, 15–16
Williams, M. J., 145

Wilson, G. D., 39
Witches, 65
Wittenbrink, B., 121
Women
   overweight, 90
   stereotypes about, 17
   workplace discrimination, 106
Wong, J. S., 161

Wood, W., 112
Word, C. O., 130
Workplace discrimination, 106
World of Difference Institute, 167
Wright, S. C., 164, 171, 172

Zagefka, H., 43
Zanna, M. P., 130

ABOUT THE AUTHOR

Lynne M. Jackson, PhD, is an associate professor in the Department of Psychology at King's University College, University of Western Ontario, in London, Ontario, Canada. Her research on intergroup relations examines links between prejudice and people's relation with the natural world, the nature and causes of prejudice between religious groups, and the role of group competition over resources in generating ethnic prejudice. She has also conducted research on contemporary sexism, the role of prejudice in jury selection, adult life transitions, and hypnosis. She teaches courses related to diversity and prejudice, psychology of religion, and human–animal relationships, as well as introductory psychology. She lives on a farm near Melbourne, Ontario, with her husband and their many four-legged friends.